INITIATION W

ENERGY
WORKS!

DR TERESA PARROTT, BM, MRCPsych. &
DR GRAHAM CROOK, MB, CHB, MRCP (UK).

FOREWORD BY PATRICK SCOTT ZEIGLER M. ARCH.
FOUNDER OF SKHM

Copyright © 2006 Dr Teresa Parrott and Dr Graham Crook
First published by O Books an imprint of The Bothy
John Hunt Publishing Ltd.,
Deershot Lodge, Park Lane, Ropley, Hants, SO24 0BE, UK
office@johnhunt-publishing.com
www.O-books.net

Distribution in:
UK
Orca Book Services
orders@orcabookservices.co.uk
Tel: 01202 665432 Fax: 01202 666219 Int. code (44)

USA AND CANADA
NBN
custserv@nbnbooks.com
Tel: 1 800 462 6420 • Fax: 1 800 338 4550

AUSTRALIA
Brumby Books
sales@brumbybooks.com
Tel: 61 3 9761 5535 • Fax: 61 3 9761 7095

SINGAPORE
STP
davidbuckland@tlp.com.sg
Tel: 65 6276 • Fax: 65 6276 7119

SOUTH AFRICA
Alternative Books
altbook@global.co.za
Tel: 27 011 792 7730 • Fax: 27 011 972 7787

Design: BookDesign™, London

ISBN 13: 978 1 905047 52 9
ISBN 10: 1 905047 52 5

A CIP catalogue record for this book is available from the
British Library.

Printed in the USA by Maple-Vail Manufacturing Group

INITIATION WITHOUT A MASTER

ENERGY WORKS!

DR TERESA PARROTT, BM, MRCPSYCH. &
DR GRAHAM CROOK, MB, CHB, MRCP (UK).

BOOKS

WINCHESTER UK
NEW YORK USA

**Foreword by
Patrick Scott Zeigler, M. Arch.**
Founder of SKHM / All-Love

DEDICATION

Teresa Parrott:
To Graham.

Graham Crook:
To my mother and father.

CONTENTS

CHAPTER ONE:
INTRODUCTION TO ALL-LOVE

CHAPTER TWO:
HEALING THE MIND, BODY AND SPIRIT

CHAPTER THREE:

WORKING WITH ALL-LOVE ENERGY

CHAPTER FOUR:

UNDERSTANDING ANGER

CHAPTER FIVE
UNDERSTANDING ANXIETY

CHAPTER SIX:
UNDERSTANDING HOW THE MIND WORKS

CHAPTER SEVEN:

CHAPTER SEVEN:
DREAMS AND SELF-HYPNOSIS

CHAPTER EIGHT:
FINAL WORDS

Foreword by Patrick Zeigler

All-Love is an energy that is within everyone. It is the energy of Love that connects you to the Universe. The All-Love system is therefore about connecting with your own energy, the energy of Source, and being in a state of oneness with the Universe. Each person can make his or her own unique connection with the Source. In a class, this is what we are helping people to do.

I am very excited about all the changes that are happening now. Twenty-five years ago, when I had the initiation experience in the Great Pyramid, I began teaching and passing the energy on to others. Initially, I called the energy Seichim, and put it out in the world originally as Seichim.

My teaching was all by word of mouth, and I didn't have a set spelling for the name of the energy, so as people heard about it they just spelled it as they wanted to – Seichim, Seichem, Sekhem. The basic root of the word is s-kh-m. Ancient Egyptian words are hard to translate into English, because the language used hieroglyphics, without specific vowels, and our alphabet does not contain the 'kh' sound.

All the different spellings are essentially alternative renderings of SKHM. There are many translations for the word SKHM, all connected to the life force, the energy of Source. The main ones are 'power of powers;' 'a place where the gods dwelt,' or 'the connection between the soul and heaven, the soul-spirit.'

The foundation for SKHM was set back in 1980, and it was adopted by various people. Over the years, more and more people worked with the energy, and developed their own symbols, methods of attunement, and different healing systems, such as Seichem and Sekhem. There were many different spellings of the word, and people used different spellings to name their systems, some of which have more of an Egyptian flair, while others work with shamanism, with angels or specific deities.

We know little about the ancient Egyptian healing methods. What we do know is that the Ancient Egyptians used healing energy; their system was hierarchical, and their healers held powerful positions; they were very secretive, so that very few people were able to find out the actual ways in which they worked. They don't seem to have worked specifically with opening the heart. Various people nowadays have been keen to learn about these systems – not an easy task!

My initial work was essentially with the energy. Gradually, I developed my methods of working with it, and developed a unique healing system. Five or six years ago I came to call it simply SKHM. Since then, my method of working with the energy has undergone a huge transition; it has moved specifically in the direction of love and of opening the heart. The energy is so different to what was taught earlier on, that I can't call it the same thing anymore. All-Love is the name that I have recently (January 2005) given to the healing system that I am now using to work with the energy. That way, people will begin to understand that it is different to all the old systems.

My view is that everyone has their own experience of the energy; it comes to us through our own filters, and we experience it in the form that we are most comfortable with. Each person working with it begins to use it in ways that are appropriate for him or her. When I started working with the energy, I used attunements, but after several years I found that there were some missing pieces, namely that of Love and opening the heart. So, I developed the Shenu meditation to focus more on those aspects, and stopped using attunements.

Some people prefer to work with a pure energy, and they will experience it as that; those who prefer to have an intermediary, such as a guide or God/Goddess, will experience that aspect. I do not associate it with any particular deity, belief system, person or place, as I do not want to place any limitation on the energy.

The All-Love energy is group energy. Each person in the group that brings the energy in makes it stronger. Once people are able to connect with the energy within the group, they can then start working to bring it in for themselves.

The group is the driving force, and this is why the energy is constantly evolving. The system is not dictated by one individual but is forming from a creative synthesis of the energies of many individuals who each bring different skills and interests. It is not a guru-based system. I recently spent three weeks in a retreat in India, and that is what they had there. They have the group energy but they focus it all on one man. That is why he is able to do miracles. But in that type of system, no one can progress beyond the guru.

It was interesting that in India they were teaching enlightenment, and people were beginning to make their own connection with the higher aspect of themselves, their divine being. Some were bringing the energy into the body, experiencing a soul-merger, which had not happened before. Of course, once this happens, the guru is no longer needed.

We want to develop a system where people are all evolving at their own pace, all experiencing their own reality without an intermediary. And I do feel that this is what will attract more and more people into our group. Because in this age you do want to have a direct connection to Source.

As each of us connects to the energy, we are linking to our own divine being. As I see it, the second coming of Christ is really all of us connecting with the Christ energy, to the divinity within ourselves; it is not the actual coming of a particular individual.

As we link to the energy of the Heavens, the Father-energy, and the energy of the Earth, the Mother-energy, we are bringing them both into the body, and we are experiencing ourselves fully, as both physical and spiritual beings. The Mother and Father energy form the basis of our primal core of love, and it may be that by experiencing them in a pure and balanced way, in a way that we may never have experienced before, we can re-set this core. And change our whole perception of love.

The main key to getting into the energy is to be able to fully experience the whole range of emotions: anger, grief, sadness, and joy. They all come together with the love, just as with the scale of music or the spectrum of light. If you have never experienced anger or grief fully, it will be hard for you to experience love and joy fully.

Each person has an area of emotion, which s/he holds in rather than expressing and fully experiencing. At times, all of us experience emotion that we do not express. We are not living fully in the moment, not fully experiencing that emotion, often because our minds are telling us that we should not, or else because our own thoughts are distracting us from our feelings.

The mind is the filter through which everything passes; it is all the time looking at the past or at the future, and this takes us away from the feeling. If we can break through this filter, we can allow ourselves to be fully in the moment. Fully experiencing the feeling, whether anger or grief or joy, can then lead into an Initiation.

It's really quite simple. It's just staying in the present moment — whether it is in the past as a child or being yourself, you are still feeling in the present. The energy can come in through the different emotional channels. However, the clearing that takes place is really just being in the moment and not letting the mind take you out of the feeling and the experience. Experiencing it, you can release it.

In order to get to that state of oneness with the Universe, you come up against some of the veils that cover the energy. Certain emotional or mental blockages make themselves known. Throughout a class, those veils may lift, and when they do, you may have a shift of consciousness - you see the world in a different way. If that is OK for you, that's great. Some may not want to see the world in a different way and that is great as well. The important thing is just to notice where you are at in the process. One of the most important things is to be with yourself. Whatever feeling comes up for you is fine. If you feel like laughing let yourself laugh, if you feel like crying let yourself cry. If you feel angry, let that come out. Allow your emotions out; don't judge them. It can get a bit wild at times; some people start to laugh and some to cry and some just feel peaceful and content. Whatever emotions come up, the idea is to just let yourself express them.

In a class, many deep emotions can emerge, and that can be a little scary. Especially right before an awakening of sorts, when things that have been covered up for years start to surface. People may not feel comfortable bringing up these emotions in a group, and that is perfectly normal. That is part of the fear. But if you allow yourself to stay with that emotion and to go into it, it may resolve and never be an issue again.

The reason that emotional blockages are there is that we have never allowed ourselves to experience the emotions fully. When we do allow ourselves to experience them completely and fully, the charge that is connected to that feeling or emotion can be removed, and whatever discomfort it is causing can be released too. Sometimes these feelings will actually cause physical problems, for instance, the tension that you hold in your shoulders can eventually cut the circulation and you can develop spinal problems and shoulder problems. From something as simple as that.

This is because the ongoing programme that is being run keeps holding back that charge or that energy. The mind is like a little computer and it has programmes. And you get viruses and spy ware and that is the way the mind works. It is going to take you right out of your heart every time. Just be aware of that. That is also how a lot of fear comes up. Since the beginning of time, the mind is programmed to protect itself at all costs. We are here to really get into our hearts more. The more we are in our heart the less we are in our head. Once you realise how the mind works then you can separate yourself from it and not let it control you.

So, if we go in and find out what that programme is, we can allow it to run its course completely. Behind that feeling, once the energy has been released, is a great sense of joy. What follows is almost like a download of divine love energy that comes in and fills that space up. As you let go of some of the fear that is associated with those spaces, the All-Love energy comes increasingly strongly into the body.

Naturally when you start to make a connection with Source, healing aspects come about, so healing is one of the by-products of connecting with Source.

One of the first healing sessions I ever did was with a lady with terminal cancer. She was in hospital on the intensive care unit, and was expected to die at any moment, but after the session, she actually made a speedy recovery, and was allowed to go home. Another of the better experiences that I had was a woman who had a tumour supposedly a little smaller than the size of a baseball and she was going to go in for surgery. In one session with the energy, it disappeared. Those things do happen. It is interesting. Healing all comes down to being happy with yourself.

That means coming to accept all the different parts, or personalities, that exist inside you. When someone asks you who you are, you might say, 'I am a teacher, a healer' – whatever you identify yourself as. But once you have identified that one aspect, it is interesting to see how it shifts – you can be a mother, a friend, a lover, or you can be the devil. And you can laugh about it. Just let yourself observe the flow of feelings coming from all the different personalities, all the different forms and ideas of who you think you are. Look at the different identities; just feel all those personalities inside of you. You have quite a circus inside of you. And notice which part of the circus wants to come in and be the ringmaster, the conductor. Feel those different identities.

And just know that these are just programmes. Programmes you have picked up along the way. Plays and dramas you have expressed along your life. Just for a few moments, see if you can identify which is the strongest at this point. Feel them and thank them. Be grateful for all the entertainment they have provided you. They have served you well. You have an internal Hollywood, right there. And, as we begin to dissolve some of these personalities, other personalities can enter. Just know that this is part of the process. You can even feel a shift into another state of consciousness as that happens.

Actually, you want to get all the feelings. To be complete you want to have experienced them all. Like a good actor, you need to express yourself fully. The most healing occurs when you get into the feeling that you are least comfortable with. Some people are very comfortable about being in anger. They break things, throw things, and beat people up. If they come to the group and start just expressing anger, they are probably not going to experience a big healing. They probably need to change gears and go into grief or one of the other emotions that they are not comfortable with. That is where the most healing is going to come.

There are natural phases, you dig up emotional stuff, then you go into a quiet phase where you just sit and watch, the witness stage, when you are up in your head again, and then we make the connection back down into the heart again.

You then bring in the higher self-aspect. Just seeing if at this time you can connect into your higher self, the part of you that is connected all the way into the divine. Your higher self comes in the form that you are most comfortable with – Jesus, Buddha, Isis, Earth Mother, whatever form or god or goddess that you relate to very strongly. If you are not sure, why don't you just ask if it has a name? Just connect with whatever form is there. Invite that aspect into you, to merge deeper than you have ever experienced before. Just allow it to come into your heart, and allow yourself to completely merge with it. We are all very much a part of a primordial essence of divine spirit.

We are all able to bring in that divine aspect. One of the reasons that people see faces, or forms, with the divine energies, is that we transpose the energy to give it a form that we are comfortable with. For some people, it is easier to connect with a face or an image; others are happier just to experience it as energy.

Many people get the impression that our class is just an emotional release class. But we can go a lot deeper than this. There is a very big difference between bringing up the emotions and having an initiation. The emotions definitely are connected with all the other energies. Emotions usually start to come up first. If you block the emotion, then you will block many of the other energies. Therefore, I encourage people to allow emotion to flow when it does surface. And if it doesn't surface then that is ok too.

A lot of us are up here in our heads. Which can be ok and peaceful, but what we are trying to encourage people to do is to make a definite shift to move down into the heart. Sometimes people like to get into the calm, peaceful place in the mind. And that is a nice place to be. Enjoy it if you are there. But know that when you are there, you can start to try to connect with the heart more, because that will give it a little more juice. The heart is where the real joy of life is, the joy of wanting to be here. If you stay in your head a lot, you can get into a dissociated body mode. Therefore, I really want to encourage everyone to move the awareness down into the heart more.

There are also some tricky emotions that are connected with people being stuck in their heads. One of those is an emotion of self-righteousness; we interpret everything we do as a good action, so that we cannot accept that we have any 'bad' energy. We all have this; it is a part of all of us. A lot of conditioning, especially on the spiritual path, is that when we feel anything negative, we think, 'I am not going to get into that. I am not going to deal with any negative feeling.' And if a negative feeling does come up then you feel you are not really connected with it. You think, 'It is really someone else's negative stuff that is coming up, and I am not associated with it.'

This happens a lot in large groups because a lot of energy comes up there in the group, and many people are very sensitive and they pick up on other people's energy. The thing is that if the energy does come up, whether it's yours or not, just go ahead and look at it, because it can help you get back into your stuff. In the group, if someone else is going through something, he or she can help you in your process. We are all connected. You can use the energy of the group to help you get in touch with your own feelings, even if you have already done a lot of work with energy. If something does come up for you do not just think, 'Oh, that can't be mine, I have already dealt with that before.' So just be aware of that, because self-righteousness is one of the most difficult energies to deal with. Listen to your mental dialogue, because that is where it is happening. If you are trying to make everything ok in your mind, telling yourself you do not have a problem, then notice that you are in your head with that dialogue rather than being in the heart. If that is what is happening, then just observe it, and eventually that will bring you down into the heart.

Sometimes when people say, 'I don't feel the energy, I am not feeling anything,' then a part of them is also saying 'I have really done a lot of work on myself and I don't need to do any more.' It is the mind playing a little trick on you. I am saying this because this is an energy that I discovered on the retreat in India and I got to know it really well! I am in the class for myself too. Once you identify that energy, you can find it within yourself. That is one of the discoveries that I made.

In the class, we normally do the meditation to allow us to get the space for the energy to work. Working with the heart, opening the crown, connecting with the Earth —all these help us to open up the different energy centres. Touch is also very helpful. Any time a person is touched, the mind and awareness will go to that part of the body. So if someone goes into process and starts to get in contact with their feelings but then gets a bit stuck, just touching them can help to unblock the process. Some people do not like to be touched, but then just being present helps them.

Sound also helps to open up a channel. Normally when we are dealing with stuck energy, the energy can't get out because it is not allowed to express itself. It wants to speak, to let itself out. This is where the self-righteous energy can come in again. It says, 'I don't really like that part of myself,' or 'I am really a good person, I am special, really spiritual. So I am just going to tuck that feeling very safely away.'

Each time we experience stuckness; there is something – a particular feeling or sensation - that we are not allowing ourselves to experience fully. Then we will need some help to identify the area of the body where we feel the energy might be stuck, or to initiate an emotional process. Once we have identified it, we can dialogue with it, to find out what it feels like, what it is about, or what it wants to say. Connecting the point of stuck energy with the throat, we can see if there is a particular sound or vibration associated with it, and encourage the person to express that sound.

We might have to work at the identification process for a prolonged period. People may need a lot of time and space before they can give permission to the part of themselves that is stuck to express itself. That may be something that they have never done before. Also, expressing emotion in front of many people can bring about a great healing as well.

With each workshop, as people bring the All-Love energy into their body, into their hearts, they are grounding the energy, bringing it to Earth, and making it easier and easier for other people to do it. People are able to experience the energy on their own, on the phone, by listening to the music, or from simply reading about the energy. You can connect with the teacher, the Shenu, the website - everything that is connected with the energy.

I think that recently there has been a big shift. Things are happening quicker; in some of the workshops we do not even get started with the meditation, we do not even finish with the introductions before initiations start happening.

For people at first, it was much more difficult, but I believe that in the future there is going to be less trauma when the energy comes in. Pretty soon, people will just go into the bliss experience rather than the emotional upset. The ideal would be that people come in, do our circle, and everybody gets the energy, instantaneously. You don't really need a teacher, you just kind of get together, hold hands and zip. No tricks!

I have always wanted to teach a twenty-one-day course. It would be good for people to be able to achieve a permanent shift in consciousness. One of the things that happens with the energy is that you make a connection in the class but then come down again. The more we work with it, the stronger the group is. The aim of a longer course would be to eventually get to feel a permanent state of connection.

Eventually, connecting with the All-Love energy, people will be able to stay in a truly very openhearted space. I know that we can get to the point where that can happen for more and more of us. That is my vision for the future.

Patrick Zeigler, June 2005.

CHAPTER ONE

Introduction to All-Love

DISCOVERING THE ALL-LOVE ENERGY

IN 1980, a twenty-five-year old American called Patrick Zeigler spent a night in the Great Pyramid in Egypt. As he lay there in the sarcophagus a brilliant blue light entered his heart and through the whole of that night he was filled with an incredible feeling of love, peace and calm; as an intense and beautiful energy moved in waves throughout his body. It was an experience that profoundly changed his life.

Now, twenty-five years on, that energy, which he calls the All-Love energy, is continuing to change his life – and the lives of many other people.

What Patrick experienced all those years ago in the Great Pyramid was a spontaneous initiation; an instantaneous, startlingly powerful, immensely joyful connection with the energy of the Source of all life and of All-Love — the God-force, if you like.

Since then, he has used his ability to connect with this energy for his own personal growth, for healing himself and others, for passing on the energy, and for teaching other people how we too can experience our own direct, personal connection with the energy that created us and the whole Universe.

The All-Love energy system that Patrick now teaches has gradually evolved over the years, as new experiences and perspectives have suggested more effective ways of connecting with and using the energy. The energy itself is constantly changing. We ourselves are constantly changing, as we come to realise more of our own unique, individual potential. Each person who makes that connection discovers for himself or herself that spirituality, or direct personal experience of the divine, is our birthright, regardless of background, culture or belief. All of us here on Earth can connect with our spiritual being. We all have a capacity for love.

Two thousand years ago, Christ spoke to us of the possibility of love. Throughout history, religious and spiritual seekers and healers have been achieving initiation, spiritual awakening, and the miracle of healing. For centuries, philosophers, artists, and poets have sought to unravel the complexities of the mind and to express the deepest longings of the human heart.

This knowledge has been with us for all time. Yet, it is only now that it is all beginning to come together in a global sense. Collectively we have the information, communication systems, and individual freedom of which our forefathers can only ever have dreamt. We can draw upon their wisdom without being constrained by the rules, definitions, and divisions of the past. We can see that our need for love, for understanding, and for spiritual awakening are not separate but intertwined questions to which each of us must find our own answers.

The All-Love system encourages each individual to experiment, to experience, and to express his or her deepest needs. Each of us has the power to make things happen. We have the freedom to choose, and, asking for help, we have the capacity to receive. The Source exists within us, love is a reality; miracles do happen.

Many people are simply not aware that we are all capable of opening ourselves up to channel spiritual healing energy and to experience an initiation. Traditionally, it was taught that a person would only be able to achieve this after years of preparation and purification, involving rigorous study, prayer, or meditative practices under the guidance of a spiritual teacher or Master.

However, Patrick's experience showed him that this could happen without years of prior preparation or study - and without any intermediary.

The All-Love system is a unique method of energy healing. It facilitates a direct personal connection with the energy of Source, or the Creator. Everyone is capable of making this connection.

It is, if you like, Initiation without a Master.

HOW THE ALL-LOVE ENERGY SYSTEM DEVELOPED

PATRICK had longed to spend the night in the Great Pyramid since childhood. When he finally visited it in 1980, he was overjoyed to find a small opening to the left of the King's Chamber. There was a narrow tunnel where thieves had tried to break through the wall, and he discovered that the gate closing the entrance was not locked. It was the perfect place to hide.

He left the Pyramid, started fasting, and returned the next day with his rucksack. When no one was looking, he crawled into the tunnel and found a small room just above the King's Chamber, where he meditated until everyone had left the Pyramid at night. He then made his way back to the King's Chamber and lay down in the sarcophagus.

He soon realised that the chamber was full of mosquitoes. Therefore, having brought a toilet roll in his rucksack, he wrapped himself in it, got back in the sarcophagus and lay there looking just like a mummy.

After meditating for a while, he heard a thumping sound like footsteps coming up from the gallery below. He lay still, thinking he would be discovered, yet no one appeared, and he suddenly realised that the sound was not human. He was terrified.

The sound entered the room, pulsating throughout the Chamber, and a swirling pattern of electric blue light appeared, hovering above him. A part of him knew that this was why he had come. He thought, 'Do what you have to do,' and at that moment, the brilliant blue light came down into his heart. For a moment, there was a total silence, and he wondered if he was still alive. Then his heart seemed to expand as the sound filled it and merged with the sound of his heartbeat. The light swirled through his heart and body in a figure-of-eight or infinity pattern. He lay there peacefully all night filled with energy and an immense feeling of joy and love.

The next morning, he returned to his hiding place, and meditated a while before coming out to join a group of tourists leaving the Pyramid. The guards started shouting at him to stop, but, ignoring them, he jumped on a bus that took him back to his hotel.

The following week, Patrick spent some time with the Brahani order of Sufism. This helped him to ground what he had experienced with the energy, gave him more understanding of it, and suggested ways in which he might teach it. He also received the final attunement of their order.

After this, whenever he put his hands on his body, he felt a powerful energy, and his pains or illnesses would disappear.

When he started working with the energy, he used it for his own personal healing. Later, he used it with other people. He had previously practised yoga and meditation, and on his return to the United States, he went to a healing school in New Mexico run by Robert March, where he learned massage and started to develop his healing skills. It was a massage school, but Robert March encouraged him to do energy work, so he did this both alone and in combination with massage. He had a session of Reiki, and realised that it was similar to what he was already doing. Intrigued, he took Reiki 1 and 2 that same weekend. That was in 1984, and a year later, he went to Georgia to study with Barbara Weber Ray, and received the Reiki Master attunement. He found that Reiki did not lead to any increase in the amount or intensity of the energy that he was already channelling. He realised that he had already connected with the energy, and that the energies, whatever they were called, were simply different aspects of the one Source.

Later, Patrick went to California, where he met a medium called Christine Gerber, who was channelling a spirit named Marat. Patrick had a lot of questions. Much of what he had been taught about Reiki – for example, that the symbols were Tibetan - did not make sense to him, and he wanted to see if Marat could give him some further insights. Through a form of automatic writing, Marat said that the energy that Patrick was channelling was not Reiki but 'Setim.' The word didn't feel quite right to Patrick so, later, meditating on what he had been told by Marat, he heard the sound 'saykhem.' He wasn't sure how sure how to spell this word. The nearest rendering seemed to be Seichim (pronounced say-keem). Later on, other spellings were used, including Sekhem and SKHM, pronounced Say-kem, which are renderings of the ancient Egyptian word meaning highest spiritual power or energy.

Initially, Patrick started teaching using a process of attunements similar to those used in Reiki. People were excited and amazed to experience the energy. The sessions that he had with Marat confirmed many of the things that he was already doing— such as passing the energy to others through attunements, and encouraged him to continue developing his own techniques.

Marat confirmed that the Infinity symbol, which Patrick had been using in his healing and Infinity Dance, was a key symbol. He also mentioned another symbol, which he called the Breath of Life. Patrick later wondered if this might have been the Reiki distance symbol, which is sometimes called the Tree of Life, but then realised that it was in fact the Ankh. He experimented using some of the Reiki symbols in his attunements, but he was not comfortable with them; and they did not always seem to work, so he returned to using the Infinity and the Ankh.

He continued to investigate other systems of energy healing, and began to use sound healing and visualisations. What he found the most effective was to guide people to visualise a brilliant sun. They brought the light from the sun down into their body forming a column of light, and he would then guide them to visualise an infinity symbol descending through that column of light.

In the early years, Seichim was often taught along with Reiki and followed a similar template, so it came to be viewed as an alternative form of Reiki; although its origins were quite distinct. In fact, many Reiki Masters decided to make Seichim a higher degree of Reiki. As more people started to use the energy, they incorporated their own images and associations and began to mould different systems according to their individual experiences. Various symbols were added and some people linked the energy to particular deities, such as Sekhmet or Isis.

Gradually, different systems were developed, including Seichim, Seichem, and Sekhem. Similar to the various Reiki systems, which require a series of attunements from a Master, they all use an attunement process, in which the teacher alters a person's energy system to allow him or her to channel the energy. An attunement connects that person with the energy, but it does not necessarily lead to an Initiation, which is a deeper integration of the energy.

Although, as mentioned previously, the energies of all spiritual healing systems are aspects of the one Source, the techniques used to connect and work with the energy vary greatly.

The system that Patrick currently uses differs in major respects to both the old Seichim and the Reiki systems. He does not use any type of attunement. His vision has always been that people can be helped to experience an initiation through their own effort, without the need for an intermediary. Over years of working with the SKHM energy, he has developed techniques and methods which enable this to happen – and which make his system unique.

In order to avoid confusion, he has now called this system All-Love.

WHAT IS ENERGY?

THE word energy, derived from the Greek words *en* – in or inside, and *ergon* – work, means force, power, effort or work. Energy is what makes us work.

So where does it come from? It comes from the sun, the water, the earth, the air that we breathe, from plants, animals and the food that we eat. In other words, all of our energy comes in one form or another from the universe around us.

The beef sandwich I ate for lunch has provided the energy to write this page; the energy from that cow came from the grass, the earth, and the light from the sun. Therefore, the energy of this writing has in part come indirectly from a star millions of miles away.

The energy of the universe is being constantly re-cycled, changed into different forms. Physics has proven that energy cannot be created or destroyed; it can only be transformed. Potential energy can be changed into mechanical energy; atomic energy can be converted into electrical energy. A generator, for instance, does not create energy; it just changes one type of energy into another. From the simplest windmill to the most complex nuclear reactor, we are merely harnessing the energy of the universe. We, as human beings, cannot create energy, we can only use, in ways of our own choosing, the energy that is given to us.

Everything that we do involves energy of one sort or another: physical, mental, emotional, spiritual energy. Quite simply, without energy nothing works.

So, in fact, whatever our spiritual beliefs, whatever our interpretation of scientific facts, it is not actually that difficult to imagine that we as human beings are able to connect with the energy of the Universe. Not indirectly, through a beef sandwich or an electrical transformer or a windmill; but directly, through our own energy system, to the energy of Source—the energy that created this wonderful universe in which we live.

ENERGY SYSTEMS OF THE BODY

MANY of us believe that nothing exists beyond what we can physically sense. We live our lives based around the inputs we receive from our five senses: sight, touch, hearing, smell and taste. The problem with this is that our senses have limits. For instance, we can only see and hear within a specific range of frequencies and wavelengths; yet we know that many species of animals can sense frequencies outside of these. We see colours from red to violet, yet waves of a different energy exist nonetheless, such as infrared and ultraviolet which, although detectable by scientific equipment, are invisible to the human eye.

Science has shown that everything, including matter, is energy. The physical body is energy vibrating at a rate which falls within the range of our physical senses.

Scientific evidence demonstrates that energy is flowing through us all the time. Electric currents are flowing through our cells constantly, and bio-magnetic fields are induced around these currents. Our whole body is immersed in an electromagnetic field, or aura, which is energy vibrating at a higher frequency than that of our physical body.

Therefore, we are in fact made up of energy. Our thoughts, our feelings and desires, our physical movements and sensations are simply different manifestations of energy. Our physical energy system is inextricably connected with our mental, emotional and spiritual energy systems.

Modern Western medicine now acknowledges the role of emotional factors in producing symptoms of both mental and physical illness. A feeling, for instance, produces chemicals, which are released from the brain to travel in the bloodstream to different parts of the body— it has an effect on our immune system; it can influence our perception of pain, and it can affect our physical health.

Just as our physical body has major organs, our energy system also has energy centres located along our central vertical axis. There is also a network of energy distribution lines, or meridians, similar to the networks of our blood vessels and nervous system.

The Eastern model of the body's energy system is that energy flows within the physical body along interconnecting pathways and is focussed at certain points, or energy centres, called chakras. Chakra is a Sanskrit word meaning a circle or a wheel. Here the energy circulates and is concentrated over an area that corresponds to particular organs of the body.

In a condition of health, energy flows freely throughout our body and the auric field; the chakras are balanced and we tend to feel good. When they are blocked, or we are low in energy, we feel 'low' or 'down' or unwell.

We all experience periods when our body's defences, including our aura, are weakened, when we feel run-down and are more vulnerable to infection. We all have energy blockages and imbalances at some time.

If we repeatedly experience painful emotions, negative thoughts, or blocked energies, and do not release them; then, over time they can contribute to the development of pathological changes, physical or emotional symptoms, and even illness.

WHAT IS HEALING?

ALL of us have been ill at some time in our lives. We have been to the doctor, we have taken medication, and we may have had to go to hospital. However, most of the time we do get better on our own.

If you start developing flu, for instance, you often go about your normal life, feeling worse and worse, until you just cannot keep going any more. Your throat is sore, it is too painful to speak, you cannot concentrate on anything, you have no energy, and all your muscles ache. Your body is urgently saying, 'Stop, I need some time to heal.' When you feel awful and completely exhausted, you finally take some time off.

Your conscious mind usually tells you what to do, but you switch it off, you just don't care any more. You go to bed, you draw the curtains, you don't talk, and you lie there for the next few days drifting in and out of sleep.

Lying quietly in the dark, not moving, not thinking, you are in a meditative state, or a trance. That is when your body heals the best.

Soon you are up and back to work and you probably do not give yourself credit for what you have just done. In fact, you have listened to your body; you have closed off from the outside world so that you can use all your energy to overcome the infection. You have healed yourself. The problem is that we often wait until we are in severe pain, until we are feeling exhausted and terrible, before we give ourselves that quiet, healing time.

Most of the time when we have aches and pains, cuts and bruises, infections and illnesses, our bodies heal beautifully. We might need antibiotics or stitches or painkillers to help that process, we feel better when other people care for us, touch us, and tend our wounds, but essentially our bodies heal themselves.

That is a miracle.

We have all had physical pain and injuries. Moreover, we have all had emotional pain and injuries too. It is just that they are harder to see and easier to ignore. Sometimes it takes us decades to even acknowledge that they exist. However, just as with the flu in the example above, we find it difficult to heal until we finally admit to ourselves that there is something wrong.

We all try, usually fairly successfully, to deny that we have unpleasant or painful feelings such as fear, anger, or sadness. In fact, many of us are ashamed of such feelings. In addition, we do not trust in our own capabilities; we reinforce negative beliefs about ourselves that constantly undermine our self-esteem. Our bodies often respond to these beliefs; our muscles become tense and our autonomic nervous system floods our body with anxiety-stimulating stress hormones.

If we do not express our emotions, if we do not modify the negative beliefs that we have about ourselves, then they become stored in our body, our energy system or our unconscious mind.

For all of us, pain from the past continues to affect the present. It hurts, and that is why most of us go to such lengths to avoid it. We turn it outwards in anger or inwards in anxiety, worry or depression. We turn it into physical illness or addiction. We take painkillers, or medication, or we self-medicate with alcohol or drugs.

Instead of holding on to that pain and anger and fear, we could use spiritual healing energy to transform and release it.

WHAT IS HEALING ENERGY?

THE words health, healing and holistic - all originate from the same Germanic root, *whole*. Healing means becoming whole; in other words being aware of yourself at all levels; accepting, expressing and integrating all that you are. As we have seen, the word energy is derived from the Greek words *en* – in or inside, and *ergon* – work. Energy therefore means inside work, or inner work.

Therefore, healing energy means doing our inner work so that we can become whole.

Being whole means being recovered or free from disease, healthy or restored to health. It also means being unhurt, free from damage or recovered from injury. Many people are physically well and feel that they do not need any healing.

However, there are few people who have not suffered emotional wounds or injuries and it is likely that, if we are honest, we have not received any help, or managed to heal these injuries.

The other important aspect of wholeness is being complete not divided or broken up; but all parts being united in a perfect system. Few of us feel complete in ourselves. We are generally not even aware of all of the different parts of ourselves, so it is not surprising that we feel there is something missing in our lives. Wholeness involves acknowledging and accepting all that we are.

Few of us love or understand ourselves enough. There are so many things that we do not accept about ourselves – memories, thoughts, feelings, desires.

The parts of ourselves that we find difficult to accept, exist in a state of conflict with those parts with which we more readily identify. The state of wholeness, or health, occurs when all aspects are integrated.

At some deep unconscious level, we know exactly what we need to learn about ourselves - and how to do it. It is not easy to start finding out about the things you have hidden for so long. It takes effort, commitment, and is painful at times.

We all need to work on ourselves; however much we might resist or talk ourselves out of it. There are many different ways of doing that work. After reading this book, it may be that you do not like this particular approach. That's fine, this isn't the only way, or the only tool that you can use. Find another that suits you. But don't stop looking.

It is our belief that the Universe wants us to progress. The energy of Source, of the universal creative life force, helps us to do it. It enables us to be more in contact with our emotions, our inner intuitive knowledge and the hidden parts of our personalities. It can facilitate powerful emotional shifts and personal transformations.

Healing is a life-long process; it enables us to learn about ourselves and to change. We can choose what to believe, we can determine our own moods and, feelings, and we can influence our own physical state: we are our own masters.

Because the fact is that, we all need to change. We all need to do our inner work, so that we can begin to accept and integrate all parts of ourselves. The wonderful thing is that by truly accepting all that we are, we will lead healthier and happier lives.

And, in becoming whole, we will be healed.

What is Source?

THE word source comes from Old French, *sourdre* – rise, spring: and Latin *surgere* – surge. It therefore means the origin, the fountainhead from which energy enters into and flows through our system — the place from which everything begins.

Belief systems vary according to customs, religions and cultures. Everyone has his or her own personal view or understanding of the Source, or the Creator. Which means that there will be as many definitions, as there are people who have ever considered the possibility. For some, that will encompass a certain set of values or characteristics, for others there is simply the view that there is some creative force or energy outside of him or her.

People who do not subscribe to any particular theories about the God force, or the Origin, must still find some way of explaining their existence, the complexity of the human organism, and the vastness of the universe. It is not without a sense of wonder that we can look around and see the beauty, variety and technological impossibility of the Creation.

Man uses all sorts of words, images and symbols to make sense of that which is inconceivable. If the Creator is viewed simply as an impersonal, limitless source of energy, then that does not exclude or contradict anyone's personal definition of God. It allows that everyone will see God through his or her own eyes. They will personify spiritual energy according to the words, images and symbols that are meaningful to them.

For this reason, spiritual energy, the energy of Source, can be to each individual whatever he or she needs it to be.

We are each created by Source; and we can each have a direct connection with that Source. There are many possible pathways. We simply need to find our own.

WHAT IS SPIRITUALITY?

THE word spiritual derives from the Latin *spiritus,* meaning breathing. The spirit is the animating or life-giving principle.

Spirit is the spark of life that we all have within us. Although we are living in our physical bodies, we are also, all of us, already spiritual beings. There is a part of us, separate from our physical body, our spiritual essence, if you like, which, throughout our lives, whether we are aware of it or not, connects us to the spiritual or life-giving energy of the Universe.

The spirit is the energy that makes up a person; the thoughts and feelings, the memories and experiences that make us what we each uniquely and individually are. As energy cannot be created or destroyed, it is also the part of us that continues to exist after we leave this physical body.

Becoming aware of our spirit, we feel that we are loved, that our lives have a purpose, that we are part of a forgiving world. Feeling the joy of the spirit, of the God force within us, everything makes sense; we are no longer separate and alone but together, connected and purposefully intertwined.

What is an Initiation?

AN initiation can be an immensely powerful and ecstatic experience, in which the whole body is vibrating with energy. We may make spontaneous sounds or movements as we release the emotions and energy that we have held as tension in our bodies. We feel intensely excited, and profoundly moved; we are flooded with emotion as we experience the immense loving energy of the Creator.

In an initiation, we experience a fully integrated connection with the energy of Source, both from above, and from the Earth. It gives an intense feeling of connectedness— of being at one with the energy of the Universe. Suddenly, we know that we have purpose here on the earth, that we are loved, and that we are not alone. Our faith has been strengthened; a burden has been lifted. It is as if we have been given a new beginning.

The word initiation itself comes from the Latin *initiare* – to begin. It is an act of beginning or originating something. To initiate means to introduce or acquaint with.

Traditionally, an initiation ceremony was a formal introduction to secret knowledge, available only to an inner circle of privileged initiates. It involved obscure concepts intelligible only to the initiated, and the rites or instruction in the elements of a spiritual or esoteric practice. The word esoteric (which comes from the Greek word *esoterikos* – inner, and *eso* – within), means secret, not openly stated or admitted.

People today do not want to be told what they can or cannot do, and they do not want secrets. They want, instead, to make their own decisions and trust their own intuition. They want to experience all that they are able to experience.

Changes in the usage of words reflect these shifts in attitudes. Pious, for example, meaning godly, religious, devout or sacred, now also means hypocritically virtuous or self-righteous. Holy, meaning devoted, morally and spiritually perfect, also colloquially means sanctimonious. What we call spirituality is now being constantly questioned and examined.

We live in exciting and fast-moving times. Information is far more accessible today; people are better informed, more knowledgeable and more aware than at any other point in history. They are much less likely to accept the authority of any given group or individual, whether spiritual teacher or religious organisation.

Organised religion, in the sense at least of a spiritual system prescribing a code of living and defining a means of achieving spiritual improvement, clearly has less appeal nowadays; in Britain today less than 8% of the population are regular church-goers.

It is not that religion has, inherently, less value than it ever did, it is more perhaps that it is not fully answering people's questions or fulfilling their current needs. Just as in the eighteenth Century period of the Enlightenment, when reason and individualism began to replace tradition and authority, now too it seems that more and more people are seeking their own individual answers.

Spirituality is no longer seen as synonymous with religion. Experience of the God force is no longer available only on prescription; enlightenment is not limited to a select few any more.

Much is changing, and things are moving in full circle. Science, having for centuries seemingly been in opposition to the concept of God, now supports it; at least in the sense of a creative force, mind or energy explaining the existence of the universe. Spiritual awareness and the responsibility for personal growth are coming back to rest upon the individual; which is where, in truth, they always were.

We live in a time of great awakening. Global, social or personal crisis are finally arousing us from the inaction or indifference of the past. But we do not need to wait for a crisis. Given an attitude of openness, a willingness to learn, and to work on ourselves, enlightenment is possible for any of us. We are collectively becoming more aware of our problems and how to solve them. We talk of 'seeing the light,' in the sense of reaching a full understanding or realisation. But, there is also an element of lightening of the burden, and lessening of the weight of personal and collective pain.

Our spirituality — our potential for enlightenment, lies within. Through our own inner work, we will find it. We are each responsible for our own spiritual development, and, when we are ready, we will choose to begin.

An initiation, a personal, life-changing experience of being in the light and of connecting with Source, is possible for all of us.

What is the difference between an attunement and an initiation?

AS we have seen, spirituality is a regard for our own spiritual essence; an awareness of the invisible, mysterious things of the spirit, as opposed to the physical, material things that we can see and touch and explain. Our normal day-to-day life tends to be dominated by our rational, logical minds and our physical senses. Our own spiritual energy vibrates at a higher frequency than our physical body, so we tend to not sense it – or the energy coming from outside of ourselves.

We are simply not attuned to spiritual energy.

To attune means to bring into harmony or accord, to make perfectly suited or receptive to. An attunement is therefore a process, which enables us to harmonise with, and receive, the energy of the universe.

In an attunement, a teacher alters a person's energy system to connect that person to the energy. As the energy flows in, people respond in a variety of ways. Some simply feel relaxed and peaceful and do not actually sense the energy. Others feel it as warmth or tingling in their body, and see it as light, colours or forms.

An attunement is not the same as an initiation. An initiation involves a deeper integration of the energy into the energy system and body than usually occurs in an attunement.

For some people, an attunement triggers an initiation; their energy system and body is filled with the energy and they have an intensely joyful and moving experience of being in the light.

When a person undergoes an attunement, he or she may not be ready at that moment to experience an initiation. He or she may have limiting beliefs, unresolved emotions, or blocked energies, which prevent enough energy from flowing into his or her energy system.

Many systems of energy healing do not focus on helping the student to overcome whatever obstacles are preventing him or her from experiencing an initiation. The teacher simply passes an attunement, which means that probably an initiation will not be experienced, and healing may or may not occur during the attunement. During the purification period over the following days or weeks, mental, emotional and energetic issues may emerge, and the student, working alone, may or may not manage to truly heal those issues.

In the All-Love system, an Initiation, or SKHM-Khet, which means energy in the body, occurs when a person makes his or her own personal connection with the energy and a spontaneous healing is experienced. The blockages or obstacles that exist at that moment are dissolved, allowing the energy to flow freely into the person's energy system. The energy from the Heavens merges with the energy from the Earth, and an Initiation occurs when the energy is integrated and grounded within the body. It is a powerful, unmistakeably intense experience, which changes the way that people view themselves and their lives.

How does All-Love connect us to Source?

EVERYONE has the ability to connect with the All-Love energy. For some people, it happens very quickly, within just a few minutes. For others, before they can make the connection, specific issues or aspects of themselves need to be dealt with, which are holding them back.

When the energy starts to enter a person's energy system, it flows into his/her physical, mental, emotional and spiritual bodies; bringing a beautiful sense of peace, joy, and unconditional love. However, it also reaches places that are holding painful emotions such as anger and sadness; physical discomfort and muscular tension; or energetic blocks.

When we are in a state of joy, the energy flows freely. When the energy encounters blocks, or triggers our feelings of pain or anger, we tend to hold our breath, our bodies become tense, and we stop the flow of energy. When this happens, we need to work through those feelings in order to release the blocks; when this is done, the energy begins to flow again.

For this reason, a teacher can help facilitate an Initiation but cannot actually give one. Firstly, the student has to open himself or herself to receive the energy. Once the energy is flowing, s/he then has to be prepared to work on his or her own personal issues, because while something within himself or herself is breaking the flow of energy, s/he will be unable to experience an Initiation.

How does All-Love energy work?

IN an All-Love workshop, the student is supported in making his or her own connection with the healing energy. When this occurs, there is a strong, direct stream of energy channelled from Source.

Working within a group, Patrick uses what he calls 'flowing meditations,' allowing and guiding the flow of energy, so that an individual opens him or herself to the energy and experiences a spontaneous initiation, from within, whenever s/he is ready to do so.

Group meditations are very effective, because the energy increases with each person present. The meditation encourages people to consciously use the breath, and to observe the changing sensations in the body; this increases awareness of the feelings, tensions and blocks that are held in the body. Toning helps to express sounds from within the body, which can enable a shift in energy and emotion, and can help to open the chakras.

The visualisations within the meditations help to keep a focussed awareness. They guide people towards the conscious opening of the heart centre— towards opening the crown and filling the heart with light, and grounding the column of light to the Earth.

The All-Love meditation that Patrick uses in his classes evolved from his own initiation experience in the Pyramid. The Infinity Dance was adapted from Sufism. The infinity symbol is a strong energetic pattern that is visualized as the breath enters, and the awareness is gradually brought more and more towards observing sensations in the body. In the Infinity Dance, physically moving in the infinity pattern also helps the energy to move through the body.

The energy usually starts to flow into a person during the group meditation. He or she may experience an initiation the moment his or her mind, body, feelings, and energy system are in balance. Resistance within the mind can be bypassed using visualisation, which focuses the conscious mind and allows the unconscious mind to take over. Energy or emotions, which are held within the body, can be freed by using physical movement and sound.

Once a person enters a state of mental, emotional, and physical harmony, s/he is able to receive more energy. The All-Love system uses various techniques to enable him or her to achieve that harmony. It encourages him or her to become aware of what he or she is feeling in his or her body and his emotions. Opening the heart centre helps a person to be more acutely aware of his or her feelings of love - or lack of them.

Many of us do not truly love ourselves, and our experiences of pain and loneliness lead us to build a protection around ourselves. Although this may have been effective in the past, enabling us to better cope with those painful feelings, it may now be no longer serving us. In the present moment, those protective defences may be preventing us from being able to receive – the love from others, and the energy of Source, which enables us to heal.

In fact, many of us have a problem with receiving – not just energy, but anything. We often feel ashamed of asking for what we need, because the need implies weakness or inadequacy. We feel guilty about getting what we want, because we feel we are being selfish or are depriving someone else. The role of the giver is generally seen as more worthy than that of 'taker,' yet in reality, we all have needs and desires, we all need to learn how both to give and to receive.

In an All-Love class, the group is a powerful source of support and love. Being able to support others through their process makes it easier for us to accept help and support ourselves. Freely giving is a catalyst to opening and receiving.

Pain needs a witness. For all of us, there are things, which need to be said, and need to be heard. We hold pain in our bodies; therefore, we need the loving touch of others to help release it. We hold emotional pain because we are frightened and ashamed, therefore we need others to give us space and support so that we can bring ourselves to express those feelings. When others listen with compassion, we have the experience – maybe for the first time – of being truly accepted by others despite our pain. This enables us to accept and love ourselves and to truly heal.

Many of us feel isolated. When others in the group listen, when we see that our pain touches them, and they touch us in a loving way and support us through that pain, we know that we are not alone. We feel other people's energy, and realise that it makes ours stronger, enabling us to do what we could not do by ourselves.

We may have thought that we had to hide our feelings and struggle on alone, yet we suddenly realise that others have felt the same pain too. When we are accepted and understood, we no longer feel set apart and isolated, but part of a whole.

Healing means accepting, not judging - both ourselves and others, as they reflect parts of us. In our infinite variety, we are not better or worse or separate. When we heal the pain that creates the illusion of separation and aloneness, when we heal the old, negative patterns that lead to divisiveness and conflict, we suddenly have a wonderful sense of being at one – with others and with the Universe.

We are each able to connect with the energy that created all of us, the Source from which we come. And, through this energy, we can also connect with each other.

HOW IS ALL-LOVE UNIQUE?

ALL-LOVE is unique in that the person opens up to the energy and allows it to enter into his or her energy system. The teacher facilitates this process by encouraging the student to become aware of the emotions and energies that are preventing the energy from fully entering the body; and which are likely to stop him or her from moving forward in life. With help, the student is then able to release and heal them. This can lead to a spontaneous initiation.

The student is less likely than in other systems to become dependent on the teacher, because s/he achieves Initiation through his or her own effort, by allowing his or her own process to unfold. If you do not experience an initiation, it is because something in you is preventing this from happening. If you do experience one, it is through your own effort – this gives you a much greater sense of your own power. An initiation is not a passive process; the teacher helps you, and the energy helps you, but you normally have to do your own inner work for an initiation to occur.

Another unique aspect of All-Love is that spiritual, mental, emotional and physical healing techniques are an integral part of the class. When a student encounters painful emotions or energy blocks, the teacher helps him or her to express these emotions and to overcome the blocks. Since these healing techniques have been incorporated into the All-Love system, more frequent and more powerful Initiations have been experienced within the group.

Traditional Reiki and Seichim courses do not focus on emotional healing in this way. Their teaching is didactic more than experiential, and any healing which comes about tends to occur later, in the purification process which may continue for several weeks following the attunement, rather than during the course itself.

The emphasis in an All-Love class is placed upon experiencing the energy for yourself; feeling how it affects you; using it to help you to overcome your own inner obstacles, and learning to work with the energy to help other people overcome theirs.

How does All-Love differ from other systems of energy healing?

IT was only in 1922, with the discovery of Reiki, that a simple method of opening to spiritual healing energy became generally known.

Reiki, from the Japanese words *rei* meaning universal, and *ki* meaning vital or life force energy, was re-discovered by Dr Mikao Usui during a twenty-one day fast and meditation on the sacred Mount Kurama in Japan. He experienced a brilliant white light entering his head, and saw a series of symbols within the light. Following this, he was able to channel universal energy to heal himself and others, and was able to pass on the energy through a process of attunements.

Dr Usui taught Reiki using the five rules of conduct that he formulated, which were: Just for today, don't get angry, don't worry, be grateful, work hard, and be kind to others. By using Reiki to work through painful emotions such as anger, sadness, anxiety and depression, we can feel much happier and more appreciative of the positive things in our lives.

It was Dr Usui's wish that Reiki should be readily available to everyone, all over the world. He died in 1926, having initiated over a thousand people in Reiki, including sixteen to the level of teacher. However, it was not until the 1980's that Reiki became widely available and affordable in the West. Now, over a million people have been attuned to Reiki, and there are thousands of Reiki Masters all over the world.

As we have already said, the All-Love and Reiki energy are both aspects of the one Source. However, the energies have a different quality, and the techniques used to connect with them and work with them are quite different.

From his personal experience, alone in the Great Pyramid, Patrick knew that it was possible to connect with spiritual healing energy, the energy of Source, directly and spontaneously, without the presence or help of anyone else.

Although the presence of an intermediary may be of great benefit, it is not always. All of us have a tendency to give our power away to others, to look to others for advice, rather than seeking it from within ourselves. And many of us would like someone else to do the work for us!

Rather than playing an active part in our own healing process, we can too easily become merely passive recipients. Receiving a healing or an attunement from someone else may have extremely positive effects, and may lead to great personal breakthroughs. Yet we need to be constantly seeking to increase our own capabilities. Dependence can quickly develop, without us even realising it, and we may end up going along another person's path rather than finding the one that truly works for us.

In Reiki, the attunements are passed from one person to another, along with each particular Master's 'rules' about using the energy. This may limit the ways in which we actually use it, rather than encouraging us to explore our own possibilities for healing. Another person's beliefs and world-views are no substitute for finding our own intuitive guidance from within. To encourage you to trust yourself, and believe in your own wisdom and natural capacity to heal yourself is the greatest gift that any teacher can give.

Dr Usui never used the title 'Master', and it is not used in Japan even today; as it creates the impression that the person is an enlightened individual. Today, the term Master is used in the West, but in fact a Reiki Master is simply someone who can teach Reiki and pass on the Reiki attunements. It does not mean that he or she is necessarily enlightened, or does not have the same problems that we all have.

In Patrick's earliest experiences with the All-Love energy, visions of pure light were associated with the words, 'No Hierarchy.' In the All-Love system, therefore, there are no rules; each person is encouraged to experience and use the energy in whatever way seems most appropriate to him or her.

In keeping with this philosophy, the All-Love system does not place too much emphasis on the use of symbols. Instead, it uses visualisation, which works by focusing the conscious awareness and forming a clear intent. To invite the energy in, you visualise a brilliant sun, or source, sending its energy down to you. The ankh, which means breath of life, and the infinity symbols are visualised simply as a means of using the mind to enhance the flow of energy.

In contrast, in an attunement, a varying number of symbols are installed into a person's energy system in order to pass the energy. The person later draws the symbols to activate the energy and to use it in different ways. Symbols are useful in the initial stages, to help a person build confidence; though a person will often realise at some later point that energy can be sent at a distance, and that the energy flows regardless of whether s/he uses the symbols. It is then a personal choice as to whether they remain an integral part of working with the energy.

In All-Love meditations, each person visualises the energy entering from above, through the crown chakra; and from below, through the feet and up to the base chakra. This means that the energy is grounded throughout the body, and does not just enter the higher chakras. When the energies merge in the heart centre, the whole body is filled with energy.

Reiki, on the other hand, does not connect a person with the Earth, and therefore can be much less grounded. In the attunements, the central energy channel is opened from the crown chakra at the top of the head to the root chakra at the base of the spine. But only the solar plexus, the heart, the throat, the third eye, and the crown chakras are connected with the Reiki healing energy. This means that when the energy enters, it may simply stay in the top five chakras, and not be connected with the earth.

This can be a problem for those people who are 'up in their heads' a lot of the time. They experience a pleasant 'spaced-out' feeling when giving or receiving the energy, but, as they may already have difficulty being totally 'in this world' with their feet on the ground; they do not fully ground themselves or the energy.

In a meditation, there are usually some people who will 'go off somewhere' in their minds; they feel a sense of space and joy and freedom, and when they 'come back,' they are not sure what happened. They can experience the joy of the energy, in the mind, only by dissociating from the painful parts, in other words from the body and the emotions that contain that pain.

In the All-Love system, by focussing on bringing the energy into the whole body, we are constantly being brought back to the earth. This process requires that we engage fully in the moment. We do not 'go off somewhere' but stay where we really are and do the work we need to do. One of the ways by which we ground ourselves is to come out of our heads and into our hearts. To feel, and not to think.

If we open our hearts, we are going to feel what is truly there. If we open our minds, we are going to become consciously aware of what we feel. When we simultaneously open our hearts and our minds, we are going to experience pain and joy in clear consciousness; when this occurs in the presence of the energy, that is when we can spontaneously heal. With love, awareness, and healing energy, pain is transformed. At that moment, the energy is integrated into the whole of our being and we experience an initiation.

WHO NEEDS HEALING?

IT has only recently become possible to measure the energy emitted from a healer's hands; to photograph the aura; and to demonstrate and quantify the increased rate of growth of tissues given healing energy. Science has finally substantiated what people have experienced and reported for centuries about healing: that something is actually happening, and that it works. It can in fact help with many different physical and emotional symptoms and illnesses.

We all have the capacity to connect with the healing energy outside ourselves, the energy of the universe, which is a constant, limitless supply of energy. We can then receive energy for ourselves and give it to others.

The main reason that we do not use the healing energy that is available to all of us is that we simply do not realise that it exists. Or even if we do, we do not know how to connect with it.

Healing energy helps us enter into a calm, relaxed, meditative state and sets healing processes in motion. Our higher self, or the intuitive mind, directs the energy to be used in whatever way we need it.

Healing energy fills you with energy vibrating at a higher frequency, balancing the chakras and allowing any energy blockages to be freed. It decreases muscular tension and relaxes you. Physical problems may spontaneously resolve. When you are in pain, it deals not only with the evident pain, but also with the cause of that pain, even if you are not aware of the cause.

The energy relieves emotional pain, and helps you to process distressing emotions, without feeling overwhelmed by them. It facilitates the release of suppressed emotions, bringing buried feelings to the surface. However, it will only do this if you are ready to deal with these emotions; therefore it is ultimately you who determines your rate of change, albeit at a subconscious or intuitive level.

Healing energy helps us to accept those emotions and memories we have judged as unacceptable, and to integrate those parts of our personalities that we have rejected and hidden. It enables us to be in better contact with our own inner intuitive knowledge, and makes us more compassionate and forgiving towards others and ourselves.

Healing energy allows us to clear our energy pathways, to transform 'negative' energies and emotions, and to release pain; leading to a feeling of well-being, harmony and equilibrium.

Who doesn't need it?

How do I choose which healing system to use?

A friend of mine, a consultant physician, said that he had a Reiki 1 attunement over a year previously, but that since he had been connected with the energy, it did not seem to have made much difference.

I said, 'How often do you give yourself Reiki?'

'Hardly ever,' he said, 'I thought that just being connected with it made it work!'

No system of healing can work if you don't use it. Once you are connected with the energy, you have to put your hands on your body, give yourself treatments, or send energy to the cause of particular problems or issues. If you do not use it regularly, the energy you are able to channel probably will not become any stronger.

After an attunement, you have the energy, but it is quite possible that you don't really know what you can do with it. You may not know how to put the Reiki principles into practice. Worry and anger, for instance, do not just disappear when you channel the energy.

Training to Reiki Master Level does not mean that a person is trained in emotional healing techniques. It does not give that person the knowledge or experience to facilitate emotional healing for others. The energy itself may bring about emotional healing; but the Reiki teaching does not. For this reason, it is important to differentiate between the energy and the techniques used to work with the energy.

It is also important to search for your inner guidance and listen to your intuition. Trust yourself. If a particular teacher says more than s/he knows, or tries to influence you or gain power over you, then find another. A Reiki practitioner is merely a channel for the energy; s/he is not directing it. The recipient uses the energy according to his needs at that particular time, although both he and the practitioner may be unaware of those needs. We just do not know what the energy will bring about for another person, in terms of specific results, or the resolution of particular symptoms.

There are teachers, however, who wish to become more active in directing the energy. This may work, but it is not necessary. If healing occurs, it is the energy, which brings it about, in conjunction with the innate, intuitive healing capacity of that person's unconscious mind and body.

Given that we all have difficulty acknowledging what our problems are, and even more difficulty in knowing what exactly we need to do about them, then the choice of which system of healing we use will to a certain extent be simply trial and error.

Knowing this, if we are drawn to one particular system, it makes sense to try it. Having worked with it for some time, if it still does not answer our questions then it also makes sense to try another. In any event, different forms of healing, including Reiki and All-Love energy, work very well together. The energies, unlike people, do not seek to compare and compete.

The All-Love system is very straightforward. When you are able to receive it, the energy comes. This means that from the outset, you are involved in an interactive process; the energy works if you let it. You are not dependent on another individual, because it is through your own effort and inner work that you become more open to the energy. This will suit some people more than others.

In reality, there are very few things that we need to know.

The first is that we are all capable of connecting with the energy of Source.

The second is that if we are open, we can receive.

The third is that if we learn to trust ourselves, and do our inner work, then we can heal ourselves.

Finally, to benefit from any system, we do have to use it!

Beyond that, there really are no rules.

CHAPTER TWO

Healing the Mind, Body and Spirit

Introduction: The Aims

HEALING, in its widest sense, has been practised for thousands of years; for as long as illnesses have existed, people have tried to cure them.

For instance, touch is one of the most effective means of relieving pain. When the body is touched, stroked, or held in a loving way, it relaxes, and healing is facilitated. If a child hurts his knee, his mother rubs it better. If you have a stomach-ache, you instinctively put your hands on your belly. When you have a tension headache, a massage helps relieve the muscle spasm and pain.

Herbal medicine and homoeopathy have identified thousands of plants and natural substances that are effective remedies for a wide range of symptoms or maladies. In the last fifty years, pharmacology has made great advances, as more and more drugs have been discovered and developed to target different cells and tissues, and to influence specific physiological and pathological processes.

Modern medicine is a wonderful example of how, through exploration of the natural world, technology and science have together yielded the knowledge and the tools to genuinely serve mankind.

Technological advances in imaging and measurement have lead in recent times to the development of incredibly accurate diagnostic techniques and treatment methods. We know more now about the human body, both at a macroscopic and sub-cellular level, than we could at any previous point in history have ever imagined possible. Yet, despite this, medicine simply cannot cure many illnesses.

The fact is that we still do not know the whole story.

Medicine - A Personal Account: Graham

WHEN I was at medical school, in the late seventies, the mind-body duality dominated medical training. Illness was explained in terms of known physical cause and effect.

Emotions were seen as unrelated to physical sensations. Patients were not supposed to have feelings – and neither were doctors. For many people, being in hospital is one of the most traumatic experiences of their lives, yet at that time doctors were given little training in how to deal with that distress.

We studied systems, not people. We saw the MI in bed six, or the Ca bladder in bed twenty-three. We learned about the anatomy, physiology and pathology of the respiratory system, the cardiovascular system, and the nervous system. The human body was being broken down increasingly into separate parts, each dealt with by a particular speciality, and disease was viewed as a disturbance of an organ or a system, not as part of the total life experience of a human being.

When I graduated, I had no sense of interrelatedness, of how the thoughts, feelings, mind, and body of a person all interacted to produce this thing that we call illness.

If a person is unhappily struggling with emotional issues, then to treat his ulcer simply with a proton pump inhibitor may relieve his symptoms, but it's not going to solve his problems. If he's constantly worrying about how to take control of his life and stand up to people, then his ulcer's quite likely to recur, whatever the state of the hydrogen-potassium adenosine tri-phosphatase enzyme system of his gastric parietal cells. Given that thoughts and feelings can release chemical molecules into the bloodstream, which affect cells and tissues around the body, it might seem more productive to help him to express and modify some of those habitual thoughts and feelings.

But that wasn't the way I was taught. He was the gastric ulcer on omeprazole to be gastroscoped, not the middle-aged man with chronic anxiety, low self-esteem and an external locus of control. Certainly not the man experiencing repeated energy blocks in his solar plexus related to issues of personal power.

The point is that you can't explain someone's individual response to his own unique life experiences with any one model, whether medical, psychiatric or even energetic. A person is a whole being; he has a mind, a body and a spirit, he has thoughts, feelings, physical sensations, and energies, all of which are constantly changing, and any reductionist model inevitably neglects vital aspects of that whole. Things are just not as simple as we would like to believe.

Medicine taught us to be logical, scientific and objective: 'If you can't prove it, it's not there.' For both patients and doctors, the lack of a physical diagnosis was an embarrassment. On medical wards, psychosomatic meant you were a waste of a bed, a whacko, or you had wished it on yourself. Medical beds were for real illness.

Medicine and surgery mainly involved drugs and procedures; the doctor's role was to diagnose and treat illnesses, not to worry about how the illness affected a particular person's life, or what it meant to that person. Doctors simply didn't have the time to listen to people.

They viewed illness as something which happened to the body, not as a process evolving out of a person's own relationship with himself, the world and life itself. Death was the ultimate treatment failure. And nobody wanted to talk about that.

I was always fascinated by the process of looking at people's symptoms and finding out what was causing them. In medicine, every patient is different, and you never know who is going to come through the door. I liked the fact that you're always learning. I also used to enjoy teaching medical students and junior doctors, not just to diagnose and treat illnesses, but to respect patients too. I liked to explain the choices to people, and get them as involved as possible in the management of their own condition.

However, I realised increasingly that, although people wanted medicine to cure them that's not what usually happened. Many people who came to see me were hoping that I could give them a drug, which would simply make their problems go away. I was confident that I could help, and it was always a great joy to see their symptoms decrease or disappear. The majority of my patients did improve, but they had to continue taking drugs; they often suffered side effects from the medication, and they frequently continued to experience some symptoms.

In fact, things were far more complicated than just a straightforward cycle of physical cause and effect. Many conditions are chronic, and the majority of illnesses are still classified as essential or idiopathic, which really means we just don't know the cause.

Medicine at that time simply explained illness from the point of view of pathological processes within the body. The link had not yet been made between a person's physical, emotional and energy systems. Years later, I realised that pain can arise from emotional symptoms, and physical symptoms can result from energetic blocks. But I didn't know that at the time.

No one in medicine ever really talked about emotions: they were seen as a sign of weakness. We used to joke that all illnesses were caused by one of two things: lack of dietary fibre or lack of moral fibre!

Shortly before I retired, I was in hospital myself, with a broken leg. I was waiting for an operation, I was upset, in pain, and at one point I started crying; it was promptly suggested I should be referred to a psychiatrist! Evidently, emotions were equated not just with weakness but with madness too.

Working with energy in recent times has allowed me to see that the physical, mental, emotional and energetic systems are all related, and must all be taken into account when considering a given individual's symptoms. A person plays an important part in his own illness, and his own recovery. But when I was practising medicine, that is not the way things were viewed. Medicine in those days treated people as if they were machines, and doctors were the mechanics.

The responsibility for diagnosis and management of illness fell completely upon the doctor, who ordered investigations, procedures and treatments and advised a patient what to do. The patient often didn't really understand what was going on, and was not involved to any great extent in the decisions made about his own treatment. In other words, the old medical model viewed illness as a physical process that happened to a patient, rather than an individual person's response to the inner and outer factors and events that occurred within his or her life.

Fortunately, this view is now changing.

I practised medicine for fourteen years in the Royal Air Force. After a year in General Practice, I moved to hospital medicine, and became a consultant physician specialising in General Medicine and Chest Medicine. My final rank was Wing Commander; I was Commanding Officer of the RAF Chest Unit, and Consultant Advisor in Chest Medicine to the Director General of the Medical Services (RAF).

I think it's fair to say I was pretty left-brained. I was a perfectionist, I tended to see things as black and white, and I liked to be in control of myself - and the situation. I didn't spend too much time worrying what I was feeling, or what my patients were feeling. I just got on with my job.

Perhaps unsurprisingly, I didn't really begin to change my views about medicine until I became ill myself. My real crisis came when medicine didn't work for me!

When I retired, at the age of thirty-eight, I developed a stomach ulcer. I had pain for several months, and tried various treatments on my own, then finally went to see a physician, who did an endoscopy and started me on the latest drugs. The pain continued. He suggested meditation. I thought I had misheard, as I was already taking medication. But I put a lot of faith in doctors, as many people do – and I was desperate— so, although it all sounded a bit bizarre to me, I tried it.

After meditating thirty minutes twice a day for ten days, my symptoms disappeared!

It was the first time in my life that I had given myself the opportunity to truly listen to my body and my thoughts. I started to feel better in all sorts of ways. I realised that I had always worried a lot. I was very critical of myself, and often took a negative reading on other people's actions. Even more surprising to me, I became aware that I had cut myself off from my own feelings.

Those things didn't change in ten days, but somehow, just giving myself time made the difference. It was about then that I realised that my doctor was not treating the ulcer, but the whole patient! The holistic approach was a completely new concept for me.

Several years passed and I continued with the meditation and without any symptoms. However, meditating led to experiences like seeing energy and feeling I was leaving my body.

I then did a psychic awareness and mediumship workshop, and was amazed to find that I was able to contact spirits. What surprised me the most was that when people died, a part of them survived, but there was no sudden transformation; their problems did not miraculously go away. That made me think I had better start sorting out my problems now!

I began having Reiki treatments. I was sceptical, but the first time the Reiki Master put her hand on my chest, I felt an incredible heat. I knew that something powerful was happening. Shortly afterwards, I was on holiday in Scotland, and a friend had a pain in his elbow, so I thought I would try healing. My hands felt hot, and so did his elbow, and the pain disappeared. I then decided to take a Reiki 1 course, as I wanted to understand more about what was happening, and to be able to set it into some sort of context.

I began to feel when there was a problem with one of my chakras. I also started feeling the same sort of sensation in my body when someone I was giving a treatment to had a blockage in one of their chakras. This became quite intrusive, to the point where I was noticing what was happening to other people when just talking to them, so I learned to switch it on and off.

I also began to wonder what caused a blockage. They often seemed to be due to unexpressed thoughts and emotions. These blockages affect the function of the chakra, the aura, and the free flow of energy; they slowly work their way in from the more subtle energy levels of the aura and after years may begin to give physical symptoms. Therefore, if we can deal with these blockages early, then we should be able to prevent certain physical symptoms and illness. Now, I can see that aspects of my own thinking and behaviour had been negative for over twenty years, long before I started getting symptoms, and this had certainly contributed to my condition.

I had always had difficulty in expressing my emotions, and felt afraid of being overwhelmed by them. When I was initiated in Reiki, I suddenly discovered that I had the ability and power to actually help myself. Not just with physical pain, but also with emotional pain. Reiki helped me to focus on, and take responsibility for, my own feelings and experiences. I liked the fact that I could do it for myself, and was not dependent on anyone else. It gave me a feeling of inner strength that I had never felt before. In addition, it enabled me to be less serious, laugh more, and enjoy life more.

I started learning Tai Chi, joined a dream group, and became a Reiki, Karuna and Seichim Master. The more I worked with the energy, the more I found that my life was changing. Instead of looking outside myself for my sense of identity and purpose, I was spending much more time looking within. Realising the connection between thoughts, feelings, energies, and physical sensations, I began to be aware of myself on many different levels.

I learned various energy and healing techniques, including psychic and intuitive work, dream techniques, toning, and focusing into the body, and began to use them in all areas of my life, to facilitate emotional – and physical – healing. Not just to deal with pain, but to enhance the joy.

When I first attended one of Patrick's workshops, I realised that my idea of working with energy fitted his All-Love system much more closely than it did the traditional Reiki systems of teaching. I was amazed at the sense of love and connectedness that came not just from experiencing the All-Love energy, but also from within the group.

It always feels like a miracle to see people open up to energy for the first time, whether through Reiki or All-Love. To me, the two energies do feel different, although they complement each other wonderfully, and are clearly aspects of the same Source. But I had a stronger connection with the energy, and felt more love, in the All-Love initiations than in any Reiki attunements I had experienced.

In the All-Love system, you have the opportunity to heal during the workshop. The teacher can help you to express and release emotions, and you have the support of the group, which makes it easier, but you still have to do your own work, and I like this, because I feel that we all have to take responsibility for our own process and our own development.

I am now an All-Love teacher, and I use Reiki and All-Love energy on a daily basis, both in my personal growth and healing and for others. I also continue to have a lot of faith in conventional medicine.

The holistic approach means that things don't have to be one or the other. There is room for all. Conventional and complementary medicine both has a great deal to offer, used separately or together.

Having spent most of my life predominantly using my left-brain, I genuinely thought I didn't have a right brain. I realise now that a lot of work in medicine is in fact done at a purely intuitive level, I just didn't give credit to my intuition for the vital part that it was playing all those years.

Thinking clearly and objectively doesn't mean you can't be intuitive. Expressing your feelings doesn't mean you're weak - or mad!

When you recognise and honour all aspects of yourself - your mind, body, and spirit – you begin to find your own balance. In addition, as your thinking becomes less black and white, the world begins to look a lot more colourful.

PSYCHIATRY - A PERSONAL ACCOUNT: TERESA

THROUGHOUT my life, I've known what it was like to be out of balance.

I came from parents who lived their lives from different ends of the spectrum. One was a thinking-type introvert and the other a sensing-feeling-type extravert. I always felt that I was hovering somewhere in the middle, unable to please both.

Looking back, I have my parents to thank that they could never really see the other's point of view, because the tension generated by that polarity between the mind, the need to understand, and the heart, the need to truly feel, propelled me to seek a way to integrate the two. It's not that difficult to see why I tended to go from one extreme to the other - or why I had to become a psychiatrist in order to learn to talk about thoughts and feelings in the same sentence.

At medical school, the mind/body and thoughts/feelings duality was further accentuated. As medical students, we had to learn an immense number of indigestible and seemingly unrelated facts. We were all pretty arrogant, intense and convinced that we could save the world. As we spent more time on the wards, and came into contact with people who were sick and in pain, we didn't really know how to cope. Medicine is very competitive, and no one wanted to appear weak or inadequate.

Feelings were a bit of a nuisance. Facts were much more dependable. Almost imperceptibly, we became increasingly left-brained, out of balance, and emotionally unavailable. During the day, we hid our feelings behind our white coats, and in the evenings, we drank or sat in our rooms cramming in a few more facts.

We came to see patients increasingly as problems to be solved. Physical pathology was diagnosed and treated, but no one asked patients why they thought they were ill, or how they felt about what was happening to them.

Gradually I realised that no one was going to ask me how I felt either. As a houseman, the first time I saw someone die, after the resuscitation failed, everyone walked off, cleaned up and got on with their job. Choking back tears, I went to tell the relatives - without a clue what to say.

Although most doctors tend to judge psychiatrists as a sandwich short of a picnic, I realised that psychiatry was the only place I was going to be able to talk about feelings – my own or anyone else's.

Psychiatry was fascinating. It was the first time that I had heard people openly and honestly talk about themselves, their feelings and experiences. I had the opportunity to talk to people about what concerned them, and to hear how they explained their symptoms and problems.

I was intrigued to find out how people's minds worked. I still remember the excitement I felt just sitting and listening to people. I began to realise how much our thoughts and feelings define our reality. I began to see how important it was to bring our minds, our hearts, and our bodies into balance. To do that, we have to look very carefully, at what we think, say, and feel, day-to-day, minute-by-minute.

In Medicine, I had come to hide not just behind my white coat but also my words. Voltaire said that 'Man uses words only to disguise his thoughts.' Maybe we should add: 'and to conceal his feelings.'

My first tutor, when I started training in psychiatry, was an internationally acclaimed authority on suicide, and a very kind and brilliant man. Whenever I said something, he would say, 'What do you mean by that?' He would sit and wait patiently while I tied myself in knots trying to justify what I had previously said without a thought. Sometimes it would really annoy me, and I would have to go away and think about it for a week before I could creep back and say, 'Well, actually I meant something else.' He knew the power of words - to inspire, or to deflate, to enlighten or to confuse. He taught me that everything we say has the capacity to affect the thoughts and feelings of those around us. A word can make the difference between life and death. He helped me to be aware of, and to take responsibility for, what I was actually saying.

Communication is the crux of the therapeutic relationship between doctor and patient. Many patients don't really understand what is going on; they are anxious, they feel upset and vulnerable, and they are dependent on a person in authority. In many respects it's just like being a child again. It's not surprising that they hand over responsibility to the doctor to sort them out.

Yet how can a person trust you if he doesn't understand what you're saying? How can he feel you care if you're constantly avoiding right-brained feelings by using left-brained verbal jargon? There's enough of it, after all; there are over fifty thousand basic medical terms, most of which are largely incomprehensible to the majority of people.

I began to realise that therapy depends far more on the personal characteristics and skills of the therapist than on particular techniques. As the song goes, 'It ain't what you do, it's the way that you do it.' At a visceral level, people sense if you're genuine or not.

I'm certain that I learned as much from my patients as they ever did from me. In those days, I could barely see what was going on in my own life. I would just keep drawing the exact same situations to me, repeating the same behaviour, feeling the same pain. And all the while trying to 'help' other people deal with theirs.

In order to help people to understand themselves better, you have to be willing to examine your own thoughts and feelings.

To help them to become more open and honest, you yourself have to be able to engage with others emotionally. And you have to like yourself. I gradually began to be aware how difficult all those things were.

Like many people, I didn't really want to admit that I had any problems. Nevertheless, at an unconscious level, I must have been drawn to psychiatry partly to find a way of solving them. Consciously, I thought I simply had to learn how to be a psychiatrist, as if that was something that could be learned from a book. But unconsciously, without realising it, I was also being propelled on my own personal journey. Reading and studying were very absorbing, and I could stay safely in my mind. However, in the face of raw emotion and anguish, words and theories aren't much use. Listening to people and feeling their pain forced me out of my head and into my heart.

What struck me was that so many people had suffered such pain. So many people were living in fear, poverty, loneliness, and misery. So many had experienced neglect, violence, and abuse. The majority of those with serious mental illness had experienced traumas that would quite literally drive anyone mad. But perhaps more alarming was the fact that it wasn't just the people who had experienced gross trauma and abuse who were depressed, desperate and in crisis.

One in ten people see a psychiatrist at some point in their lives. Some of those have serious, definable mental illness. But there are also many people whose lives are simply not adding up; who feel completely lost. They worry, they are angry and frustrated, and they never seem to feel truly happy or at peace. They know there's something missing, yet they don't know what it is. Some of these people see a psychiatrist; many more don't. The longer I worked in psychiatry, the more I realised that emotional turmoil and mental confusion, far from being limited to a minority, were actually pretty much the norm. There are many people who are not in contact with their feelings, they don't understand how their thoughts affect their lives, and they have no sense of their own spiritual centre. They're simply not aware of their own potential, and they're not living their lives to the full.

Plenty of attractive, educated, successful people, who I would have looked at from afar and admired or even envied, used to come into my office and break down in tears. They just didn't have anyone in their lives who would listen to all the things they needed to say; or to challenge the front they tried so hard to maintain.

Yet, however much they suffered, most people were extremely reluctant to ask for help. Most of us want to pretend we're fine, we don't have any problems, and we don't need to do any work on ourselves. That's the game we've been playing for so long we've ended up believing it. If you're unhappy, there must be something wrong with you. So who's going to own up to anything?

People say, 'I had a really happy childhood, my parents were fantastic, I've got a lovely wife and kids, a nice house, and my job's great.'

Yeah, and I look like Claudia Schiffer, write like Shakespeare and was Cleopatra in a past life.

In a world where the best, fastest, and biggest is the most desirable, where beauty, wealth and success are the yardsticks by which we are all measured, it's not surprising that no one goes round boasting how it feels to be poor, miserable, or in pain.

There is still a huge stigma attached to seeing a psychiatrist, yet some of the basic tools used in psychiatry – learning to identify and express your emotions, learning to relax, learning to manage your anger and to assert yourself, and learning to like yourself more – would benefit us all. Most of us could use a bit more self-esteem.

Of course, nowadays, there are many different things on offer; pop psychology, New Age, life coaching, Self-help and How-to books on everything from being a better parent to getting more sex. People are finally realising that life itself, just existing, interacting with others and living through your own moods and personal crises, is not easy. We're at last able to say we're hurt, we're unhappy and we'd like things to change, without being seen as some kind of nut.

But even just twenty years ago, that was not the case at all. People were frightened. They were not particularly happy, yet they struggled on, thinking that they couldn't do anything about it, and that they could not expect any more from life.

I know that for years I was anxious, self-conscious, and intensely lonely at times. I was desperate to please others rather than genuinely be myself. I had great difficulty expressing my true feelings, knowing what I wanted, and stating my own needs. I liked to think of myself as reasonably sorted-out, self-aware, and symptom-free, but in fact, I was pretty much jumbled, uncomfortable and confused.

Now, I know that a lot of people feel the same way too. But then I didn't. I never talked about it because no one else ever talked about it. Everyone was desperately trying to make out they were 'normal;' to create the impression that they were coping, having fun, and that everything was ok.

This concept of normality is one of the things that work most powerfully to keep us where we are. It took me a long time to grapple with it. In psychiatry, I was fascinated to find out what constituted 'madness.' It struck me that you could only talk about what was abnormal if you had a clear idea of what was normal. What thoughts go through a person's head in a day? How many changes of mood does he experience? What does his happiness feel like? How much does his pain hurt? What are his relationships like?

Psychology talked a lot about rats and conditioning; psychiatry talked about neurophysiology and pharmacology, but the basic facts - about what it was like to be a human being, with a mind, body, emotions and spirit - nobody really seemed to know.

Many mentally ill people are viewed with prejudice and suspicion. They look odd, they say weird things, they often don't work, and they don't behave in a socially acceptable way. People are embarrassed by them, maybe because they reflect aspects of themselves which they do not want to see, or perhaps simply because they don't fit in.

I found many mentally ill people to be likeable, imaginative and ingenuous. They blurt things out, they say what they feel, they're spontaneous, direct, and uninhibited. The normal controls simply aren't operating. Which can lead to problems, not just in the outside world, but also in how they are able to make sense of their inner world.

The fact is that the society we live in does not place much value on the things of the mind, the emotions and the spirit – in other words, on the inner world of the individual. It focuses instead on the physical and the material, on appearance, money and possessions. We have come to accept as normal a way of life that fosters greed and egotism rather than personal values such as love and honesty; that demands productivity and conventionality rather than creativity and individualism.

So we're actually all in trouble. Our socialisation leads us to ignore our inner world, yet how then can we be truly happy? Depression, anxiety, addiction, lack of self-esteem and a sense of pointlessness are symptoms of mental illness, but they can also be seen as symptoms of an age of disenchantment, in other words as social, not mental illness. The society we are living in, as a whole, is not actually conducive to mental health. In many respects, psychiatry is just the stopgap arrangement. It plasters over the cracks when we should all, collectively and individually, be rebuilding the foundations.

In order to be happy and at peace, to find our true purpose in life, we have to be ourselves – and that is not easy. We all live with contradictions and ambivalent feelings. We all have to deal with the conflict between what we really are inside (our true self) and what we show to the external world (our pseudo-self). We all need to face these issues at some point in our lives.

I often used to wonder how patients actually got better. At times, of course, drugs played an important part, but often it would be possible to stabilise people and help them to recover merely by showing interest, seeing them frequently, and talking to them about whatever they needed to talk about.

When people are genuinely listened to— and given space to be themselves, when they are treated with compassion and respect, they are encouraged to find their own inner resources. For a person to work on him or herself takes an enormous amount of courage and energy. Yet, we all have the innate potential and drive towards growth. All of us can heal ourselves. Many people came in crisis or pain or desperation, and, in the resulting condition of honesty and humility, they opened themselves to grace. That is when healing came about. In psychiatry, we didn't call it that, but that's what was happening.

HOW EMOTIONAL HEALING TECHNIQUES DEVELOPED

THE Greek word *psyche* means life, soul or mind; *iatros* means healer. The term psychiatry was first used by Johann Christian Reil (1759-1813), an anatomist, a religious man and a mystic. Tom Walmsley writes: 'It is quite clear what he had in mind: a new kind of medical treatment in which the doctor used his psyche as the therapeutic agent.'[1]

Historically, not just psychiatry, but medicine, philosophy, religion, and latterly psychology and science have been searching for ways to better understand the human condition and to explain the meaning of consciousness.

We are all a product of our own history. In fact, it is the past, which holds the key to the present. Both in individual terms, the legacy of our own personal memories, experiences, patterns and programmes, and in collective terms, the universal knowledge handed down through time in stories, myths, and gospels. Discovering where we have come from, we understand where we are. In this sense, therapy is history in the unmaking.

FREUD: WHY ARE WE ALL NEUROTIC?

IT'S almost impossible to imagine how anyone else is feeling; unless you ask them. Sigmund Freud (1856-1939) was one of the first people ever to do that. An Austrian neurologist and psychiatrist, and one of the most brilliant and innovative thinkers of modern times, he founded psychoanalysis based on what his patients told him.

Freud simply listened to people talking about themselves, their dreams, their thoughts, their feelings and fantasies. His method of free association encouraged a person to talk about whatever came into his mind, openly and honestly, without censoring anything.

From this, he made some exciting discoveries. Firstly, that if you let people talk long enough, they will tell you what's wrong with them. Everything they say leads in some way to the core issues. Secondly, that psychological symptoms - such as anxiety and depression - occur for a reason. They mask emotional traumas that have not been resolved. Thirdly, Freud realised that we actually benefit in some way from our symptoms. The primary gain is that these symptoms help us to avoid things that we do not want to face. The secondary gain is the attention or advantages that we gain from others through our symptoms.

He came to see that almost without exception, patients were avoiding, or rather, were simply unable to consciously access, vast areas of unresolved emotional distress. In 1895, he put forward the idea that we automatically defend ourselves against painful thoughts, memories, and emotions by excluding them from conscious awareness, by making them unconscious. We repress things that have hurt us.

And we also repress things we think we should not feel such as certain sexual, violent, or destructive urges which have come to be associated with guilt and shame. In other words, we are routinely denying and suppressing powerful emotions and indeed entire parts of ourselves in order to fit in with what is socially acceptable.

It is not just psychiatrically disturbed patients with problems who repress their emotions: it is all of us. Repression is a universal phenomenon, which causes problems universally. We cannot constantly push feelings down without them re-emerging somewhere in our lives. They can emerge as neurotic symptoms such as anxiety or obsession, as moods, or simply as strongly held irrational beliefs. For example, a man may express a strong opinion about all women being untrustworthy, without realising that this belief arose from his own sense of betrayal and abandonment by his mother as a child.

As Freud himself wrote, 'How neurotic our whole civilised life is.'[2] In other words, how repressed we all are. Neurosis is a word that simply means a symptom or group of symptoms that is distressing to the individual. Nearly everyone has neurotic symptoms such as anxiety and depression at some time. In a significant minority, a constellation of symptoms produces a neurotic disorder. However, there is no loss of contact with reality. This distinguishes it from psychosis - more serious mental disorder such as schizophrenia and manic depression - which does involve a loss of contact with reality.

Freud came to see that there was no clear boundary between 'health' and 'illness.' We all have inner conflict between what we would like to do and what we think we ought to do, between the parts of us that can express themselves and those that cannot. Most of us repress these conflicts to such an extent that we are not even aware that they are there. It is only when we feel sufficiently bad, when our inner turmoil finally produces symptoms, which we cannot ignore, that we admit that we have any problems. This is the point at which we finally become disturbed. But it is an arbitrary point.

David Smith writes: 'Disturbed people know that they are disturbed but do not know what, at bottom, is disturbing them. The normal person is not conscious of any disturbance. The Freudian psychotherapist seeks to help a person become more self-aware than those who are normal, and better able to cope with this awareness than those who are disturbed.' [3]

At the time, Freud's discoveries themselves were startling and disturbing. Yet, they had far-reaching effects, and the vast majority of psychologically effective therapies currently used today draw upon at least some elements of his work.

Freudian therapy allows people to express their thoughts and feelings, to discover things that they have been concealing, and to integrate parts of themselves, which they have disowned. It acts, in other words, 'to make the unconscious conscious.'

'The therapist must spend long periods quietly listening; he does not offer advice on how clients should live their lives, and does not play the role of expert or 'guru.' The basic Freudian skills are creating an atmosphere of safety and keeping out of the client's way… to create a situation in which clients can authentically be themselves without fear of censure or interference.' [4]

JUNG: THE LINK BETWEEN PSYCHOLOGY AND SPIRITUALITY

CARL Jung (1875-1961) was a Swiss psychiatrist who collaborated with Freud from 1907, but then broke away from him in 1913 to develop his own system of analytical psychology.

Jung's most exciting discovery was the coexistence of the personal and the collective unconscious. The personal unconscious, or shadow, contains repressed personal material. The collective unconscious contains a transpersonal dimension. It is a source of images and symbols, of creativity and intuitive wisdom, which can access the knowledge of the Universe.

A religious and deeply spiritual man, Jung was fascinated by the interrelationship of the mind, body and spirit. He saw the psyche as dynamic, in constant movement. To him, the aim of therapy, indeed of life, was becoming whole, realising one's innate potential; he called this process individuation, and viewed it as an ongoing spiritual journey. So much so that he said that 'he had never seen a patient past the age of thirty-five who was cured without finding a religious attitude to life.' [5]

'He sometimes compared his work to Gnosticism. One of its teachings is that initially there was a primordial oneness of all reality and existence and that there is an inherent longing for a return to this unity. The Gnostics also held that wisdom comes through direct experience leading to individual insight rather than through received dogma backed up by authority.'[6]

Jung believed that the individual is linked inextricably with the rest of mankind by archetypal figures, which have symbolic significance and occur in dreams, myths and intuitive images throughout history, all over the world. He described various archetypes. The persona is the mask or false self we present to the world, which hides our true identity. The anima is the unconscious feminine element of a man, while the animus is the unconscious masculine element of a woman. Other archetypes include the old wise man; the earth mother; and the Self, a new centre of personality, which is balanced, integrated and whole.

When we are suffering from distressing neurotic symptoms, our psyche produces – for example in dreams - archetypal images which help us to see the conflicts which are unconsciously being played out, so that we can begin to consciously address the underlying issues.

One of the techniques, which Jung frequently used, was active imagination, which he described as dreaming with open eyes. Frieda Fordham writes: 'Many of the dream figures recurred; Jung gave them names and talked to them even when awake, because he thought that a new aspect of his personality was trying to form itself and become part of his conscious life and he tried to assist the process in this way............

'Talking to the dream images was a method Jung evolved for dealing with them: in this way he tried to link them up with his conscious viewpoint; at the same time he took them seriously enough to allow them to modify or alter this if it seemed necessary. He also made conscious efforts to evoke imagery, especially when he found himself in an inexplicably disturbed state; he found that if he could crystallize an image, i.e. find a psychic representation for his emotion, he was immediately relieved and calmed. The image also gave him some means of understanding what gave rise to the emotion or what it meant.' [7]

'In Jung's view, every neurosis has an aim; it is an attempt to compensate for a one-sided attitude to life, and a voice, as it were, drawing attention to a side of personality that has been neglected or repressed.' [8] In other words, although symptoms may have originated in the past, they are also linked with changes that have to be made in the present. Jung was always looking beyond symptoms to the purpose and meaning they had in a person's life.

Anxiety or depression often occurs when something in our life has to change. We begin to feel dissatisfied, unhappy; no longer fulfilled, for instance in a relationship which we need to end. We try to ignore these feelings at first, because we want things to remain as they were. Nevertheless, in fact, they have already changed. We become withdrawn, preoccupied, focussed inwards as we struggle with the implications of those feelings. Gradually, we become consciously aware of what those feelings are about, and what we are going to have to do about them. At this point, if we act, that is, if we leave the relationship, we know it is going to take effort, energy, and will probably involve emotional upset. We are going to need some time to adjust to a new state of being, to recover our equilibrium. If we do not act, the dissatisfaction and unhappiness persist, and it is quite likely that the anxiety or depression will become chronic.

Once we are consciously aware of the conflict within ourselves, we have no further need of the symptoms: they have served their purpose, which was to make us listen to our inner feelings and act according to our need. Each time that we become more aware of our true nature, or identify more clearly our inner needs, we experience conflict between the part of us that wants to change and the part that resists this. It is only by experiencing this paradox: of two conflicting feelings existing simultaneously, that we grow into our next stage of awareness.

To achieve individuation, a person must come to some understanding and resolution, or creative synthesis, of the many paradoxes, or opposites within human experience— for example good and evil, arrogance and inferiority, creativity and destructiveness. S/he must also come to accept all aspects of him or herself.

To accept ourselves, we have to know ourselves, and much of Jung's work was aimed at helping people to identify certain characteristics within themselves. People differ in their attitude to the world, and their ways of functioning within it. His scale measuring attitude ranges from extroversion to introversion. Extroverts 'tend to focus on the outer world ... they need to experience the world in order to understand it and thus tend to like action. Introverts focus more on their inner world. They like to understand the world before experiencing it, and so often think about what they are doing before acting.'[9]

'There are four functions which we use to orientate ourselves in the world (and also to our own inner world): sensation, which is perception through our senses; thinking, which gives meaning and understanding; feeling, which weighs and values; and intuition, which tells of future possibilities and gives us information of the atmosphere which surrounds all our experience.[10] Each of us tends to rely on one or two more differentiated functions; we develop these and almost completely ignore the others, so we need to work with the function we find most difficult. For example, I consciously use mainly intuition and thinking, so I feel comfortable with them. Sensation and feeling are more difficult. To me they are unfamiliar and slightly uncomfortable. I am less conscious of them, and therefore trying to focus on sensing and feeling brings up all sorts of unconscious emotions. Jung found that, 'a great deal can be learned from the least differentiated function.'[11]

Becoming whole means moving away from the extremes within our personalities; finding a balance between different aspects of ourselves. As we develop the Self, we become more adept at dealing with our emotions and conflicts, and more aware of transpersonal values and energies, which lead to a sense of oneness with all of life. As Edinger writes, 'The Self is the point where God and man meet.'[12]

Fordham writes, 'The aim of therapy ... is for the patient to explore the latent possibilities in himself, to find out what kind of a person he really is, and to learn to live accordingly.......

'The emphasis lies not on "treatment," but on the relationship between analyst and patient, for neither knows the answer or can predict the outcome.......

'Jung has likened this meeting of two personalities to the contact of two chemical substances; if there is any reaction both are transformed.'[13]

Gerhard Adler said the therapist must have what he called 'the four H's: honesty, humanity, humility and humour.'[14] He must also have been through his own personal therapy in order to understand his own shadow; otherwise, patients will simply trigger his own unhealed wounds.

PERLS: 'ALL THERAPY IS PLAY.'[15]

FRITZ Perls (1893-1970) was a German neuropsychiatrist and psychoanalyst who, with his wife Laura, founded Gestalt Therapy, the word Gestalt meaning form or shape.

When we look at an incomplete circle, we see it as a whole; automatically, the mind completes the image. The view in Gestalt therapy is that the same is true of all personal experiences; we naturally attempt to organise our perceptions and thoughts into wholes. Like in a child's dot-to-dot picture, when the pattern is completed, separate parts are integrated, and the experience is concluded; the cycle of that gestalt has ended.

In fact, most of the time, our gestalts are interrupted before their cycles are completed. This means that most of our business is unfinished; there is no closure, which is not only unsatisfying but can also be disturbing. It's like rushing around trying to do ten different tasks, being distracted from each, and ending up not finishing any of them.

'Health' is seen as the ability to respond creatively in the present; rather than hanging on to old patterns, or 'fixed gestalts.' The person is seen as a whole, constantly changing, continuously moving towards a state of greater balance and equilibrium.

Feeling states are complex and difficult to accurately describe. When we experience a feeling, it is actually a combination of a physical sensation in the body and an emotion. Yet, many people are not consciously aware either of their physical sensations, or their thoughts and feelings. They do not take much notice of the messages that their bodies are giving them, and they do not necessarily relate physical tension or discomfort in particular areas with accompanying emotions.

'A Gestalt therapist will want most to observe how aware a person is of his own process – i.e. of the current direction of his interest, bodily state, physical and social needs, and how capable he is of externalising his inner experience.'[16]

Gestalt therapy is concerned with how we each recognise our needs, and how, through the formation and completion of a gestalt cycle, those needs are fulfilled. This process consists of various stages.

'Recognition of the dominant need or imbalance rests on the person's being able to sense and feel and then to allow these feelings and sensations into awareness. To explain why may be less important than noticing and acting on the need, the somatic truth, of her experience. Many people need to be invited to recognise bodily sensations – they do not naturally notice them or attend to them 'consciously.'

'The person mobilises himself, using physical energy … to take action. The next stage is when the person is fully engaged in whatever she needs to do; she is sensorily, emotionally and physically involved … concentrating on what she is doing. At some point, engagement may reach a high point of 'final contact' after which she stops. The need has dissipated. Then follows a crucial stage of integrating, or taking in fully, what has happened. This is often the time when there are cognitive insights … or she may simply be noticing with relief the loss of felt tension.

'The final stage involves letting go; it is marked by loss of interest and concentration, the end of the cycle of this gestalt, and a return to equilibrium in which temporarily no need or imbalance is registered. The person is clearly satisfied … she may experience a temporary 'void,' a time of natural quietness and lack of particular focus.'[17]

The cycle may be interrupted, or get stuck, at any of these stages; with the result, that the initial drive or need is not fulfilled. We each tend to acquire our own particular sticking points, therefore understanding the necessary flow of a gestalt shows us ways in which we can modify our attitudes or behaviour in order to allow it to emerge, complete, and finally dissolve.

For example, I talk with my boss. He says something, which I take to be critical. I feel upset, and become anxious. I do not tell him my point of view, and later I get a headache and feel in a bad mood. I have interrupted the cycle right at the start; at the point at which I become aware of my feelings of upset, I tell myself 'He thinks I'm useless, he won't listen.' I don't act to explain the situation. I want to get the conversation over as quickly as possible, so I don't engage fully. Later, when I have the headache, I take an aspirin and don't ask myself what it is about, so I don't get any insight. The next day I suddenly think of what I should have said to him, but he is away for a week and when he gets back, I have 'forgotten' all about it. There are two gestalts here, both of which are still incomplete, so my needs in each have not been met. The first is the external situation; I did not clarify things with my boss. The second is my internal situation; I did not explore my anxiety about criticism or my tension headache. In fact, everything is connected, and our interactions with the external world are constantly affecting our internal responses.

In Gestalt, the relationship between a person and a situation is described as the 'contact boundary.' We have different ways of maintaining our boundaries:

We may tend to take in (introject) everything that comes at us, or reject most of it.

We may tend to constantly hold our feelings in, or we may be unable to contain them, crying or getting in a rage at the slightest provocation.

If we do not own our own feelings, then we project them onto others, in which case we are not distinguishing clearly between others and ourselves.

In relation to a group, we may be too much of an 'insider' and lose our own identity, or we may find it hard to relate to others and always feel an 'outsider.'

If our boundaries are too rigid, we are unlikely to satisfactorily connect with others, or to the situations we find ourselves in. If our boundaries are flexible, we can sometimes let go and sometimes hold back; we can express our feelings when appropriate, and control them when appropriate. The whole point is to develop a range of possible strategies or behaviours rather than always using the same ones. The more we unconsciously repeat old habits, the more we are living in the past.

Living in the moment, being fully present in the here and now, means being adaptable and responsive, being aware of ourselves and our feelings, recognising our needs, and being able to choose how we act and react at any point in time: it is in fact living consciously.

The gestalt cycle is the prototype for our experiences in life and therefore the means by which a therapist helps a client to extend his repertoire of possible responses and gain more satisfaction from his life. Therapy reinforces and accelerates our own natural capacities for learning and growth. 'Beisser, 1970, says that change occurs when a person becomes what he is, not when he tries to become what he is not.'[18]

'Even though a person's pattern of disturbed functioning may have originated in the past, the manifestation of the disturbance is played out and witnessed in the present, and can only be undone (deconstructed) by first living it in the present and changing it in the present.'[19] In this way, fixed gestalts are freed.

The focus in a gestalt therapy session is on current experience – the 'what and how' rather than the 'why.' The person is encouraged to become aware of what he is feeling – mentally, physically, emotionally and energetically. Firstly, through the bodily 'felt sense.' We do not tend to notice our non-verbal behaviour: for instance, a man might clench his fists every time he talks of his father, or when talking about her depression a woman might hunch over. The therapist notices the person's non-verbal behaviour and body posture, and draws his attention to it; he might get him to repeat or exaggerate certain movements or positions in order to expand the feelings associated with them. On the other hand, he might ask the person to try out the opposite body stance, in order to notice the difference in feeling and energy between the two positions. The aim is to help the person to become more aware of how physical sensations and feeling states are linked.

'Individuals are effectively acquiring a "biofeedback system:" by more accurately attuning themselves to their actual physical and emotional experience, moment by moment, they can recognise more accurately when they are tensing up, withdrawing, suppressing a feeling. Further, with this additional information, they can choose to relax, breathe differently, speak out or withdraw, or whatever they need to do in order to feel more balanced and satisfied.'[20] The person begins to see how emotional tension is held in the body; by bringing awareness into that part of the body, relaxing, breathing into that area, and allowing the emotion greater expression, perhaps by giving it a voice, s/he can experience the emotion more fully and release the associated physical tension.

We often avoid our feelings or interrupt our awareness of what is going on inside us by holding our breath, becoming tense, changing the subject, or distracting our attention in numerous other ways. Once a person sees how s/he is doing this, s/he can more readily focus awareness to a particular area of discomfort that may represent a feeling needing to be noticed; and become more adept at expressing physical sensations and feelings. Emotional problems are bound in with physical tension; exploring both in this way helps to uncover the underlying issue or uncompleted gestalt.

The next stage is working with polarities. For instance, I am still upset at not standing up to my boss. There is a part of me that feels weak, inadequate and afraid. I shall call it The Wimp. In Perls' famous 'two-chair work,' the therapist encourages me to talk to The Wimp; I imagine him sitting in a chair opposite me, and I start a dialogue with him. In this way, I can let him express how he feels and better understand his point of view. However, there is also a part of me that is strong, capable and confident. I call him The Warrior, and I now imagine him sitting in the chair and I talk to him. Dialoguing with The Wimp and The Warrior helps me to see that they are each a part of my personality. They are polar opposites; and by setting up this confrontation between them, I can fully experience the feelings associated with each. Doing this, I am likely to tap into a past traumatic experience involving this particular polarity, including the thoughts, feelings, and body sensations that are all wrapped up with that event.

As the conflict between the opposites rises to conscious awareness, a powerful emotional release can be experienced. In a full spontaneous integration, a person may experience uncontrolled tears or laughter, and a sudden surge of energy as inner blocks are dissolved.

Once the pain and anger I felt towards these particular parts of me have been expressed, I come to accept them; I can see that they each have something to offer; they each have qualities that can be of use to me in different situations.

If I cannot easily imagine these different parts of me, then the experiment could instead involve a dialogue between me and the person who triggered my painful feelings, in this case my boss, or, going back in time, a parent. I express my feelings, and then go to the empty chair and allow that other person to respond. By speaking in imagination directly to the person with whom I have unfinished business, the gestalt can be completed.

The purpose of all of these methods is to bring about greater awareness of different parts of the self, and to facilitate greater communication between them (or between self and the other). Integration is a continuous, ongoing process; with each integration that occurs, we become more in touch with ourselves; we feel more energetic, joyful and alive.

Gestalt therapy helps people to make changes in their lives and to discover and realise their own potential. 'Gestalt therapists let themselves be themselves and encourage those they work with to do the same.'[21] 'They are continuously seeking a real as opposed to a transferential relationship… inviting clients to use their eyes and ears to see and listen to the actual person behind their projections.'[22]

'The achievement of a supportive relationship is perhaps the most important single feature of the approach. We exist, and grow, in relationship. The other techniques simply contribute to establishing the relationship as a real one based on a level of respectfulness equivalent to love, and therefore as intrinsically healing (Latner, 1995).'[23]

CONCLUSION: THE REWARDS

MANY people today are searching for ways to make positive changes for themselves; to become healthier, happier and in more control of their own lives. Many of us are now realising that acknowledging and expressing our emotions is a vitally important part of that process.

Most of us are adept at controlling our emotions. After a lifetime of hearing, 'Don't show yourself up,' 'Stop making a scene,' it's not surprising that we are ashamed and embarrassed about expressing them.

In fact, emotionally, we're still living out the fear of past generations - that if you lost control, the men in white coats would come to get you. Shouting your anger, wailing your pain, and breaking down your inhibitions got far too close to 'nervous breakdown' for comfort.

As little children, we used to sulk and have tantrums and scream. Growing up, though, we're not allowed to do that any more. Public displays of emotion are frowned upon; people get embarrassed and don't know how to respond. Or they assume that it's aimed at them, in which case they become defensive or aggressive. Screaming and crying, stamping your feet and shouting obscenities don't go down that well in most situations. Yet, that's exactly what many of us desperately need to do.

We keep quiet at work while the boss rants and raves over the slightest thing. We secretly cried when parents took out their feelings on us yet never said what was upsetting them. We have learned that those in power get to act out their emotions; the rest of us develop ulcers, depression, and a chronic perception of unfairness.

Most of us fear that if we open the floodgates, we will be overwhelmed. But the more we try to control our emotions, the more intense, insistent and ready to spark off at the slightest provocation they become. Holding them in, the pressure builds, and we become increasingly tense and exhausted. Or we may cut off totally and end up with a feeling of numbness, of no longer being fully alive. It's a high price to pay.

The fact is that most of us have to seek therapy of some sort, whether problem-centred, person-centred or energy-based, simply to start to feel again.

When I left psychiatry, I had nightmares for six months, I spent the next year grieving what I had lost: status, money, friends, identity, and then I got premenstrual syndrome. Finally, when I was nearing crisis point, I had six sessions of Reiki, and the PMS disappeared completely. I continued therapy for eighteen months, including dream-work, neurolinguistic programming (NLP), and hypnosis.

At first, it felt very odd being on the other side of the table, hearing someone saying the same kind of things to me that I had said to so many of my patients. But it made me realise that, whatever you call it - psychotherapy, energy work, or personal growth - the basic process is all the same.

A therapist is a person who accepts you as you are, without judging or giving false reassurance. S/he allows you to express whatever it is that you need to express, and quietly encourages you to keep on looking at yourself, despite the pain. A therapist does not give advice; s/he encourages you to trust yourself, giving you time and space, holding a place of love while you find out what it is you need to do.

You learn not from being told, but from being asked. You realise what you're not doing well by seeing how it's better done. Being met with warmth and genuineness, you become more open and compassionate yourself. Startlingly, you find that being honest is more important than being nice. By expressing what you really feel, you start to genuinely be yourself.

Therapy provides you with a new relationship in which you change old patterns of acting and reacting and learn new ways of relating to others. You do that in the moment, as they arise, because the therapist gives you honest and immediate feedback; you become aware of your automatic, non-productive attitudes and behaviours; the therapist shows you ways in which you could respond differently, and you begin to realise that you have a choice.

I learned a lot in that time. Firstly, that until you do something, you haven't done it. I knew how to help other people believe in themselves and find out who they truly were; I just hadn't done it for myself. To love myself, I had to do my own work.

I wanted my therapist to tell me all about myself, my problems, and what I should do. I wanted to hand over responsibility to her and get a quick fix. Of course, she didn't let me. So, the second thing I learned was that doing your own work means doing your own work.

Thirdly, I realised that to change means to change. Not to think about it, or dream about it, or feel you could do it, but to actually do it.

Those were hard things to learn.

Through therapy, most of us will find that, in the main, we are not who we thought we were. We are, without exception, far more capable, with more potential and inherent goodness than we ever imagined ourselves to be. There is a part of us that is desperately trying to break out of the old painful patterns, that wants us to learn, to progress and to become more aware.

As the song goes, 'Everybody hurts.' No one grows up, exists in this world, and lives a life, without being hurt. Rather than trying to avoid or deny that pain, we need to do something about it.

Therapy helps us to stay with the pain long enough to look at it, to fully experience it, to bring it to some kind of release. In therapy the aim is not to avoid pain or to seek to foreshorten it, on the contrary, it is to allow what you are currently feeling to expand so that you feel all that is there. Doing this, you can then let it go. The good news is that the more you do it, the easier it gets.

Many psychotherapeutic, cognitive and dream techniques bring about great personal breakthroughs and healing. But there are still some missing pieces. One of which is the sense of joy that is experienced when connecting strongly to our own spiritual energy.

The All-Love energy system leads to very powerful effects because it combines therapeutic techniques for emotional clearing with a direct connection with the energy of Source, the energy of our own spiritual or divine being.

When a person connects to the All-Love energy, he feels a joy and a feeling of love that he may never have felt before - and an excitement that he himself has made it happen. However much pain he has suffered, and however much work he still has to do, he knows that joy is possible for him. Of course, feeling the joy does not stop our resistance to looking at the pain. But it does make the whole process easier.

Connecting with the energy also speeds up the process of bringing unconscious emotions into conscious awareness. It allows us to more readily access painful and negative emotions held within the energy system and the body; working with whatever issues and emotions come up then facilitates their release.

The All-Love system uses techniques such as focusing into the body, conscious breathing, toning, touch, dialoguing with sub-personalities and inner child work, all of which enable you to overcome your resistance, heal your pain, and release those blocks which are preventing the flow of energy. The energy can then more fully enter your energy system and body.

Healing the emotional pain that is holding you back, at the same time as feeling the joy of connecting with the energy, leads to an experience of enlightenment, in the true sense; both of seeing, feeling or sensing the energy of the Source, or light, and also of lightening the inner burden, or weight of personal pain.

Becoming aware of what we are feeling is the first step to changing our whole view of life. When you ask yourself, 'What am I feeling? Why do I feel that way? What am I going to do about it?' you are taking responsibility for yourself in a way that you simply have not done before. You start to own your own feelings instead of projecting them on to others; you tell people how you feel instead of resenting the fact that they don't seem to know; you say no instead of agreeing to things that you know won't make you feel good. Taking responsibility for yourself means dealing with your own pain – that of the past and that of the present. Doing this, you become able to truly look after yourself, protect yourself – and love yourself.

In other words, you have become your own therapist.

CHAPTER THREE

Working with All-Love Energy

THE HISTORY AND ORIGINS OF ALL-LOVE

PATRICK had been fascinated by the pyramids, hieroglyphics and the culture of Ancient Egypt since the age of twelve. He also felt connected to Imhotep, the first architect and physician in recorded history. Imhotep designed the world's oldest standing step pyramid, and was later deified as the Egyptian God of medicine and healing.

When Patrick studied Architecture at College, he incorporated the principles of sacred geometry and pyramid symbology into his thesis. In 1978, he studied with Christopher Bird, whose book, with co-author Peter Tompkins: 'The Secrets of the Great Pyramids,' inspired him to spend the night in the Great Pyramid.

Four and a half thousand years ago, the Great Pyramid was constructed on a site of powerful natural energy, in accordance with the principles of sacred geometry. A pyramid is a structure that concentrates energy, and the most powerful point within the Great Pyramid was the King's Chamber.

In ancient times, the sarcophagus in the King's Chamber was used as a place of initiation. An initiation, brought about by an intense shift both emotionally and energetically, represented transformation from one state of consciousness to another.

Alone, in the dark, an individual was left to face his fears. Exposed to powerful energies of immensely greater magnitude and frequency than his own, the vibration of his energy system and body would suddenly be dramatically raised. It was said that he would either go mad or die, or emerge re-born.

Patrick's first experiences with energetic healing occurred in Egypt, his first initiation experience occurred in the Great Pyramid, and he was guided to call the energy some rendering of the Ancient Egyptian word SKHM, meaning highest spiritual power or energy. This gave his teaching, and the systems which originally developed from it – the first of which was Seichim - an 'Egyptian' feel. However, Patrick does not promote his teaching as such, because 'that in itself begins to define what the energy is. Once it is defined, it becomes very difficult for it to grow and expand. I am well aware that it came to me from within, even though there were some incredible outside experiences that facilitated my inward experience.'

Patrick wrote in 1998; 'It has been my experience that whatever image you are most comfortable with, the energy can take that physical form. I do not wish to see ancient Gods or Goddesses fully associated with the energy to the point where they become the main focus.'

Some people experiencing the energy associated it specifically with Egyptian deities such as Isis; others have said they have had Sekhmet appear to them. In 2000, Patrick wrote: 'This has not been my experience. It has been my experience that the energy will take on any form that a person feels comfortable with. I had only visions of pure light that manifested at first with a deep cobalt blue and eventually encompassed the whole spectrum of light.'

Patrick's All-Love classes now combine working with the energy to enable people to make their own connection with Source, and working with emotional clearing techniques, which facilitate the initiation experience.

The energy is constantly evolving, and the system that Patrick is currently teaching has come a long way from its original conception twenty-five years ago. He does not use attunements, and he does not place much emphasis on symbols.

Patrick has studied vibrational healing and polarity, breath work, visualisation, sound healing, energy healing, Vipassana and inner child work. He has trained in, and taught, massage, yoga, Reiki, hypnotherapy, Chinese medicine, toning, channelling, Zikr and many different forms of meditation. Over many years, he has used the All-Love energy in his own personal growth and in working with others.

He has received many attunements, including Reiki Master, Kundalini Yoga, Sufi, Native American, and Divine Unity. Yet, as he says, 'it is the opening to Love that brings about the initiation that people are longing for.'

Patrick: 'The All-Love system is very different from what I taught in the past. There are now many diverging systems, for instance the Seichim system that I started out with. People need to know that there is a lot of variety out there.

'At the beginning of a class, I often say that we are going to go in and identify the emotions, and that at times anger or sadness might come up. I ask if everyone is willing to do that, or if there are people who have reservations about looking at what is inside themselves.'

If people are unaware that an All-Love class involves working with emotions, then they may feel angry or frustrated when they find that it does. They may not be able to allow themselves to benefit fully from the experience because they are focussed on trying to learn something else.

If people simply come in an open state, without preconceptions or expectations, they often end up having a very powerful experience.

All-Love classes aim to empower people, so that they can become more aware of themselves and their emotional issues, and take responsibility – and credit – for their own healing. All of us tend to give our power away – whether to an inanimate object such as a crystal, or to another person, such as a teacher or parent. We all need to find a balance between being helped by others and helping ourselves. Sometimes we focus on particular systems or personalities or accessories – all of which are simply tools - and lose sight of the fact that each of us is actually healing themselves.

As Patrick says: 'The most powerful tool is Love. If the heart is not full of Love then other tools are like a dead end. You already have everything you need within yourself. If you can open up to the energy of a crystal, or another person, then you can also open up to your own heart.'

That is what All-Love is all about.

What does All-Love Energy Do? Personal Experiences

FOR many people, the All-Love energy has brought about life-changing events. Some were expecting this to happen – others were not! Many people have reported positive changes in their lives because of the workshops.

Michael Heemskerk writes: 'In 1999, I was searching the Internet one day for the 'original' Reiki symbols. Many different versions existed, so I wanted to find the correct way to draw them. I stumbled across a site that showed a symbol I had never seen before.

'It was one of the Reiki symbols, the Cho Ku Rei, with an Infinity symbol added on. Apparently, it was called Cho Ku Ret, and the website associated it with someone called Patrick Zeigler.

'Reading further, I discovered that he had created a new system called Seichim, after experiencing a spontaneous initiation in the Great Pyramid in Egypt. I must admit that my initial reaction was, "Here's another guy who's trying to change Reiki just to create the impression that he is somebody special!" So, I forgot all about it.

'But every time I looked on the Internet for the Reiki symbols, I came across this man's name. I began to feel that there was actually something about him. I found his email address and wrote asking if he could tell me about the Cho Ku Ret.

'He wrote back, simply saying that he did not use symbols anymore.

'No symbols? I could not understand it! I was so caught up in the way the Reiki system was traditionally taught, that it had never crossed my mind that we did not need to use the symbols.

'I asked him how he initiated people, and he told me that, instead of an initiation, he used a flowing meditation.

'I thought "A flowing what?" I wrote back, asking him how that went, and he sent me a short, one-page meditation, and a picture of the Seichim Shenu.

'I remember thinking that it was very strange that he gave me this for free, because at that time it was very expensive to obtain information about the Reiki Master level. But I printed it out, and asked him if I could call him sometime. He agreed, and we exchanged phone numbers.

'That evening, lying in my bedroom, I decided to read the meditation he had sent me. But, as I picked it up, I thought, "Why not just do it?" So, I started to read the first lines aloud.

'Suddenly my crown Chakra popped open, a huge energy came in, and went through the whole of my body. It took me completely by surprise!

'I was swept away in a really unbelievable "sea of love." Everything from my past, the times when I had started to hate myself, all the things that had happened to me - all these feelings came passing by, encompassing me, and filling me totally with this "feeling of Love." I found it an incredibly moving experience.

'I stayed like this all night, lying there totally in bliss. I was in awe of what was happening to me, but at the same time, it all felt so natural.

'At six o'clock in the morning, still awake, I started to wonder how I could give this to my students. I was already teaching Reiki and doing spiritual healing with groups. Suddenly, a vision appeared before me, a woman with a beautiful white dress and wild, floating, white hair. She was drawing a symbol that looked like the outline of a vase.

'I didn't understand, and asked, "Can you give me a symbol to initiate people with this energy?" Again, she drew the vase symbol.

'I still did not understand what she was doing, so I just let it go, and kept on feeling this unbelievable feeling of love.

'In the morning I had to get up to take my daughter to school. Although I was still feeling the energy, I decided, because of the time difference between Europe and the US, to wait until the afternoon to call Patrick.

'When I told him what had happened, he said, "Well, that's it. This is how it works - this is the initiation!"

'I said, "Well, it's a bit simple," and he replied, "Yes, that's how it goes. If you're ready for it, it will happen."

'I told him about the woman, and the vase, and at first he didn't understand what I was saying. Then he replied, "Oh, the symbol is the kelb. In Egypt, the vase is the symbol for the heart."

'Suddenly I understood what the woman in white had meant. To give this to my students, I just had to open their hearts!

'I was so impressed by what had happened, and I felt so good, that I asked Patrick if he would be interested in coming to Europe. It was something that he had been wanting to do for a long time, so, in March 2000, Patrick came to Holland to give the first SKHM class in Europe.

'Before I met Patrick, when treating people with hands-on healing, I was already using the image of the sun coming into the head, the body, lighting up everything, taking away the painful things and forming a column of light. In the workshop, I saw that what he was doing was very similar. Afterwards, when I was working with the Reiki energy with people, they would start processing things and I was never able to do a Reiki course normally from that point on! I didn't really force it, it just happened. I decided that it would be better to spend my time with SKHM, so I changed to what he was doing, it evolved a little bit more, and I developed the website.'

Teresa writes: 'When I read about Patrick lying in the sarcophagus wrapped in toilet roll, I thought, "This guy is fascinating, I have to meet him!" I was excited about going to his workshop in Delft in April 2004. I had spent some months before trying to heal the period pain I had had for twenty-five years. So, I went with the intention of dealing with this problem as much as I could. When Patrick asked for a volunteer to demonstrate his healing methods, I jumped at the chance. With his help, I was able to do some important healing work.

'When I met Patrick, I was impressed by his humility and integrity. It was obvious that he was deeply committed to healing. He had spent years mastering different systems, he had studied with some excellent teachers, and, while developing his own system, had been constantly working on himself. I could see that he knew what he was talking about.

'I was looking forward very much to what might happen. During one of the meditations, listening to Patrick's soothing voice and Michael's beautiful music, I was surrounded by green and violet light, and I saw the Shenu symbol, in brilliant purple, coming from above down into my heart. It was absolutely wonderful. I sat motionless, with tears streaming down my face, and was amazed at the sense of peace and love that I felt. In that moment, I felt complete.

'The following day, I simply wanted to experience that wonderful feeling again. I sat quietly, waiting for it to happen. As the energy started to come in, a woman right in front of me started to make the most horrible noise: a loud, repetitive, wailing scream. It just went on and on. The energy had stopped, so I closed my eyes and tried to connect with it again. But I couldn't. Boy, did I wish she would shut up. I sat there for a few minutes taking deep breaths and telling myself, "You're calm, you're not angry, just let the energy flow." Nothing happened at all. No calm. No energy. Nothing.

'I was getting more and more annoyed at all the noise around me as people were shouting and crying, I felt frustrated that I wasn't getting anywhere, and was envious of those who seemed to be experiencing bigger and bigger initiations, shaking and moaning and leaping all over the place. In fact, I was close to tears. I had really wanted to feel what it was like for the energy to go down from my heart into the rest of my body.

'Suddenly I said to myself, "I'm f***ing angry. I feel bloody pissed off." At that exact moment, the energy shot into the crown of my head in a stream of brilliant white light. And I realised the importance of being honest about my own feelings. I didn't need to know what the anger was about, whether the woman's feeling was triggering something for me, whether some time in the past I'd felt someone had stopped me doing something I really wanted to do. No, it was very simple. The message was, just tell yourself what you are really feeling.

'I sat there for a few minutes experimenting, telling myself different things, some I knew weren't true, and others I knew were. Every time I said something in my head that I knew was a lie, the energy instantly stopped. In addition, every time I told the truth, the energy came into me in a wonderful stream of brilliant, joyful, shining light. It still didn't go down past my heart, but it didn't need to. It had already showed me what I needed to know.

'I was amazed, and realised that I had learned something very important – that to be honest about what I was feeling, without judging it or trying to pretend it was something else, was the key.

'I also learned that there is no point in assuming things about other people's experiences or comparing them with mine. Some people are dramatic others are not. We all need to cry and shout at times, other times we need to be quiet. Sometimes the energy is strong, other times it isn't. The important thing is accepting whatever is happening, without judgement or comparison - doing what I need to do and allowing others to do what they need to do. That is love.

'In that first workshop, not knowing exactly how the process worked, I had been more reserved and felt that I had to sit there and try to get the energy flowing on my own. In the second workshop I attended, I realised that it actually works much better to become more involved with other people: their energy helps your own. It was important for me to realise that I find it difficult to ask for help, and it was a wonderful experience when, asking, people gave so freely and with such love. Touching and being touched, toning together, and letting different people's energy merge with my own, was a lovely experience. At one point, Graham had a very strong connection with the energy, and was bringing it up from the Earth with several people gathered around, touching him. As we did so, the energy became much more grounded for all of us, and I could feel it in my feet, rising through the whole of my body.

'In fact this felt similar to what I had experienced seven years previously, when I started writing. I would sit at the dining table writing longhand – before I got a computer – and I was filled with joy, excitement, and an incredible sense of aliveness. My head felt hot, especially on the left side, and waves of energy kept rushing up from my root chakra, it was like being on the edge of an orgasm, and it would go on for hours. At that time I had never heard of Kundalini or energy or chakras, it just seemed that writing was a wonderful thing to be doing!

'I have found that each workshop is different, and in each I have had some beautiful experiences and gained some important insights. One thing's for sure, something always surprises me!'

Graham writes: 'In the first workshop I attended, the energy came in but I felt very spaced out; as if I was floating. I started getting a pain in my knee, and Patrick just said, "See if that wants to make a sound. Do what your body needs to do." I ended up on the floor all curled up, and I made some sound, and amazingly, the pain seemed to go away. I was quite impressed with that. When Teresa had her session, something happened in my sacral chakra. Trying to get that out started me retching so much that my contact lens flew into a bucket. Afterwards, I felt much more grounded. I was able to feel the connection with the energy from Earth much stronger than before and I felt present, here, connected to Earth instead of floating. At the time, I thought, I've had an initiation because I've felt the energy stronger than I have ever felt it before.

'At the second workshop, without Patrick, I wondered if the energy would be as strong. If anything it was stronger, and the feeling of love I felt was absolutely incredible. In the past, I would have associated that feeling of love with being in love, but it was happening towards various members of the group, both male and female, so I realised in some way it was different.

'When we did the workshop in Malaga, with Patrick and Michael, one of the things I found about the energy is that it is quite gentle. Although it can bring up difficult issues, it often brings them up in a slow and stepwise manner that allows you to deal with it at your own pace. One of the issues that came up in October for me was not fully resolved until three workshops later in February, and that lead to the strongest initiation that I have ever had.

'We were doing the Infinity Dance, I was translating for Michael, and at the end, when there was less to translate, I actually had time to think about what Michael was saying. He asked if we really wanted to receive love. I thought about it for a minute and I said, "Yes I do," and suddenly the most powerful energy that I have ever felt poured into my body. I felt wonderful, completely loved in a way that I'd never felt before, but not just loved, supported, as if I was being looked after.

'For me personally, what I like most about All-Love is the fact that since I have started doing it, I have felt that there is more love in my life. I am actually able to give and receive love in a way that I was not able to before. I am still learning, and there is probably still a long way to go, but I am very glad that I started on this path. It has been painful at times, but the advantages have far outweighed the disadvantages.

'Although it is called All-Love energy, it can actually bring up a variety of emotions; sadness, grief, jealousy, anger, and you have to work through those other feelings before you get back to the feeling of love.

'The other thing that I have found is that All-Love has affected how I channel energy. Previously, I had done Reiki and Karuna and I felt the energy in a particular way. It feels different now; the All-Love energy has made the energy I channel much stronger, and it seems to increase after each workshop.

'I was amazed when I first found out about All-Love, that it included so many of the things that my intuition had led me to do on my own. It didn't feel as if I was finding a new system, it was as if I was coming home. I love toning, and I found that this helped a great deal in releasing emotions held in various parts of the body. It enabled energy to shift, and made me feel a lot better.

'All-Love also seems to have helped me to develop other abilities. When I put my hands on a person's bones, I can feel the bones moving under my fingers. They slip back into place. It is not I that is moving them, it is the energy that seems to be giving them permission to return to where they should be. For instance, I put my hand on Patrick's foot, as he said he felt as if a bone was out of place, and I felt the energy shifting. I didn't feel the bone moving at that time, but then he got up, flexed his foot, and he felt the bone pop back into place.

'The other thing that's happened is that I've felt that when I am doing healing, I have been helped by very strong energies. It's as if I am merging with a powerful energy that allows me to do things that I would not be able to do on my own. I am still not entirely clear what's happening. I do know that my intuition is guiding me much more. Each treatment is different, and people experience very positive effects. It's very exciting.'

Marcus Vinnicombe writes: 'From a hypnotherapist's point of view, at the workshop, I was witnessing around me people getting to places in a matter of a few hours, that under normal circumstances could take months to arrive at.

'Every tear you cry in an All-Love session is like a million you've cried in the past without ever getting to the real source of the pain. Things that have been held down for so long finally escape. Crying and expressing emotions under these conditions seems to lead to a permanent release, as if the emotion has been uprooted, and the space it occupied has been filled with, dare I say it, love.

'I also experienced some very interesting physical sensations when I was working with people. I would feel a surge of energy through my arms and the person I was touching would all of a sudden feel the energy and seemed to be having a very intense experience. You can almost see the energy flowing through them at an immense rate, causing the muscles to vibrate at a high frequency. I must admit I found that quite disturbing when it first happened, as I am a bit of a sceptic, but I felt there was an energy present, an actual tangible physical energy.

'In the breaks, you could see that something very profound had happened to people, and was still happening. When you look in their eyes and smile, the smile that comes back, even through tears, is one of "I know I am going to be alright now."

'I suppose what I am trying to say is that there was a feeling of love. But not love as I'd thought of it before - not the love that you say, but the love that you do, that has no embarrassment any more because it is pure, untarnished. It's the love you might feel for a baby, when you make eye contact with him for the first time. And you can see infinity in his eyes, space and stars and a window to the Creator, whatever that is.

'I went to the weekend under the guise of picking up some new tools to use with my clients - I didn't really think all this sort of thing was for me. Just when I thought I was going to get out without making an arse of myself in front of all these people, blubbing and carrying on the way they seemed to be enjoying, Patrick spotted me and let me know that in the last session, after the break, whatever happened, I was going to get my turn.

'I thought, "Good, now I can blame him." Sure enough when we came back there was one chair in the middle of the room. Everyone was looking at it. The walk to the chair seemed to take forever. I sat down. It reminded me of school, of always feeling an outsider. He encouraged me to stay with those feelings. And simply would not let up.

'Finally, I felt a rush, my body started to vibrate, and the tears began. I found myself viewing a memory of my mother's face from when I was eight years old and feeling that I wasn't sure that she knew I loved her. Teresa got me to speak to her. Now, that eight-year-old boy knows that his mother knew he loved her. He smiles at me sometimes when I am drifting off to sleep, that part of me, and then goes back to playing.

'The other part of my experience was having a very clear visual image, which I don't normally get. I was viewing a tree from above, and there was a nest about half way down. I felt the peace and quiet of the countryside. Then I was next to the nest, viewing it from the side, and in the nest there was an egg, coloured red like everything else with the sunrise. Just as I was thinking how warm it looked, I found myself inside the egg, peering out through a crack, and then climbing out, emerging from the warmth inside out into the sunlight.

'That was the point at which I let go. I was coming out of my shell, on a whole life level. I realised that my life and the bird's life were identical, and that I was just an animal, and any fear I held - that did not involve death or injury - was unwarranted, and unwanted. Who would think that such a seemingly small realisation could lead to such a feeling of strength?

'During my experience at the workshop, I had belief changes that influence my life to this day. I feel that I can step back on situations and view them from a completely new angle, which has no fear. Expressing myself in front of all those people allowed me to be a lot more open. In hypnotherapy, I am used to watching people duck and dive away from the source of their pain, but I am now much more able to see when I am doing it myself. My internal dialogue has shifted, and I feel I am starting to be truly honest with myself. Since then, my relationships with people have changed, and they have noticed, to my irritation, how much calmer I am! Actually, even that irritation dissolves.

'In my work, I use the All-Love technique whenever appropriate to help people clear their emotional blockages, and it works. It bypasses the left-brain, which is what we need at times, and goes directly to the core of the blockage. I think the most important thing for me is that I now have uninterrupted concentration, whereas, before, my mind was a constant Moroccan marketplace of questions scrambling for answers. A lot of the questions have disappeared because I think they all needed the same answer - they just didn't realise it till now.'

Vicky Barnes: 'I had definitely experienced initiations before any Reiki or All-Love attunements. Several months after these, I was introduced to Reiki, and later read Patrick's story. On the first day of the first All-Love class, I had a very powerful initiation, the difference being that I had the assistance of Patrick to help me relax into that process, which I hadn't on previous occasions. He also explained the spontaneous initiations that I had already experienced, which had scared me a little; as I had thought I might be having a heart attack; combined with shaking and palpitations it was a little daunting.

'In relation to having an initiation, intent is the key. The label we give it is immaterial, as it just is - and as Patrick often states we will all interpret it in our own way; giving it a shape and form that we are most comfortable with. I personally feel more comfortable with using All-Love!

'I believe intent must be the key, this combined with a willingness to give up something that no longer serves you, as each of these events, like the classes, were combined with a conscious surrendering of something I no longer wanted to be embroiled in or to experience as my reality.

'My first experience quite literally rocked my world. I was talking on the phone to the previous owners of our house — a wonderful lady called Helen who is a born-again Christian. We were experiencing a few problems with the parking at our property, and at first I was quite enraged by the injustice of having to approach her for help, when halfway through the conversation I thought, "What am I doing? This really isn't serving me!" Almost instantaneously, it felt like I was in a spinning vortex, bands of energy from my feet all the way up to my throat, which seemed to be spinning. I understand this to be a Kundalini rising, which is relevant to the initiations that followed.

'I started crying and I did not stop for nearly a month continuously. It was an amazing experience, although traumatic for all concerned. It felt like a life review, all these events flashing before my eyes. I would then enter the emotion and the tears would flow but what amazed me more was as I cried and emptied myself of events I had long forgotten and the trauma they had caused, I was filled with this immense sense of peace and appreciation and joy. I likened it to liquid love, and I was Love. Everything and everyone seemed brighter, more alive, through this new perspective; I would then cry, totally overwhelmed by life and its beauty.

'Helen was incredibly supportive during this time and invited me to go to a Christian evening with the Five Gospel Brothers. The guest speaker was Jimmy Davro. That night my heart was so alive. I had all this love just welling up inside, I was almost at a point of combusting.

'After the talk, my friend Wendy asked if I would come with her to ask for healing. Jimmy placed a hand on her head and proceeded to speak in this most beautiful language, I was compelled to pray for this beautiful lady and that is when the initiation energy really got me. My eyes twitched rapidly, it felt like an electrical current, which entered my crown and proceeded by running through every blood vessel and vein in my body. I was shaking and was aware of this immense golden light that engulfed me. Needless to say, my attention soon shifted from prayer to this amazing experience for which I had no answers! This process lasted for between five and ten minutes and I was totally bemused.

'My second initiation experience was at a sharing of healing with my dear friend Stephen and two other people. I started to shake and I shook and shook, again combined with the twitching and the light starting at the crown and spreading all the way down to my toes. I spent almost two hours totally immersed in bliss.

'Experience of the energy initially was akin to being plugged into the mains. Normally it starts with tingly sensations around the crown then I can sense an expansion around my head, my eyes tend to flick, rapid eye movement, and then a surge of vibrational energy and uncontrollable shaking. I am able to relax more now and the energy finds it easier to move through me so the shaking is considerably gentler, until I get an upgrade or downloading of finer energy. I find I notice it more in my hands, which shake a lot. When the surge has integrated and shifted any blockages I feel totally supported in a shaft - I liken this to the tree trunk feeling, totally grounded and a state of complete being, very nice.

'I have attended five classes in Cornwall now. I find the healings taking place build up to the workshops and invariably I would feel rough leading up to a class, but that is not so noticeable now. Nothing prepared me for the shift that took place because of holding a class though. The class that Keith and I organised in October was so powerful for me personally. My whole world caved in on me, it felt like my heart had been split in two and I could not eat or sleep for five days. The waves of emotion were so deep, they hurt. I am still not quite sure how I came through it but I did, a major shift had taken place. Sometimes the completion or assimilation can take a while, it really felt like I had undergone an initiation.

'For me personally, the benefits of All-Love have been that I am now able to cope in this reality, I feel more alive and content with my life. I have learnt to love who I am and have been able to break many of the thought forms that prevented me from moving forward. I know that the All-Love energy is constantly at work on me and as a result those around me.'

Katja Kaiser writes: 'Just at the beginning of the first workshop, I noticed that my whole body was crying inside, there was something that wanted to be liberated, that wanted to cry and scream. Suddenly I noticed a tremendous stream of energy entering my crown chakra, which started to move a deep pain. I was starting to "peel the onion," just being in my pain: feeling this deep sadness caused by many cumulated experiences in my life. I just let it go, let it be liberated, giving my body what it needed in this moment, being myself and in this way being in contact with a very deep emotional part of myself that I never knew before. After this first All-Love experience, I felt much better.

'The next morning, I started again with a deep movement in my body, and I entered again into an emotional liberation process. But this time it was different, I entered in a different world, feeling the union with the universe, and seeing a bright, pure, divine light coming down and surrounding me. My whole body was filled by this brilliant light, and I felt as if I was floating and flying, being connected with the Earth by my feet and to Heaven by my head, feeling the flow of energy inside myself. It was a wonderful and peaceful moment. I felt such happiness that I blessed the Universe for giving me so much peace. And then I began singing; chanting with the angels.

'Just after this wonderful moment, it seemed that the energy was again touching a deep pain inside my heart, but this time it was going deeper than before. It was as if the Universe was showing me how to liberate my body and soul, of all the emotions accumulated over years, and I was able to cry again.

'Each emotional process seemed to last less time than the one before. I came out of them much faster, and entered again into a wonderful moment of peace and tranquillity, being in harmony with the Universe, feeling the union between Earth and Heaven.

'That workshop definitively changed my life. It gave me the opportunity to come in contact with my deeper emotions, and to work out emotional blocks for myself. I was able to forgive people who had hurt me, and to heal an important part of my inner being. Finally, I was crying because of such happiness, being grateful to the Universe for giving me the opportunity to experience a love that I had never felt before; to love and accept myself, and to give and receive love from everyone around me. I felt like a new person.

'Now, one month after the Workshop I can see the changes in my life; feeling more peace and being aware of everything beautiful that happens. Above all, recognising my own value and knowing that this is the path I have to follow. Now, I trust myself much more, accepting myself as I am, and as a consequence taking away the power of the pain and fear that I felt before, knowing that everything that happens in my life is right. ALL-LOVE.'

Silvia Morales Alonso writes: 'Now that I am back in Madrid, having assimilated the powerful experience that I had at the workshop - powerful is the word that characterises it - I will tell you in the clearest way that I can. Beginning at the beginning, my experience began the instant that I said goodbye to my parents at the bus station in Madrid on Friday the 22nd October 2004. I note it because it is something that I will never forget. I got onto the bus feeling nervous, not really knowing what was going to happen; but disposed to do what was necessary.

'I arrived at Torremolinos at 6pm and decided to walk the 8 km to the hotel in Benalmadena. The temperature was as if it was the month of August, the streets full of people who were going from bar to bar. At 8:30pm, I started walking again and after taking some photos and watching the sea for a while, I arrived at the hotel. I started feeling nervous again.

'At 9:30 the next morning, we went down to the room where the course was taking place. Once I was there, we sat down in a circle of seats, about thirty people from different places. Everyone expectant before a door that was going to open and nobody knew very well what to expect.

'Patrick decided that we should introduce ourselves, each one of us saying our name around the circle; with the intention of us getting to know each other. You had to breathe deeply and enjoy your name…. And after the presentation of only four people, what happened was incredible: people started to lose control, some cried, others sang, some vomited, others laughed and I was stuck to my seat. I thought that these people were mad or acting or I don't know what, and suddenly someone started to scream, an amazing scream that seemed to go into my heart.

'I felt as if the muscles of my body were contracting increasingly. It was something that I felt but my head could not control it. Someone moved me onto the floor and there my body continued to shrink until I was in the foetal position. It was very confusing, being conscious, hearing everything happening around me but I could not stop crying and getting smaller. I felt afraid, terrified. This happened for about thirty minutes. When I was able to relax my left hand had a strong intense pain and I couldn't feel it. In this moment, I felt real anguish. I am left-handed and my left hand is the most important tool that I have. After a while, it began to move and I was glad of that. That was how my first experience ended.

'In the afternoon, after lunch we continued around the circle introducing ourselves. After three people had introduced themselves, the same thing happened again. Everyone had a different reaction and this time my body began to go rigid, my back began to stretch out backwards and someone again decided to move me onto the floor and I began to kick and I felt menaced. They left me on the floor and I began to hit myself and pull my hair without any control. I don't know why it happened but suddenly I felt really ashamed of all that I had done and I ran out of the room. I was thinking about not coming back, this was for mad people; and I was becoming mad.

'The following day when I got up, I kept repeating in my mind that I would control the situation and that I wouldn't let myself go as I had the previous day. The exercise that day was to find a partner and start an All-Love session. I preferred to give and then I could avoid the explosions of uncontrolled feelings. And in the morning, I succeeded.

'After lunch, we had to change partner and so I did, with the intention once more of controlling the situation. I was going back to Madrid on the bus alone and I did not want to feel bad on the trip back. At that moment, Graham came over to me and I am sure that he knew that there was still something to come out. I began to feel menaced again, frightened and I hit him, it was only for a moment, but I felt awful. I have never been aggressive and have never hit anyone. I tried to run away, to find a corner, I felt really ashamed. They brought me down to the floor again and I felt I was shrinking again and crying, but that ended when Graham hugged me.

'I decided to miss the bus in order to experience what I had to experience and the journey was very enjoyable. When we were 80 km from Madrid, my hands were burning and Katja, someone I love a lot, advised me to use this energy. I decided to send it to my brother. In the middle of the session my hands began to move apart and I started to cry again, I felt sad, although I wasn't alone, the people I was travelling with, Paco and Katja were with me. After a little I began to feel afraid again and I continued crying. I saw my mother and spoke to her. The conversation ended with us hugging each other and suddenly I began to laugh as I have never laughed before. The laughter came from my stomach and I couldn't control it. I was not laughing at anything but I felt really happy.

'This is my experience that I want to share with you all. I have to say that I am a very rational person who always doubts everything and that I need to experience things before I believe in them.

'If I had to sum up what happened to me I would say that my head, my rational part, became disconnected and I was just controlled by my feelings and sensations. And it was something that I will never forget.

'I have to thank Patrick, Michael, Graham and Teresa who made me feel protected amongst so much fear, pain, shame and sadness. And of course those others who helped, giving me their support, and caring, Marilú, Katja, Paco, Marisa.... and a long list. And I carry a part of each of them in my heart.

'A really big kiss. I love you all.'

The Shenu Meditation

PATRICK: 'Just allow yourself to be comfortable. Let yourself be quiet, go inside, close your eyes for a moment. Just notice what is going on inside.

'Feel your breath. Just allow yourself to watch that. Notice your feelings; notice your emotions. Just relax.

'Take a few deep breaths, and allow yourself to feel the breath all the way deep down into your belly. Feel the areas within the chest that might be a little more restricted than the others. Breathe and feel. And begin to be aware of all the sensations in your body. Notice how you are feeling, from the top of your head down to your toes.

'Now bring your awareness to your spiritual heart centre, this is the place between the physical heart and the throat. Begin to feel into this area, bring your consciousness there, and as you breathe, allow the awareness to move deeper and deeper into the heart centre. Allow yourself to feel all the different sensations that are there. Let your breath and your awareness become one. So, with each breath you allow yourself to feel deeper and deeper into your heart.

'Just imagine this heart centre opening and creating a space within your heart. Breathe in and fill that space. Let it keep coming in. Allow yourself to feel all the different sensations within this space. Begin to connect the sensations of breath and feeling as one. Breathing and feeling. Allow the feeling to come in. Let it come in. And as the heart chamber expands, begin to feel all the different sensations, just completely relaxing into the breath and feeling all that is there, not putting any judgement, not trying to figure out what's there, just experiencing the feeling for what it is. And know that whatever you are feeling is absolutely perfect for you.

'As you open your heart, just begin to feel the rooms within the heart centre. Open up those rooms that have not been opened up before. If the sound needs to come in, let the sound come in. Speak from this space, if there is something you would like to express. Let the heart sing.

'If your body wants to move, let it move. Notice what your body wants to do. Whatever is happening for you is absolutely perfect.

'And now imagine that there is a connection from your heart up to the top of your head. There is a flower on the top of your head, and its petals are just beginning to open.

'Above the top of your head, visualise a brilliant, beautiful sun that is radiating its light. Imagine the light coming all the way down to the flower on the top of your head, and just invite the rays of that brilliant sun to come down into your heart.

'Take the light in, breathe it in, from that brilliant, beautiful sun above your head, and breathe it right down into the heart centre. Allow it to move into all the different areas. Within the heart there are little doors off to the side, and just allow yourself to begin to open those doors and allow the light to move into those areas, where this light may not have ever been before. Just begin to feel all the different sensations there are behind those doors. Open the little closed doors in your heart that may never have been opened before, and allow yourself to feel deeper and deeper whatever is there.

'Imagine a column of light from that sun coming down from Heaven, through your whole body, and connecting into the Earth. Bring the column of light all the way down to your heart, and into your belly, to your solar plexus, filling your belly, moving down to your sacral chakra, down to your root chakra, and going all the way down your legs to your feet.

'Under your feet, imagine your roots going deep down into the Earth, into the core, connecting your heart with the heart of the Earth, and allow the Earth to feel your presence as you receive the presence of the Earth. Feel all that is there within the Earth.

'Feel the support, the Earth supporting your column of light, and at this time, if you wish, you can make a commitment to fully be present at this time, it doesn't mean for eternity but just for this moment of time, you can say "Yes" to being here and being fully on this planet.

'At this time, if you wish, invite all of your essence, all of your light, all of who you are, into your heart centre, and root it deeply within the heart of the Earth.

'Now bring the Earth energies up into your feet, up your legs and all the way up into your heart, and in your heart let them merge with the energies from the Heavens. Feel the energy mixing and merging in your heart, feel it coming out of your shoulders and into your hands. And the vertical column of energy and the energy coming horizontally out from your heart form a cross. Just feel that. Breathe with it. Breathe into it and feel.

'Just imagine you are standing on the top of a mountain looking out over a brilliant sea, and feel your energy moving out all across the planet, touching the heart of all beings. Feel the column that is forming and if you wish at this time you may stand in this column, stand in your light. And be completely aware of who you are and what you are and allow yourself to remember why you have come here on this planet, what your true purpose is here on Earth.

'Now connect back up to the brilliant golden sun above your head. Bring that sun down into your heart, so that the sun is sitting on the top of the cross that you have made, forming the sign of the ankh. Feel your connection with that. Feel yourself completely in the present, completely connected to Source.

'Just stay for a few minutes in this space; and know that you can come back to this space whenever you want, for as long as you want. Just slowly start to open your eyes and look around from this space.'

Patrick: 'I do not use a fixed format for the meditations. Sometimes I get people to visualise pyramids, but other times I don't. A pyramid is simply a structure that focuses energy, that's all. It's nice when they come together and form a star. The ankh is the connection of Heaven and Earth, the sphere is eternal life and the cross is the Earth, the physical. The infinity symbol is a natural energy pattern. Really, the whole thing is just giving people time to connect with the energy. We are telling a story while you are in the energy and it just allows you to connect. So, that way, people will not be caught up in whether I missed a pyramid. Because really the key is, getting that feeling in the heart, opening your crown, bringing the energy down and connecting it to the Earth.'

The Shenu meditation encourages a person to enter into a relaxed and receptive state, in which s/he can invite the energy to enter, both from the Heavens, through the crown chakra, and from the Earth, through the feet and up through the base chakra. Once this connection is made, the All-Love energy starts to flow into a person's energy system.

When it encounters energetic blocks, or areas of tension, where emotional pain is held within the body, the flow of energy stops. So, the aim is also to open up each of the seven chakras to allow the energy to flow freely between them, and to release any blocks that may be stopping the energy from fully entering the body.

The crown chakra on the top of the head is the place of our connection with the Universe, the Creator, Source, God – or whatever we like to call those higher energies outside of ourselves. The crown chakra is associated with understanding, spiritual consciousness and integration of the higher self.

We connect with the energy of the Heavens through our crown chakra, and bring it down to the third eye, in the middle of the forehead. The third eye is the seat of self-awareness and intuition. It connects us with other beings and higher knowledge, and allows us to see things more clearly.

The throat chakra is the connection between our minds and our hearts. It has been described as the centre of truth; accepting what we see in ourselves, including our shadow, and expressing what we truly feel. When we make a sound, when we connect the throat with an area of blocked energy, we allow that blocked energy to express itself.

The heart chakra is where we feel joy, compassion, and love - of self, of others, and of God. It is also where we feel pain, heartache, and lack of self-love. When we open our hearts, we allow ourselves to feel all the conflicting feelings that are there.

The solar plexus is described as the power centre. It is involved in intuition (our gut feeling), and in perceiving and processing emotions. It is also associated with the will, and the drive to control – us or other people. When we let go of conscious control, we allow the energy to go wherever it needs to go.

The sacral chakra is associated with sexuality, creativity, and our relationship to others. When we release the energy that gets trapped in this area, we find we can relate more openly to others, with more spontaneity and less fear.

The root or base chakra, situated at the base of the spine, connects us to the energy of the Earth. It is the centre of our sense of strength, security and self-esteem, and it also grounds us, allowing us to make our creative ideas into reality. It contains the creative energy of the Kundalini, which rises during orgasm and can help remove blockages.

We all have a spirit, or essence, our life force, which connects us to the energy of the Source, or Creator. As Patrick says; 'We are all already connected to Source. It is only our limited awareness that gives us the illusion that we are not.'

Most of us need quiet time and space in order to break out of our normal state of awareness and become aware of ourselves on all levels. When we visualise the sun, we imagine a brilliant source of light; it helps us to see more clearly, and it brings us the energy we need to help us to grow. We feel warmed in our body and our feelings.

Opening our heart centre, we begin to feel, and we also allow ourselves to receive. When we invite our divine essence into ourselves, we feel connected to a source of power and energy outside of ourselves – but also within us. When we fully ground ourselves, we are fully present in our moment, in our body, and in our sense of connectedness to the Earth. Connecting with the Earth and to the Heavens, you feel the energy merging in your heart, you feel the connection with other beings, to the Universe and to yourself, your own spirit.

As mentioned previously, spirituality is an appreciation that we exist on many different levels simultaneously; we are mind, body and spirit. A spiritual initiation, or awakening, therefore involves coming to fully experience the self, in clear consciousness, as emotion, physical sensation, thought, energy and spirit. In other words, it means that at that moment we are truly whole; aware, integrated, and fully present in the here and now.

THE INFINITY DANCE

PATRICK: 'The first step is getting out of the head. A lot of us are very uncomfortable about getting the energy all the way down. That is why we use movement to get the energy through the whole of our bodies.

You can begin to start to unwind the energy that is in the body, because that is where a lot of stuff is stuck. Just allow yourself to let the energy come into your body. Draw the infinity pattern with your head, and then it comes down to your shoulders, to each of your chakras. You can do whatever you want with this.

The way you move says a lot about yourself and what you think and feel about your body. As you start to move, it helps to you to unwind.

Listen to your body and just let it flow.

Take a few deep breaths. Breathe it in and feel.

Just imagine a beautiful star way above your head. Visualise that star and begin to move in the infinity pattern. Let your body begin to connect with the infinity pattern. Bring it down so that it is about two feet above your head. Let your head begin to follow the pattern and relax. Feel all the tension in your head and your jaw relaxing.

Let the infinity pattern come down to your crown like the petals of a flower.

Now begin to move it down to your third eye area. Feel it opening your third eye.

Let your head move a little bit more. Let it flow.

Bring it down into the throat area. Feel all the different sensations there.

While we are in the throat area start saying "All-Love."

Move that sound down into your heart. Let the infinity expand in the heart. Let it expand out to the shoulders. Let the shoulders move.

Feel the movement.

Take it down into the solar plexus.

Now move it down into the pelvis.

Take it down into your legs.

Go deep into the heart of the Earth.

Begin to draw the infinity up from the centre of the Earth.

Let your body do what it needs to do. Move the parts that seem to be stuck, let it unwind.

Now let your body slow down, let the movements become more gentle and soft. And notice how your body feels.

Just stay in that space, in that feeling.

When you are ready, open your eyes and look around.'

What happens in an All-Love workshop?

THE aim of an All-Love class is to establish a direct connection with the energy of the Source, or creator. The workshop provides a safe environment, in which we can experience the joy of our own direct connection with Source, and in which we can heal those physical, emotional, and mental issues which are preventing us from fully being ourselves.

People often find that they start to experience the effects of the energy before they even get to the workshop. Simply talking on the phone, looking at the All-Love website, or listening to the Shenu meditation on a CD, they feel the energy. An experience of the energy, and even an initiation, does not have to be linked to another individual.

Jayne Forsyth writes: 'When I first communicated with Patrick ... a feeling from that email that I had known him for eternity, and the developing presence of crystal clear, brightly coloured but fragmented patches of light in my third eye area, primarily electric blue, but also sometimes magenta or bright emerald green.'

Many people are not sure what to expect at a workshop. Linda Newman says; 'I came to the seminar on a gut feeling that I should be here. I am dyslexic so I have never read much in my life. So, I had never read about this course, about the people involved in it. And really did not know their names either. Coming here and not knowing quite what to expect and what happened to me blew my mind. To experience what I have experienced here in the last few days is quite awesome ... to say the least.'

At the beginning of a class, people simply introduce themselves and invite the energy to come in and sometimes the energy is experienced so powerfully that people start to go into emotional processing and initiations immediately. In some workshops, it is impossible to even get round to doing the meditation.

Patrick writes: 'Lately, I am finding that the introductions can be the most powerful part of the class. In Malaga, we got around to about the sixth name in the circle before the energy started to flow and initiations were happening.'

A workshop is an opportunity for people to express themselves in whatever way they need to, crying, shouting, moving, dancing, and laughing. It can come as something of a surprise for people who are expecting a quiet meditation!

Janie Forbes says: 'This is the first workshop I have done of this sort and although I had been to four All-Love meditation sessions I was not sure what was going to happen. Wish I had read the article about Workshop Experiences in the All-Love magazine before I went!

For the energy to enter within you have to go through/allow a cleansing process which can be quite traumatic. Before we had time to start the meditation, people began processing ... screaming, crying, vomiting. My daughter and her friend were a bit shocked by all this. I have seen this before and also experienced it but not to the extent that some of these people did.'

If you do not get involved in the class and you are just looking at it from the outside, then All-Love classes can look really weird. But when you are in the energy, and becoming involved in your own process, just doing what you need to for yourself, you are not really aware of anything outside of what you are experiencing. It all seems perfectly natural.

Patrick: 'Looking on the outside it is always a little different. It's a bit like sex. A child watching sex would think it was a terrible thing. People are moaning and doing all kinds of contortions, and a child would be frightened. In the same sense, when you see people throwing up, screaming and yelling, you get frightened, but when a person is actually in it, it is actually a very enjoyable experience.'

The energy helps to bring the emotions to the surface. People start to spontaneously express their feelings. Seeing and feeling what's going on around them helps others to get in touch with their own unexpressed emotions.

Shaila Hernández González says: 'I can't explain why I went to the workshop, but similar to when I started Reiki, I simply knew I had to do it. I didn't know what we were going to do there, but in no way was I expecting what happened when all we'd done was start to introduce ourselves. The person next to me started to shout, an intense and piercing shout. I thought I was hallucinating. What on earth was happening here? Various people entered into process, but I didn't really understand what was happening. After a while I started to feel bad, I felt sad. I wanted to cry, but the tears wouldn't come out. I felt emotions were stuck in my throat, my solar plexus and my belly, but I wasn't able to get them out because I was afraid.'

For many people, experiencing painful feelings that they have been holding within them, sometimes for many years, can be frightening. Often, we stop the flow of energy when we try to control what is happening within us. We stay in our minds, rather than allowing ourselves to feel what is happening in our bodies and hearts. Losing control, truly feeling our feelings, is something that most of us fear. The energy flows strongly when we allow ourselves to feel what is happening in our bodies, when we open our hearts, and become consciously aware of the feelings that we have been blocking.

People are naturally drawn to help others. When one person gets upset, another supports her, being with her, touching her, encouraging her to express the pain that she is feeling. This occurs quite spontaneously, and it often happens that the helper begins to get in contact with her own feelings more. Instinctively, we often give to others what we are most in need of ourselves.

Crying, shouting, laughing or screaming often occurs within a workshop, as people are suddenly able to express what exists inside themselves. Again, this can be disturbing for people who are used to strictly containing their emotions and upset. However, for each individual, the feelings of others act as a trigger for his or her own feelings. It can be extremely enlightening to find out why you are affected in some way by someone else's emotion – it often means that somewhere, within yourself, that same emotion is waiting to be expressed. A kind of knock-on effect can occur, where various people are each triggering other people's unresolved emotional issues. This is one reason why emotional processing within a group setting can be so powerful.

Likewise, feelings of joy and love that are experienced as the energy comes in are also magnified many times. The group energy is stronger than each individual could experience alone.

You invite the energy to enter into your body, both from the Heavens above and the Earth below, and you often have to start to heal some emotional or energetic blocks before you develop a strong connection. Each person is encouraged to allow him or herself to fully experience the tensions held within his or her body, and to express the emotions associated with these. When painful emotions are fully felt and expressed, blockages and old patterns are released. Insights often arise about the origin of that pain. We become aware of the meaning of that pain, when and how it first arose, what personal significance it has for us.

Graham: 'I was helping someone, and I suddenly felt the pain in her heart, and I started to cry, partly for her, and partly for me. Then I lay on the floor, and started sobbing and my body started to jerk uncontrollably. I became aware that I was feeling upset because a close friend of mine was going back to England, but then I realised that the sense of loss was also related to the death of my father many years ago. In both situations, I was feeling that they were about to leave me and I felt helpless to do anything about it.'

Patrick: 'About one in ten people have spontaneous body movements with the energy. It is quite common to have involuntary movements in areas that have blockages.' Movement helps to release energy blockages and emotions held within the body.'

In the class, people are encouraged to start to learn the process of leading someone else through the meditation, getting them to focus into their body, to allow feelings and sensations to emerge, and to express them in whatever way they need to.

Janie Forbes: 'We did a one-to-one meditation, and I was the doer/giver. We followed the instructions of the teacher. It was not long before my friend began to open up and her process started. During the session the teachers (there were four of them) went round helping/supporting us all and giving advice. But I found that when she opened up, so did I, so my process started too, and we both ended up giving to each other and doing our own thing.'

Patrick: 'You might feel like going to help another person but you're really not sure exactly what to do. The best thing to do is to be with the person. Connect with them. Let them know that you are there for them. That can help the whole process itself. Ideally, this energy is so simple; you do not really have to say anything. Some people go into an initiation without any of the techniques — on the phone.'

Shaila Hernández González: 'I was lying on the floor, and a woman was at my side, giving me help and love. I felt like a four-year old child, sad because she felt that nobody loved her. It was good to feel loved, I began to feel happy, I laughed a little. When we sat down in the circle again, I was feeling very good. I could feel the energy vibrating and moving very subtly through my body. It made me feel very happy, full of peace and, above all, love for all those who were there.'

Much of the emotional processing that takes place, and the support that members of the group give to each other, occurs at a non-verbal level. Much of our pain comes from a time when we had no words to express it. So, we cannot access it simply through words. To release it from our emotional energy system, or our body, we need to fully experience it within our bodies.

Janie Forbes: 'The second day it did not take long for my process to start. The tears started to flow...this is my normal way of cleansing my hurt but today they seemed to be coming from way deep down within me. While processing, the teachers ask you to voice your emotions in words or in a sound. I find this very difficult, although I have no problem chanting or singing. I had this terrible pain in my heart chakra, and this horrible sound came out of it ... well it sounded horrible to me ... like an animal in pain. Also my hands started to tense up into fists. One of the male teachers came over to me and I begged him to hug me because if he didn't I was going to floor him! I am not usually a violent person but the feeling of violence that I have against men is frightening and though I have been working on it for years it seems to be deeply rooted. While being hugged by the teacher, I had this beautiful sensation of warmth entering me from above and I felt so much at peace afterwards and the pain in my heart went. I was also able to voice my feelings in sound. It is very difficult to describe how I felt afterwards ... very calm and peaceful ... but full to bursting with love.'

Sometimes emotional pain is accompanied by intense physical pain. It is as if the emotions are stuck in the body and are struggling to get out. For some people, as the energy comes in, it hits areas of longstanding tension or blockage, where painful emotions or memories are held within the body. The energy helps these blockages to shift, and the pain to be released.

Paz: 'During the Infinity Dance, lying on the floor, I felt a vibration in my vertebral column, as if something was cleaning it. Then I heard a man shouting very loudly, and I started to shake and to have strong feelings of wanting to disappear. I covered my ears so I couldn't hear anybody, then I could hear my breathing and I started taking it to the areas of pain. I felt as if I was diving, listening to my breathing through a regulator. It was good, because I always forget to breathe, I hold my breath. I took the breath to the muscles which had seized up. I had to do it. And they started to stretch. Then, somone touched me on the solar plexus and I felt a lot of pain, so I breathed into it and managed to move the pain down to the abdomen but I couldn't go any further. Graham told me that there was a part of me that could do it, and to trust in that part, and I began to push down to get it out of me. Afterwards, I felt good.'

For many people, to be able to support someone else through their pain is a very positive and healing experience. They realise, maybe for the first time, that they have something valuable to offer to others.

Shaila Hernández González: 'In the afternoon we did another meditation. In the first, I had received, and in this one, I was giving. There was a woman who was feeling bad, and to do the meditation with her was for me an unforgettable experience. I was able to leave my blocks and my fears on one side and be there for her with all my heart. For me it was a lovely experience to hug this person and to feel her in my arms crying like a child. It made me see that I am able to help and to give love and affection. It made me very happy to have been able to help her.'

Touch is very important. It helps us to relax and to heal – and to feel that we are cared for. When we are touched by someone else's pain, we naturally reach out to them. Yet many of us have felt very alone when we have been upset in the past. When painful feelings emerge, it is very comforting to have someone with you, holding you. Without words, they are saying, 'I am here with you.'

Shaila Hernández González: 'I think that before the workshop I could count on one hand the number of times I'd been hugged. Now, five months later, I would need a hundred hands to count them all. To hug people has become something quite natural for me. Since the workshop there has been more love in my life and my heart is more open to give and receive love.'

The support from the group is an important part of the healing process. Throughout our lives, many of us have felt rejected or ashamed when we have expressed our anger and pain to others - which is one reason we continue to hold it in. When we are able to acknowledge the emotional pain within us, to express it and still be accepted by others, we experience love in a way that we may not have experienced it before. This can be a powerful healing experience.

When supporting another person through their emotional process, it is a good idea to ask that person if s/he would like you to be there. You must be sensitive to other people's needs, not pressurising them but allowing them to take their time to do whatever they need to do and not thinking that you know what that is! You can help a person enormously just by touching, giving encouragement, and allowing him time and space. People will do as much as they are able at that time. Sometimes asking them if they would like to try to bring the energy and the light into their pain can be helpful if they are feeling stuck and not sure what to do about it. This may help them feel better, or may trigger an emotional shift so that they can come to express more of what they are feeling.

Katja Kaiser: 'In a workshop, people are vulnerable and sensitive, and I think the best help you can give is to touch someone, keep quiet, not say too much and above all, not tell a person why s/he is feeling the way s/he is, even if you think you know why. No one has the right to say what's happening to someone else. For me that is the most sacred law of healing – as well as realising that we are all simply channels for the energy, we personally cannot take the credit for what we are doing.

'Now I am getting to know the procedure in All-Love workshops, I think it is important to attend as many as possible in order to learn how to help someone in process. I think it is a very delicate business, firstly to make sure that you do not say anything that could hurt a person, or give false leads, and on the other hand to be prepared to enter into your own process at any point.'

We need to be constantly aware that when people are in an open, vulnerable condition, things that we say, perhaps inadvertently, can be hurtful.

Shaila Hernández González: 'At one point, I was feeling very sad, frightened and confused. I was lying down and crying. There were a few people with me. One of them suddenly said, "You have a problem with your mother." She said it with great certainty, as if she knew what she was talking about. I did not like that much, I still felt stuck. Okay, maybe there was a problem with my mother, but at that moment I was having a problem with the world in general! She should have kept quiet.

'I felt very bad. After she'd said that, another woman started arguing with her, saying she shouldn't have said something like that. I wasn't in a state to say anything, I didn't even have the strength to get up off the floor. They carried on arguing and I felt a bit abandoned. I was still stuck, feeling very bad and I didn't know what to do about it. Another woman came over and simply hugged me. I held on to her, and started crying disconsolately, letting all this sadness come out. After that I felt a lot better.'

In a workshop, we are trying to move away from our heads and into our hearts – or at least to connect the two! We do not really know the whys and wherefores of anyone else's experience; we are looking to offer not interpretations but interested concern. It is a challenge, to stop our minds from trying to explain things – for ourselves or others - and instead to simply feel, to hold a place not of judgement but of love.

Katja Kaiser: 'At the start of the workshop, I was helping a person who had a serious depression and a feeling of wanting to be dead. It is a situation that I have known myself, and I could really feel for her. I could relive this situation, and, if I hadn't healed it properly, I could have started hurting a great deal again, and entered into strong emotional processes. I didn't though, I think because I have got over this episode of my life, and it doesn't cause me pain because I have accepted this part of me and taken away its power.

'In the break, after helping this person, I went outside on the terrace. I was simply standing enjoying the warmth of the sun on my face. I wasn't thinking of anything, it was a quiet, peaceful moment with no distractions. I noticed that something was happening. The energy was coming up my legs, and my legs became rooted strongly to the ground, and the energy came down from the Heavens, and I was flooded with heat. I simply sent the message to my mind: "Enjoy it, go with the flow, let it happen, don't be afraid." My whole body was filled with a strong current of energy, especially in my feet and my arms, and finally formed a cross. My heart was opening more and more. I felt genuine gladness to be alive, and I enjoyed a feeling of inner peace and quiet that I'd never felt before.

'Going back into the workshop, I continued feeling this strong connection with the energy, as much from the Earth as from the Heaven. Sitting in the room, I simply felt my heart very open. I felt a lot of love, and my whole body was vibrating with the energy. It made me feel profoundly at peace with myself.'

Patrick: 'The grounding aspect is a very good sign of an initiation. You don't have to have that. But if all of a sudden you have these huge roots and you feel that being on the Earth is effortless, it's a wonderful experience. I liken an initiation to an orgasm – if you have to ask whether you have had one, then you probably haven't!'

When a direct energy connection is made to both the Heavens, or Source, and the Earth, the energy is grounded within a person, the chakras are balanced and connected, and the person feels the energy throughout his body and energy system. As Patrick says; 'It is as if you are one big unified chakra.'

Once we have expressed our pain, we feel so much lighter, as if a weight has been taken away from us. Many of us have forgotten how to play, to laugh, to truly feel all the pleasurable sensations and emotions that we are capable of experiencing. Once we have let go of our own rigid control, we can allow our joy to come out.

Pilar Holgado Catalán: 'For me this has been a really powerful experience beyond what I thought possible in two days…

'Another load of energy came and I felt so much heat. I started to shake again and… started to laugh…to laugh in a way that I don't remember having done before, for I don't know how long, without knowing why, but with an immense pleasure running through me…

'I would like to deeply thank everyone who was there, those who supported me and those that let me support them. And above all, thanks to the Universe for having given me this opportunity to find myself and reconcile myself with what is inside me.'

Shaila Hernández González: 'The meditation was very nice, very peaceful. I felt very good, very connected with the energy. But I also felt something stuck in my throat. I volunteered to work with this blockage. It was as if I wanted to vomit, but nothing came out however much I tried. I hunched over with my arms round my knees and my fists clenched tightly across my chest. Graham suggested I sat up with my back straight, so I could open my chest and breathe deeply, and see if I could feel the difference. When I did it, something happened, it was like an explosion of happiness, I started to laugh and I couldn't stop. Suddenly the block in my throat disappeared and the laughter came up from my solar plexus. Later I don't know where it came from, I only know it was coming from somewhere deep inside. I felt very happy, I wanted to laugh and I didn't hold back. I threw myself on the floor and let the laughter take over. It was great!'

The energy does whatever we need it to do. It helps us to gain insights into ourselves, and to become aware of our own true purpose.

Teresa Arias Alonso: 'I have been waiting for this SKHM workshop for some time because I knew perfectly well that my life was going to change after it. I knew that I wasn't completely grounded on the Earth. In some way I was still floating on the higher levels. It has helped me to ground myself in order to do the work that I have to do. I have come to do something but I couldn't collect myself, root myself sufficiently to gain the strength, the courage and the bravery to do what I had come to do. I felt really good. I felt the energy flowing through my body, channelling it. I feel complete in this moment.'

Janie Forbes: 'In the Infinity Dance, we all stood, with enough room between us and a space in front of us to lie down afterwards. The music began and we had to visualize the sign of Infinity, which is like a number eight sideways. We had to do the sign with our head and imagine it above us. As we were swaying to the music, we had to visualize the sign entering our crown chakra ... then down to our third eye.... throat chakra ..... heart chakra .... solar plexus .... abdomen ... root chakra ... then down into the Earth. We then had to visualize the Infinity sign coming up through the roots from the centre of the Earth, through our feet and all the way up our body. The energy coming up through my body was so strong it knocked me off my feet and I thought I was going to faint, but then I felt this beautiful warmth coming down through me from above and the two energies met at my heart chakra. I then felt myself transforming ... I was wearing my blue Sari, and someone painted a Bindi (a red dot) on my third- eye chakra ... I think one of the teachers actually touched my third-eye at the time ... it felt like it but so much was happening I'm not sure.

'I started to sway to the music again but with my hands clasped. I started from above my crown chakra bringing them down to my third-eye ... then to my throat and to my heart chakra.

I then began to feel this beautiful warm feeling rising from the bottom of my spine coming up to meet the energy at my heart chakra. I was no longer me ... I had become a Cobra and the sensation I had was of rising out of a basket to the music of a snake-charmer. I then lay down on the floor and just breathed in all the sensations.

'All in all it was a great weekend. Apart from experiencing the Initiation and the Kundalini rising, I met a lot of lovely people, have made a lot of new friends and feel renewed.'

Patrick does not try too precisely to define the energy, or how it can be used. His view is that each person experiences the energy in their own way and defines it for themselves: 'If we all work with the energy, it's just amazing what can happen.'

It can work a bit like a tuning fork. When a person connects strongly to the energy, his vibrational energy is raised. If he stands next to, or touches, a person who is vibrating at that moment at a lower rate, then that other person's energy can start to increase until s/he vibrates at that higher level too. When people are experiencing intense emotions, they often have a good connection with the energy, so if you go near them, you may also feel that energy.

Patrick: 'One of the reasons that I encourage people to go over and support is because they get more out of it sometimes than the person that is getting the healing. Many people say, "Oh my gosh, when I was facilitating, I could feel my crown opening and my hands glowing." People processing their emotions are more connected with the energy, the ones supporting are not necessarily but then they get into it through the person's processing. That is actually one of the tricks. I see someone in process and I see someone who feels a little stuck, and I say, "Go over there and help them," and they get involved in it. One of the nice things is that everybody is helping and sharing and getting into it. There's a ping-pong; one person would be in process, someone would go to help, then they would be in process. There would be a switch.'

Sometimes, if one person experiences an initiation, the energy can spread to those around.

Jayne Forsyth: 'My initiation was on the second weekend in Cyprus – it started after lunch on Sunday when I'd gone up to my hotel room for a little rest! I recall stepping on to the balcony and looking out across the sea, feeling very content and then saying aloud (I am sorry if this sounds like plagiarism but this is how it is and it worked!!) "I am ready, if you want to do what you need to." As soon as I lay down, patches of electric blue light appeared in my third eye area but this time they had lightning strike patterns, in a different colour, going vertically through the centre. Then I had a few mild "judders" that went the lengths of my arms and then my legs. Wondering if this was it, I had that anticipatory feeling of a "rite of passage" and what the **** happens next, particularly as I was on the fifth floor of a hotel and had to get to the first in a lift that was sometimes as shaky as I was by now feeling. So I asked it to give me a few minutes to get some help and I just continued to have waves of shaking and as it did my heart area just kept expanding.

'Everyone wanted to hug me afterwards to see if they could "catch" it but my heart was so big, and they all hugged me so tight, I felt as if I would suffocate. However, my initiation did create the house of cards effect with about the five or six people next to me in the circle going into spontaneous initiation. I remember being very, very hot, and I had what felt like real "growing pains" all over my chest all night.'

Patrick: 'Once a person has had an initiation, they will vibrate at a particular level, and when they come into contact with another person they will help that person to vibrate at that level. You really don't have to do anything, it just happens. When you go home and meet the family, it could start to happen. Like after the Malaga workshop when one person went home and gave someone a hug and they went into an initiation. It might be that the person they come into contact with has a strong resonance with them, but also when a person is in that initiation state they are beaming a lot of light and that can affect a lot of people.'

In a class, many people feel a strong connection with the energy within a very short time; for others, more emotional processing is necessary before the energy can be more fully integrated. Whether an initiation takes place or not, it may still take weeks or months for the full effects of the energy to be experienced and integrated. Memories, feelings and images may emerge over a period of time, as people continue to process their emotions. It is important that teachers are available to provide support during this time, including for people who have spontaneous initiations outside the workshop, as some people find that when simply recounting their experiences to others, both they themselves and the listeners feel the energy, and suppressed emotions can suddenly surface.

Shaila Hernández González: 'In the weeks and months following the first workshop, I experienced many ups and downs. There were many times that I felt immensely happy, but behind this happiness I could feel a shadow; the sadness was still there, hidden underneath the happiness. I had to get to those feelings, but I couldn't. Four months later, the week before the next workshop was very difficult. I felt terrible: sad, confused, and hopeless. I spent the whole week feeling very depressed. The only thing that stopped me from slipping completely into this sadness was remembering the moments of intense happiness that I had come to experience, and the certainty that I would feel them again. I went to the second workshop determined that I would release the painful emotions. But I knew it would be very difficult because I had never been able to express my emotions in front of anyone, I'd spent years hiding my tears so that no one could see me crying.'

Patrick: 'Some people do get depressed afterwards. But that is really common when a person has had a really high peak experience. When you come down, it is very depressing. It's like you are in Heaven for a few hours, and all of a sudden you are back down on Earth.'

When we have seen something clearly, and realised our true feelings about ourselves, or about some other person or situation, it can be very difficult to then go back into our normal lives and carry on as before. Seeing something clearly means that you then have a choice whether to act on it or not, and sometimes we are simply not ready, or we are fearful of the consequences. Then we need to give ourselves time and space to feel what's really right for us.

Rachel McCormack: 'In the months following my first workshop I felt rather blown away. It was an incredibly strong spiritual experience and I couldn't sleep or eat properly for a couple of weeks afterwards and would end up in tears whenever I meditated. It also began to change my view of life. It has made me try much more to do what is right rather than simply what I want. I would say that since my later initiations - at home and at the following workshop in Cornwall - I have been much more able to wait and see, rather than feel the need to control everything, my life has moved forward very fast in terms of my work and my personal spiritual life.'

An initiation is not a one-off event. At the point that we experience an initiation, we are in balance. Yet healing is an ongoing process, and our energy and emotions are constantly changing as we move towards our next point of balance. When we experience another initiation, we may bring in a different aspect of the higher parts of ourselves.

Rachel McCormack; 'My first initiation was at the first workshop I went to. I felt filled with golden light and I just didn't want to move. It blew me away but I now realise that I was dipping my toes in the baby pool.'

Some people, although they may not have experienced anything particularly dramatic during the class, begin to be aware later that things are shifting, that they are more sensitive to the energy, or that they feel more peaceful and forgiving towards themselves. They may take up new interests or begin to feel more creative.

Every workshop is different. And every person is different, in how he responds to the energy. Each person is on his own individual path, and what happens will be what he needs to happen at that time. The energy is very powerful; it brings an incredible sense of joy and harmony, an inner knowing that there is some loving force outside of you that connects you with the Universe – and with others. Just to feel it – with or without an initiation - is the beginning of a wonderful and exciting new journey of discovery.

Not everyone experiences an initiation in the first workshop they attend. Even if you do, it still takes time for the energy to fully integrate into your energy system and body.

Pedro De las Heras Garcia: 'I think that both those who did not experience an initiation, and those who did, have received a wonderful gift. I know that All-Love has changed some people's lives, and I know that it will also change our lives as well.

'Now we have to work, but I feel so fortunate, it is as if I have won the lottery – I only have to dare to pick up the prize.

'But it is there waiting until I am ready. And Patrick, along with Michael and the group have showed me how to get it. It is free and marvellous, I know.'

Once you have experienced the energy, you can bring it in for yourself after the workshop, by opening your heart and crown and visualising the column of light.

Patrick: 'It is always easier when you have help, but you do eventually need to start working on bringing it in on your own. Visualise that golden brilliance and remember your connection with the Creator, bring it into the now. Movement can also have the same effect. Moving in the infinity pattern brings up many experiences. When we are in that state of joy, the energy begins to flow.'

You can use the energy for self-healing. You may wish to put your hands on your body, or you can visualise bringing the infinity symbol throughout your body. Some people simply think of the energy, and it starts to flow. In the same way, using your intent and the power of your mind, you can send the energy to other people at a distance or to situations in your life.

Many people will also experience an increase in their healing abilities. Many people come to an All-Love workshop having already done Reiki or some other form of energy work. Those who already have Reiki often find that after a workshop, the power of the energy that they are channelling increases. Both Reiki and the All-Love energy can be used to continue to heal issues that have been brought up in the workshop. People often find that they are not using one or the other, but a mixture of the two. All-Love encompasses healing, personal development and energy work, and can therefore be used in combination with any other method of energy healing or personal growth work.

Rachel McCormack: 'At the moment, I principally use the energy on myself, but I do Reiki treatments and I do not distinguish or use any symbols; whatever comes out comes out. But it has changed the way I view others and myself so I suppose I also use it everyday all day in my relation to others. It has helped me to form a completely different view of the world, my place in it, and myself. It is most recently helping to establish how I feel about things rather than my usual monkey mind unleashing a torrent of thoughts and ideas.'

Jayne Forsyth: 'After the first workshop I was feeling very ill as my "old" energy system and the blueprint of the new one were causing the brain to get confusing signals. Now, to connect with the energy, I just put my hand on my heart chakra or imagine the column of light. If I feel a bit blocked, I play the Shenu Meditation CD. All-Love has helped me to reclaim me for myself without losing compassion for others.'

For many people, a SKHM workshop provides a powerful source of unconditional love; the joy of connecting with the energy, of healing painful emotions, and the opportunity of receiving the compassion and support of the group make it a truly unforgettable experience.

Techniques used in All-Love

THERE are two main aspects of working with the All-Love system. The first is enabling people to have an experience of the energy; the second is helping them to deal with the emotions that frequently arise as a result.

Teachers must be able to deal with both of these aspects. The teacher-training programme for All-Love requires that people have attended at least four or five workshops. Once they have experienced an initiation, they will be more familiar with some of the different ways in which the energy acts and is experienced. They must be able to work with people on an individual level and also within a group, guiding people through the meditations, bringing the energy in, facilitating the process for others so that they can open themselves to the energy. They must also learn how to help people to work through emotional blocks.

The Shenu meditation focuses on opening the crown, opening the spiritual heart centre, and connecting with the Earth. The Infinity Dance combines movement with active visualisation. They both encourage a person to become more open and ready to receive; to become more aware of themselves and what is happening in their body, and to begin to relate emotions to the physical sensations and tensions felt within the body. A person as a result feels more connected with his body and becomes aware of himself on different levels; mentally, emotionally, physically, energetically and spiritually.

Once a connection has been made with the energy, the person invites his spiritual essence to enter more fully into the body. This is a very important part of the process. This is the point at which we make the connection with our divine essence, to the part of us, which is spiritually connected to the Creator. It has many names, and each person will describe or visualise it in different ways. For some, it is simply the part of themselves which knows the intuitive self or inner wisdom. For others, it is the higher self.

Patrick: 'Many people see this connection with Source in the form of some divine being; for a Christian it would be the Christ consciousness; a Buddhist would bring in Buddha. The Christ energy is more heart centred, whereas the Buddha energy is more in the head. In India, they would encourage you to bring in Ganesh, Vishnu, Krishna, the Indian divine beings. Each individual personifies the energy in whatever form s/he feels most comfortable with.

'But really, in this process of personifying the energy as something outside of yourself, you are just essentially working with archetypal energies. For instance, the Native Americans, instead of working with half animal, half human forms as many of the older religions did, worked with just animal forms. If they wanted to work with a feeling of power, they would bring in the bear, which has a lot of strength. If they wanted to bring in a feeling of expansiveness, they would bring in the energy of the eagle, up in the sky and feeling completely expanded. I have used these images – the heart of the lion, the strength of the bear, the sensitivity of the deer – a lot in the past, and they work very well. As long as people don't get caught up in it and start worshipping animals. People will have an image and they begin to worship it; that is how idol worship started. They would develop a connection with Source through these animals. Soon that animal becomes sacred, and then a god, and then it sometimes becomes replaced by a man.

'Christ and Buddha did not promote it, but people began worshipping them. Then religion and the Church said that they had that lineage of light on the Earth. In the Catholic religion, the Pope becomes that living God. The split that happened in the Church was that the Protestants did not want someone to be pretending to be their connection with God. If you look, every major religion has that split.

'I see our higher essence, which I would essentially call our eternal soul, as being very connected with our higher self. This is what we are bringing in more fully. I do not see it as a divine being who is separate from ourselves. That is where your ideas of separation begin to come in. Once you begin to break down these feelings, perceptions and concepts of being separate, then that essence begins to descend and come into your body more fully. It feels like it descends, but really it is there all the time, it's just that your awareness is now growing.'

In All-Love, we are making our own connection with the Creator, without any intermediary. Patrick: 'In other systems, such as the one I experienced in India, you are relying on someone else to alter your energy field; whereas with our approach you are pretty much opening things up on your own. If you come up against an energy block then we work through it.'

A teacher needs to be familiar with the energy, and be able to use it for his own personal growth, so that he can help a person work through energetic and emotional blocks. He learns by experiencing the process first hand through individual sessions with a teacher, and by practising individual sessions with another person under supervision.

During a workshop, there are times when many people are processing their emotions, or experiencing initiations and so the energy within the group is strong. Other times, the energy falls off, and the teacher needs be able to get it moving again, by encouraging people to share their experiences in the group, or by demonstrating healing techniques if someone feels stuck and volunteers to work in front of the group.

The energy can release some very powerful emotions, and the teacher needs to know how to guide a person to work with these. Merely to access painful feelings without helping a person through the emotional work that is necessary in order to truly transform that pain may simply re-traumatise that person and leave him or her feeling worse than before.

Patrick: 'I have learned that there is a very strong relationship between emotional clearing work and initiation; this is why I have incorporated emotional healing as an integral part of my classes. It does require more extensive training and a deeper level of participation. Some people want to get the energy, have the certificate, become a teacher - but don't want to do the work. You have to do the work in order to understand what it is all about. Otherwise you can't really help other people.'

The All-Love system that Patrick has developed is an eclectic mix of techniques drawn from energy healing, sound healing and body-centred psychotherapy, such as conscious breathing, focussing into the body, and inner child work.

When the energy enters a person's energy field, it tends to start shifting any energetic blocks it encounters.

Patrick uses a variety of techniques to help the person become aware of these blocks and to identify their origin. Directing a person's awareness into their body enables them to locate areas of physical tension or pain, which may be associated with blocked energy or emotion. Simply to touch a person lightly in that area helps them to focus awareness in that area and to begin to feel what is happening both in their body and in their feelings.

In emotional clearing work, there is a cycle, which moves through identification and expression of pain, to fuller integration of self and then finally to forgiveness and gratitude.

Patrick: 'The technique is to initiate the process if the person is not in an emotional state. If the person is already in a process then you can start a dialogue. This first stage, of Identification and Expression, is common to most emotional healing work, except that many systems do not then lead on to an initiation. I usually do the meditation and then would go into the identification process.' The following is an example of Patrick doing this with Graham.

'Just be comfortable and become aware of your breathing. Feel your physical body, from your head to your toes. Scan your body. You may notice an area of discomfort, or tension, where you feel the energy may be a bit stuck. Bring your full awareness to that point and simply observe.'

'Let yourself feel whatever is there. Just feel it, remember it is a part of you.'

'Tell me the area of your body, and bring your awareness into that area.'

'We want to start an identification process: Where is it? How big is it? What shape is it? Does it have a colour? A smell or taste? What is it made of? That is the first step.'

'Breathe into it, give it space. Just let yourself feel it, without judging it. Once it is identified then it can be given a voice.'

'Connect this point with the throat.'

'Is there a particular sound or a particular vibration connected with this? Go into that, feel the vibration. If it wants to speak, to let itself out, allow it to come out. Try to get a sound.'

'Now go back into that area, how does it feel?' (G: "It feels quite sharp.")

'Just feel the sharpness, feel the points.'

'Go back to the sound again. See how the sound has changed – maybe now it is higher pitched. You are giving it permission to express itself. Maybe that is something it has not done before.'

'How old is this energy? When did you first feel it? What purpose was it serving?'

'Go back to the time when you first felt this energy. What is happening?' (G: "I was being bullied at school.")

'If anyone is connecting with this energy, come up and help. Just feel what is going on in the group.'

'Maybe there are some words that are associated with this energy.' (G: "Stop!")

'How are you feeling?' (G: "Frightened.")

'Feel the fear. Feel that sensation.'

'Let your body move. Do what it needs to do. Let the voice come out. Drop right down into that.' (G: Shouting, screaming, low-pitched.)

'Let yourself feel. Let it speak if it wants to speak. Stay with it. Let yourself feel it. Notice what is going on. Let it come out. Whatever you are feeling let yourself feel, just let it come through. You might feel a little restless.'

'Is this energy associated with a person?' (G: "Other kids at school, taunting me.")

'What do you want to say to this person? Say it.' (G: "Go away! Leave me alone.")

'Breathe in. Let it come through. Cough it out. Right down in the gut. Just let yourself feel it. Breathe it in. Let yourself feel.'

'Does that person want to say anything to you?'

'Let it speak. Give it a voice if you can. And it's ok if you can't.'

'Connect with the feeling that is behind that. Just notice how you are feeling.'

'Listen to your body, what does your body want to do?'

'Now bring the light in. Bring it all the way in. Once the energy fully expresses itself and is heard, the transformation to light can begin.'

Let us look at an example of a phone session. Patrick is working with Teresa, and Graham is supporting her.

T: 'I have been a bit unsettled, worrying about whether I have to move back to the UK.'

P: 'You probably need to do a little bit of screaming now, Teresa.'

T: 'Probably.'

P: 'Let it out. How are you doing?'

G: 'She is crying.'

P: 'Let it come out. Breathe into it. Let a little sound out…
What is it that you are feeling? What is the connection with this?'

T: 'It's talking about leaving here and not knowing what I shall be doing.'

P: 'Just feel that. Really connect with that. Leaving here and not knowing what you are doing. Just really experience that. I realise that some of this is a projection of the future, but what is the projection from the past? Of what else does this remind you? When did you feel this before? How old is this fear of not knowing what you are doing?'

T: 'It's like starting at medical school, or going back earlier, like when I was little, going to school. I never knew what the f*** anybody was doing really.'

P: 'Okay let's get to the first one, school. How old are you?'

T: 'Five.'

P: 'Feel five-year old Teresa. Breathe into it, feel it.'

T: 'It's just like I am always an outsider, I am always on my own, I am always lonely, I don't know what anyone else is talking about.'

P: 'Just feel the aloneness. Breathe into it. Is there something that you need to say to anybody? Who do you need to speak to?'

T: 'It's just like wanting to say that I do exist.'

P: 'Good, say that.'

T: Cries.

G: 'Just say it, say it out loud.'

P: 'Breathe into that.'

T: 'I do exist.'

P: 'Let yourself feel. Is there anyone connected to this feeling that you need to speak to?'

T: 'I don't know.'

P: 'Who would you like to speak to? Breathe into it. Come from little five-year old Teresa. Do you need to talk to someone? Who would you like to have hold you just now?'

T: 'I don't know, my mum I guess.'

P: 'Ask your mum to come and hold you. Ask her.'

T: 'Come and hold me. Yes, I feel a bit more peaceful now. Yes, I feel better.'

P: 'This is one of the things that we want to work on. Breathe that peace in; just keep feeling the peace in the same way that you were feeling the fear of being on your own. Just breathe that peace in. We want to do this; we want to anchor this love and this peace. Where do you feel the peace anchoring into your body?'

Pause.

G: 'Where do you feel the peace in your body?'

T: 'In my heart.'

P: 'Let's connect it with your heart. And bring it into the present now. Feel the present, of that peace, bring it in there. And now bring it into the whole situation, getting ready, and the possibility of leaving. Project it into the future as well. Feel that real calmness. Feeling the whole situation. Breathe it in.

'How does that feel?'

T: 'It feels all glowing now.'

P: 'Just let it glow. Keep bringing it through, feeling it in your body. Start in the heart, feel it expand through the whole chest, get it down into your whole torso, your arms and legs, your fingers and your toes, the top of your head, tip of your nose.

'Just breathe into that. Really begin to feel the cycle of what you went through in the last hour. The feelings that you felt, of how they came in, and then how you felt the fear, but feel the result of being in the space that you are in now. And know that this is all your creation.

'Once you begin to connect it fully with your body, then begin to fill the whole room up. Radiating it and filling the whole room up. And Graham just allow yourself to receive. As Teresa begins to radiate it, feel that, be able to receive.

'How are you feeling now Teresa?'

T: 'I feel nice.'

P: 'Stay with it. How are you feeling Graham?'

G: 'I feel good too.'

P: 'Just bring in the All-Love, ask the All-Love energy to come in now. Work with the infinity too, coming in through your crown. Bring it down into your hearts. Really feel All-Love in your hearts.

'I am going to get off the phone now. Just stay with that.'

Focussing into the body, allowing yourself to feel what sensations and tensions exist in particular areas of the body, helps you to become more aware of your inner reality. Breathing into that area, sending sound vibrations into it, and allowing the part of the body to make its own sounds, are all powerful ways of shifting emotional energy. Once you bring your consciousness fully to the area that is holding emotional pain, you can feel what is truly there.

Patrick: 'Often the shadow self will emerge and want to express itself. Once the shadow is engaged, it can create a polarity and the energy can help a person to go even deeper.'

The release stage involves fully expressing your feelings and giving them a voice. This enables you to identify what part of you is in pain, for example the child part. You are helped to discover how your feelings - of grief, shame, anger or whatever - in the present link back to painful experiences in the past.

Tracing present emotions back to their origins in the past is the most difficult part of emotional processing work, and the one that requires the most skill on the part of the teacher. It involves setting up a conscious verbal dialogue with the felt pain, so that the pain of the present can be followed back to its roots in the past.

Entering into a dialogue with the part of you that was hurt shows it that you accept it, despite its hurt or angry feelings. You stop judging and rejecting it, you start listening to it, so that it can say what it needs to say to whoever was involved at that time. This leads to an important shift in emotional energy. The felt wrong can be righted; the held pain can be released, and you start to integrate that part of you into yourself.

Patrick: 'Sometimes when you are in tears, it's like, "Who do you need to talk to?" and maybe you need to say something to Mom, and it helps clear the energy.'

Talking to a part of you, to people in your past, or to the energy itself that you need to clear, can be very effective.

After the Identification and Expression stage, there is the Integration stage. Patrick: 'Usually during the integration stage the higher self will come in and a knowing and a realisation may come in that will help the person better understand the emotion. In most cases, a person will come to the realisation that they are responsible for their own feelings. That, through their own projections and holding on to past trauma, they are the one responsible, not really the person they are projecting the emotion on to.'

If there is a person associated with that feeling, for example a parent, then entering into further dialogue with that person may lead to increased understanding of how each felt at the time. Seeing the other's point of view may give you a different perspective on the relationship or situation in which the painful feelings arose.

This is the Forgiveness stage, when, having accepted, understood and released your pain, you are able to integrate a part of yourself, and you experience a great sense of relief. Releasing the block, the energy can flow more freely into your body and energy system, bringing a feeling of love, peace and forgiveness.

Patrick: 'This is not something that can be taught, but is a natural experience of the heart opening. Once this phase is complete, the stage of Gratitude will begin to flow and the cycle is complete. It is usually at this time that an initiation may occur; it can be very spontaneous. It is not something that someone else can give to another, but truly an opening of the heart from within. Once you can truly love all of who you are, the grace of forgiveness rises up into the heart. The heart begins to open and is filled with love. At this point if enough of the self-hatred is cleared away, the crown opens and the energy floods in.'

Sound healing is another very effective method of shifting energy. Sound helps to move energy through the body and the chakras, and helps to restore harmony.

Patrick: 'I use overtones and a technique that brings awareness of the suppressed sounds within the body. Once these sounds are expressed, it may help to open up closed chakra centres and eventually lead to a spontaneous initiation.'

Breath work can also be used if a person is having difficulty in getting in contact with his emotions or is unable to feel anything at all.

Patrick: 'Conscious breathing is one of the most beautiful experiences. I still remember my first breath work session. My body was filled with so much joy and love. I could hardly believe all this energy was possible by just using the breath. In a class, if the energy is not moving and the class is really, really stuck, then I get them to lie down and do deep breathing from the abdomen for an hour. That will open them up.'

'One of the aspects I have been researching is the group that does not feel. With proper training, I have increasingly been able to help the non-feelers to start to feel. The key is a more focussed awareness in the body. Most non-feelers tend to be very mental and out of touch with their bodies. By bringing their awareness into their body a spiritual experience or possibly an initiation occurs. With the combination of awareness, and a willingness to heal, very deep wounds can be healed in an instant, that otherwise might take a lifetime to heal.'

When the body, mind and heart unite, a powerful healing may result. Working through pain in a loving environment enables the body to express itself, the mind comes to a conscious awareness of the root of the pain, and the heart allows compassion and forgiveness to replace that pain with love.

Patrick: 'Working with these processes over a period of time, sometimes over a year, usually an initiation will occur.'

We learn about the energy through experiencing it. We are healed by the energy through allowing it to help us to release the emotions and energies within ourselves that have brought us pain and held us back in our lives.

Healing involves release of the old, and transformation of that which no longer serves us, so that new connections can be made within the mind, body and energy system.

How the All-Love energy works in a group

WE have all learned how to interact in a group. Throughout our lives, we have learned not to show what we feel and not to say what we think – sometimes not even to ourselves. For many people, an All-Love workshop is actually the first opportunity they have had to express what they feel in a safe environment.

A group has a dynamics of its own. We may feel anxiety or fear as soon as we enter the room. We find ourselves drawn to certain people, while we might feel repelled by others. As people start saying things, doing things, expressing themselves in whatever way, we naturally start to react. In a workshop, someone might start screaming, another might shout, another could cry, others might do nothing. Whatever happens, you will react to each of them. Maybe not consciously – you may not be aware of your reaction as it is happening – but you will react.

Physically, your body may become tense in some particular area, you might start breathing more quickly, you might move away, clench your fists, get a headache, or feel sick. These reactions are telling you something about yourself. As you sense them and become aware of them, you need to let yourself feel them fully. They will bring you into your own process.

When other people get angry or upset, it affects us because all of us have been in situations, for instance as children, where we witnessed anger and pain, maybe a father getting drunk and shouting and lashing out, or a depressed mother crying and saying she wished she was dead, and we have felt angry, upset and powerless. One woman put her hands over her ears, crouched on the floor and said, 'I can't stand the screaming.' For her, it was triggering intensely upsetting feelings and memories, which at that time she was having great difficulty dealing with.

Other people's emotions trigger our own. When a person cries, you may want to cry too. You may go over and touch her, support her, and let yourself cry too. When someone starts shouting, you may feel intensely angry yourself and want to shout, 'For f***'s sake, STOP!' You might find yourself backing away, going somewhere else to avoid those uncomfortable feelings. It's important to notice how you are reacting. You might look at someone else wailing and crying and feel totally unmoved; you think, 'What's she making such a fuss about?' All of these reactions are important. Especially as we are probably going to suppress and censor most of them.

We tell ourselves all sorts of things in our minds to shut ourselves off from the feelings in us that those events are triggering. You might look around at everyone else expressing their emotions and think, 'You're a bunch of whackos, and this is really silly.' You sit on the edge of the group feeling slightly resentful and bored, and say nothing. Whereas if you actually expressed what you were thinking, it could lead you into your own feelings. If you allowed yourself to say aloud, 'This is a load of bollocks!' you would feel something, for sure, frustration or anger or relief, and you could then let that feeling expand so that you could express and explore it further.

Our mind always tries to project our own state of mind, mood or feelings onto others; it is always talking about 'that out there' rather than 'this in here.' We sit and think, 'this workshop has cost me a lot of money and it's a waste of time,' instead of recognising the feeling behind that thought and saying, 'I am feeling disappointed.' Once you have a feeling, you have something to work with. Our mind stops us from feeling - that is one of its jobs - and it does it very well. That's why most of the time we never express what we are truly feeling.

Within a group, any group, we play out the old roles and behaviours that we are familiar with. You might listen to someone and think, 'She talks too much, and I wish she would shut up.' She goes on and on, yet you say nothing. All of us avoid conflict; we switch off instead of dealing with the situation we are a part of. We tell ourselves all sorts of things – that we're being nice, we don't want to hurt the other person's feelings (or make them angry), it's not worth the hassle - while playing out an old role of 'victim' who suffers in silence and does not express what's going on for him. It is always frightening to break out of an old pattern of behaviour, to say, 'I'm sick of hearing this,' and to realise how often you may have felt neglected, ignored, or bullied, yet done nothing about it. That simple statement can help you towards a personal realisation, to break what may be the pattern of a lifetime.

Nearly everything that we say, do and feel is about us, not about anyone else. The point of a workshop is to become more aware of what you are feeling, to express it without judging it or explaining it away, and to engage more fully in your own moment. Particular people in the group may represent different parts of ourselves, they may express an emotion that enables us to get in touch with our own feeling, or they may give us an opportunity to externalise an internal conflict. So, whatever is happening can help us. We learn about ourselves through what others reflect back to us about ourselves.

In the Cornwall 2005 workshop, Patrick said; 'We are stirring up all kinds of sensations. I would encourage you to go in, have a look on the inside, and see what is happening. The group creates these dynamics, and if you do not participate, then you will miss the opportunity for something else to happen. So just allow that to come out. Allow yourself to express it. You are holding it in; you are not expressing it. That is what you do most of your life. You have the opportunity to change that just for this weekend and then you can go and shut it down again afterwards. Sometimes it can get you in a lot of trouble. We go through life capping it, capping it, capping it. It builds up, builds up, and builds up. This weekend can be the time to allow you to start to let it out, to give you relief. Let it expand, and then maybe it can change your whole perspective on things, so that you can start to live life a little bit more.'

Fundamental to making a connection with Source is opening the heart and allowing yourself to receive. To do this, we have to allow ourselves to fully feel. We have to get involved expressing, experiencing, and supporting others. If we stay on the edge of the group, then we tend to stay on the edge of our own experience. Connecting with the energy makes you feel that you are not alone; it connects you to Source, but also to others.

Patrick: 'An energy shift has been happening. The energy is becoming much more spontaneous even in the smaller groups. I have been focusing more and more on just keeping it simple and focusing more on All-Love. I realize that there are always going to be a few people who are disappointed - in the simplicity of the class, or by the fact that what they perceive is not the love and light they wanted to experience. This is one of the biggest blocks that class participants run into. All-Love is experiencing all of who we are. That means looking at those parts of ourselves that we have hidden away. These parts are put into a sense of separation.

'Some of the most powerful healings for those in our class have been based on going into the pain and separation. Yet there always seems to be one or two people in each class that feel it is not necessary to look at those parts of ourselves and don't participate in class fully. This not only affects the individual, but others in the class.

'Sometimes it is very difficult to look at feelings such as anger, rage and grief, but once we realize that these feelings are very much a part of the healing process, the healing transformation and Initiations come much quicker. I have really been amazed at times, how quickly the Initiations are consistently coming in for people. I also feel that the Initiations are going to a much deeper level. As our group energy becomes stronger, I feel that we will begin to see even greater shifts in our awareness and consciousness.'

CONCLUSION

THE only limitations that we really have are the ones that we place upon ourselves. This is a very encouraging thought. It means that if we are restricting ourselves, then we can also free ourselves. Conflicts – inner or outer - can be resolved.

And let's face it; life is full of them. It is full of contradictions, ambiguities, and uncertainties. One of the major doubts that most of us have is that we can do anything to make it better. That is one of the reasons why we go to such lengths to deny our pain. We simply do not believe that we can do anything about it. Actually, it's not just a belief, it's also borne out by experience; looking around, there does not seem much evidence that pain ever really goes away.

We will only really believe it when we experience it for ourselves. At the moment that we face what we'd previously considered to be an unbearable and irresolvable pain, and we find that we can actually let go of it; when we shout and scream and rage and realise that we do not need to do that any more. When the inner tension and self-doubt is replaced by a feeling of calm and relief; when we come to understand why we were confused; when we can love what we previously judged unlovable. That is when we are going to believe it.

When we experience a sense of a vast and powerful energy extending from within us to immeasurably far beyond, we suddenly change. Whatever our beliefs may have been, however we may have tried to explain that experience, the fact is that our perception – and hence our reality – is suddenly transformed. We are likely to start living our lives in a very different way.

There is usually a battle going on inside each of us. At the very least, our hearts and minds are each trying to overrule or undermine the other. Part of us yearns to touch our eternal spirit; the other part says it doesn't even exist. Our hearts long to fly, while our minds tell us we can't.

All-Love listens to both. Both are right. We are here on Earth in a physical body for a reason – which we each need to find out for ourselves - yet at the same time we also exist as spirit. All-Love does not try to find a glib answer or a quick solution to that unquestionable and essentially unsolvable paradox. It helps us to achieve a balance between our minds and our hearts, between our spirits and our bodies, by connecting the two, by showing us how we can experience both the bliss of Heaven and the groundedness of Earth.

All-Love enables us to experience our own experiences more fully, to know – and like ourselves better, to deal with our pain so that we can experience our joy. It shows us how to go inwards, to reconcile the opposing forces within us, and to reach outwards, to overcome the barriers that separate us from others. Becoming aware of what we truly are, loving ourselves becomes a possibility. Loving ourselves, God becomes a possibility.

We all want a connection with Source. We all want to feel happy. We would prefer to feel oneness rather than aloneness. In order to do this, we have to work through the pain - the anger, worry, sadness and grief.

All-Love shows us the way.

CHAPTER FOUR

Understanding Anger

Don't get angry; get even
— Anonymous.

I may have my faults, but being wrong is not one of them.
— Anonymous.

WHY ANGER IS A PROBLEM

HOW often, in our stressful, chaotic lives, does a whole day pass without getting angry at something? How much of that anger do we simply bury or deny? How many times, after ranting, raving, and dumping our anger out on someone else, do we later wish we hadn't?

As a society, we have become desensitized to anger. We are bombarded by media images of war, racial intolerance, violence, and crime; collectively we have come to tolerate incredibly high levels of anger, therefore individually we see no reason to give it up.

Yet, everyone has a problem with anger. It's not just you, or me, or that guy at the traffic lights who does his nut when the car up ahead forgets to indicate. Anger is endemic to modern life, it's everywhere, and this fact alone makes it much more likely that we'll put up with it – with all sorts of horrible consequences for ourselves and others – rather than do something about it.

It's almost certainly true that we can't prevent anger arising, but we certainly can change our attitude to it when it does – and we can change how we deal with it. Most of us feed our anger. We rage at feeling out of control and then blame others for our sense of powerlessness. Therefore, the anger never really goes. It's stored away, unchanged, in our memories, our energy systems, and the cells of our bodies. But there has to be a better way of dealing with anger than merely going onto automatic and either bitterly swallowing it or spewing it back out in uncontrolled fury.

Perhaps, instead, we could talk to it. Listen to what it's trying to tell us: because anger always has its own unique message. It's a warning system. Red alert. Stop, it says, something's wrong; some work has to be done here.

'Work?' you say, 'I don't like the sound of that.' Nobody does. Generally speaking, we'd all like to avoid the work even though that means staying angry. However, the point is that we do have choices. Anger is a learned response, and it can be unlearned. It is a complex, self-perpetuating, negative cycle of events, thoughts, feelings and physical sensations - yet this cycle can be broken.

We do this firstly by acknowledging that we're angry, then by expressing that anger in some appropriate form. We do it by taking responsibility for our anger; exploring its origins, and getting the message it's trying to tell us. And, finally, breaking the cycle of anger means letting it go.

Defining Anger

THE word anger is derived from three roots: 'anguish' from Latin; an Old High German word for 'narrow;' and the Old Norse word for 'grief.'

Anguish literally means distress, squeeze, or strangle. Angina is another word with this same root. Part of anger then is feeling constricted, suffocated or oppressed, which makes us want to fight free, to break out of that restriction. It may be the sense that someone or something is interfering in our lives, invading our space, and imposing their will upon us. We feel powerless, and struggle to re-assert ourselves, to win back control of the situation and free ourselves from discomfort.

If Jim, next door, is three years older and a foot taller than you, and he grabs you in a headlock, odds are you are going to struggle to get free. And the more you struggle the tighter he holds, and the tighter he holds the madder you get, until he is really hurting you; and you start getting desperate, terrified that he might strangle you.

You're angry. Your body is angry, ready for action, ready to attack. Your heart's racing, your blood is pounding, your muscles are tense, adrenaline's rushing round your body spreading 'Fight or Flight!' propaganda. The voice inside your head, usually rational and calm, is shouting, 'Get lost, you weasel! I HATE YOU!' Sounds familiar?

The second root of anger means narrow: 'Rigid in views, intolerant.' It also has the sense of driving or pressing people closer together. People are pushing too close for comfort, close enough for us to see very clearly, what it is we don't like about them. Moreover, if we are honest about it, showing us those things that we dislike in ourselves. From this point of view, anger is potentially very useful.

When we feel threatened, constricted within a situation, or pressured by someone, our attention is instantly focused. The stressor may be concentrated on one area of our body, as with Jim's arm around your throat, or the band of muscle spasm around your head in a tension headache. Our thinking narrows down to a single train of thought. Nothing can distract us from the person or situation that provoked our anger. As in the situation with Jim, you are busy thinking up reasons why you hate him, remembering every despicable thing he ever did (and all the other similar injustices you ever suffered) and wishing something horrible would happen to him.

We go over and over in our minds everything that was said and done, completely disregarding any positive feelings we may have had for that person, and endlessly repeating to ourselves how bad he has made us feel. It is as if we cannot turn it off, however much our rational mind attempts to bring some distraction or relief.

When our awareness is focused to a point in such a way, two things happen. The first is that particular emotional states remember each other. In other words, the anger of now triggers the anger of then – and then, and then. It is as if we have walked through a distorting mirror and come out in Angryland, home place of all of our past anger, the place where we store the unresolved thoughts and feelings of a lifetime of frustrated desires, disappointed hopes, and broken dreams. They are all in there, of course, the people who have hurt us, or stopped us from being ourselves, those who humiliated us or laughed at us, and the ones who never listened.

This explains how anger is the sunken mass in the 'tip of the iceberg' analogy. When we come to deal with our anger, things are always more complicated than they seem. For, it is likely that our present anger is only partly related to that other person and what they said or did now. The remainder of our anger comes from the past; the present event has triggered anger from a past event, and it is this anger that we need to recognise and explore.

However, if we do not realise that our present anger is a message of something deeper about ourselves, then we won't explore it, and we will blame that one person standing in front of us just now for the huge weight of anger, frustration and rage that we are experiencing. This, apart from being a little unfair, is also historically incorrect.

The second thing that happens in anger is that our thinking becomes very one-sided and rigid. We are not even aware that it is happening. Just as the triggering of an emotional state accesses the energy of past memories and similar emotional scenarios, so too does the mental state, or mind-set that forms the invisible framework behind the emotion. Once we have entered into that particular mind-set, it becomes very difficult to get out of it.

It usually involves a combination of self-justification and putting the blame onto someone else: 'You shouldn't have done that.

I didn't do anything wrong. You've made me feel bad. It's all your fault.' We are not willing to consider alternative explanations, to see the situation from the other's point of view, or to take responsibility for our own feelings.

From here, we can take two roads. The first is to express the anger to the person concerned. As we have already built it up into far more than the situation deserves, we are likely to overreact. If we are used to having our own way, this is probably what we will do. Then later, when we have calmed down after our outburst, we will maybe feel guilty about how we acted.

The second is not to express it. If we are scared of anger and do not know how to express it safely, we hide it rather than risk losing the acceptance or approval of others. We feel bad about the other person, and bad about ourselves for not saying anything to him.

Sadly, both roads are going nowhere.

The third root of anger is grief: 'Sorrow caused by loss, regret or remorse.' It is this aspect that is probably the most difficult to bring to mind when we are in the grip of anger.

It makes sense that when we are hurt, when we lose something, or are disappointed by someone; we experience pain. When we feel bereft, or cheated, or badly treated, it is understandable that we feel angry with that. We think, 'Why did this have to happen? What have I done to deserve this?' Of course, most of the time, these questions have no answer, and then we are angry with that too. Then, if we do not express and release the pain in some way, it will become buried, along with the anger we feel, both at having experienced the pain, and at not having had that pain acknowledged or relieved.

When we feel angry, actually, we are in pain. Anger is one of the ways by which we unconsciously draw attention to the pain that we need to heal. So, perhaps it is time now to throw out some of our old beliefs about anger, such as 'Anger is bad,' or 'I cannot / must not express my anger.'

Instead, perhaps, we could say that anger is telling us something about ourselves that we need to know. It is a gift, albeit usually unwanted, because it points us in the direction of the underlying pain that we need to acknowledge; and it also brings with it the energy that we can use to do something about that pain. Anger is a message, conveying vital information in a way that compels our attention.

The problem is that the message is usually in code.

Breaking the Anger Code

ANGER is a very powerful emotion. Often, it is not immediately obvious what it is really about. It does not arrive all neatly packaged with labels, cross-references, and helpful how-to hints. We may not even be sure that we are angry. People cut themselves off from their anger because they cannot own it as a living, shouting, fighting, and powerful part of them.

On the other hand, they try to reason it away. 'There must be some logical conclusion,' they say, (like I am right and he was wrong so I was justified all along). Forget it. Anger cannot be defused simply by thinking about it or by thinking yourself out of it, or by denying that it exists.

Anger is held in many places: in words and thoughts, in memories and feelings and in the body. It exists in our subconscious mind, the recycle bin that we keep dumping stuff into, hoping it will go away, but that never gets emptied until we start working through it. Anger is never just an isolated thought, devoid of emotional energy, free from physical accompaniments. It is a multi-system event. And it demands action.

How anger affects the body

ANGER is physical: we experience it at the physical level, through our senses, and deep within the cells of our bodies. It is a racing of the heart, a tensing of the muscles, a pushing forward of the head, a thrusting of the jaw, a clenching of the fists, a stamping and a banging and a shouting. It is a body overloaded with sensations, straining to act, wanting to fight, demanding some physical expression of its force.

As you sit there reading this, let your body take up this angry stance, clench your fists, snarl, throw the book across the room, shout an obscenity. What do you feel? Silly? Strange? – Not something you normally do. Embarrassed? – For sure, if you are in the middle of a crowded railway carriage. Overall, overriding these other concerns, I bet that what you mainly feel is angry. Try it out a few times, if you are not convinced.

Now, when you are nicely cranking it up, just as suddenly, cut it. Switch it off. Relax the show's over. But is it? How does your body feel now? Frustrated? Disorientated? Deflated? (These are just mind-words for body-states.) It is a bit like when you are just about to have an orgasm, you've been trying for ages, building up to it, finally you are right there on the edge, yes, that's it, it's coming, just a moment more – and the doorbell rings. You've lost it. The moment is gone. Talk about all revved up with no place to go.

Your whole body is pulsing, throbbing, straining – and suddenly - nothing. That is an ugly feeling. All that energy gets suddenly pushed down, choked off, stifled. Your body is almost in a state of shock; you are aching so much it is painful. And it is not as irrelevant to the anger scenario as it might seem, because much of our anger-energy comes from the same place as our sexual energy. We store a lot of anger in our root chakra.

So, that's what your body feels like when it cannot express itself. It happens once, that's bad luck. But chronically, over time, your body's going to start holding a grudge. Chronic non-expression of anger means holding it somewhere. It might be in your stomach, so ulcers start sprouting, or your joints, so they start gnawing away at themselves, or you get the strangled heart of angina. That grudge becomes engraved in your cellular memory.

All of us have been at the receiving end of other people's anger. Flinching, cowering, saucer-eyed, shaking, smarting in anticipation or in actual pain. Violence, hurt, fear, terror – for some more than others; these are all carved into our senses. Physical injuries lead to body wounds, but mind-injuries and damaged feelings lead to body wounds too – at least at a cellular or energetic level. The body does not just experience sensations; it remembers them too. Somewhere, your body will store that pain.

If anger is related to your basic needs or survival it is often stored in the root chakra; anger related to creativity or trust affects your sacral chakra; anger arising from issues of personal will and power target the solar plexus. Anger deriving from relationships or lack of self-love affects your heart chakra, while that arising from inability to accept and express yourself affects the throat chakra.

So, then, viewing anger as just another expression of pain: what does your body normally do with your anger? Most of us have a habitual way of dealing with it, or a special place in our bodies that we store it.

Personally, I eat mine. I chew it over, ruminating obsessively, and it can make me feel physically sick. For most of my life, I have smoked it too. Get angry, quickly reach for a cigarette; light up and inwardly fume. Self-medicate and say nothing. But I don't let it go. It doesn't nicely burn away and go up the chimney in a cloud of smoke. Oh, no. I hang on to it. I store it in my pelvis. Painful periods, premenstrual syndrome, even pre-cancerous changes; it has all been there, pain and anger stewing in its own juice. I pretend most of the time it's not there, and then cyclically explode.

There is a story my mother tells that still makes her angry. In wartime England, when she was about nine, she had no shoes, because when her last pair fell apart, there was no money to buy any more. So, one day she wore a pair of Wellington boots to school. When the teacher saw them, she threw a wobbly: 'Who do you think you are? Don't you ever come here dressed like that again.' Totally powerless to say anything in her own defence, humiliated and horribly ashamed, the eyes of the whole class on her, my mother just about managed to choke back her tears.

So, take a few minutes to think back to one of your own childhood memories, perhaps a time when you were at school, a time when you were singled out or punished unfairly. Go back into that memory. Imagine yourself standing there. See yourself dressed in your uniform, what age were you? How did you feel? Can you see the image clearly in your mind? As you go back to that moment, it is as if the whole situation exists there within you. You can feel the eyes of the other kids on you, you can see your face going red in embarrassment, hear the anger of the voice telling you off, feel your heart pounding, remember wishing you could just disappear and never be seen again.

Visualizations of specific moments like this are interesting because they show how real it all is. Twenty, thirty, forty years later, it is as powerful and vivid and painful as it was when it happened. That is because in some sense, it still exists. We carry all of our experiences with us. The thoughts, the feelings, the physical sensations, are all stored somewhere in our energy system.

Holding that image, you feel the pain as well as the anger; maybe in your heart, racing and pounding in your chest, a band of constriction, a feeling of emptiness, a sense that no one cares. Put your hands on your heart chakra for a few minutes, and imagine energy flooding into your heart; healing, soothing the heartache, helping release the pain. Perhaps you can cry, let out those tears that you have held inside so long.

You begin to feel more peaceful; but there is still anger boiling up. Sit with it, do not try to stop the thoughts, do not fight the feelings; just accept them, and stay with them. You could send energy to the cause of that anger, letting that energy go back to that distant time, gradually freeing you from its pain.

Maybe you feel that anger in your solar plexus, as butterflies churning in your stomach, as hunger or emptiness or a feeling of sickness. You feel your confidence is being attacked, your self-esteem undermined; you feel inadequate and powerless. You are that child again, frustrated and vulnerable. The memories of that event are held in your stomach area. Invite the All-Love energy now into that present feeling. Slowly, in your stomach, and in your mood, you feel something shift.

WHAT WE CAN DO ABOUT ANGER

THE body is vitally important when we start to heal anger. Our physical sensations give us clues as to where we feel it or where we store it. Listening to the pain in our bodies can help us to access memories of past and forgotten anger. However, when we are actually experiencing that anger, we have to give recognition to its physical components too. Somehow, we have to express our body anger.

For example, in the past, Graham never used to say what he really felt. He could not acknowledge his feelings, and did not want to try to understand them; he just wanted to feel better. So, when he was feeling tense, angry or frustrated, he used to play squash. Focusing on the game took his mind away from the events that might have contributed to his mood; after running around and hitting hard drives for forty-five minutes, he would feel less uptight and more relaxed. However, he ended up having to play squash most days.

When anger builds up, it blocks energy within it. Physical activity bypasses the mental part of the anger cycle, diverting energy, expending some of the built-up energy and at least partially releasing the block. This physical expression makes you feel less tense, but it will not necessarily lead to insight about what caused the anger.

Many people dissipate anger through sport; a heavy workout or a 5km run. However, this may merely rid you of the frustration that arose from not expressing the anger in the first place. It is actually just a way of displacing the energy, of working off excess energy or free-floating aggression or redirecting the anger from the true cause to a less threatening situation. It is a safety valve.

Often it is not enough, because the conditions of sport are not always conducive to tuning in to the source of that particular anger. You need to physically express your anger at the same moment that you access those feelings, and that usually means being alone with no distractions, with time to really work out what you are feeling – in all senses. Hit a punch bag when you are closely in touch with your anger and you will know the difference.

For example, I might say to myself, 'I am bloody angry with Rob. He's a selfish bastard and just takes me completely for granted. I do plenty of things for him and the one thing I ask him to do for me he finds lots of excuses not to. I am sick of him taking advantage of me.' Then I attack whatever I am doing with the force of this anger behind the action. I can feel the energy rising in hot waves from my base chakra as I do it, and I hold the image of Rob in my mind, and keep repeating, almost like a mantra, whatever expletives most capture the mood. I find chopping wood while shouting, 'You f****** c*** I hate you,' is quite effective. Or punching the punch bag imagining it's his face is good too. Finally, hot, sweaty, exhausted and, if it is working well, almost in tears, I feel the anger leaving my body. Then I feel peaceful.

To some people this might sound excessive or overly aggressive. Are the things I am telling myself in my angry outburst actually true? At that moment, it's the way I am feeling, though it is not the whole truth; the angry feelings are not the only feelings I have towards him, but they're blocking out all the others. He is actually probably no more selfish than I am. I do not really hate him. However, in Angryspeak it sums up nicely what is going on in my head. And I am not saying it to him in a frustrated torrent that I might later regret. Another concern might be that the negative waves of energy I am feeling for him at that moment might be reaching him or having some adverse effect upon him. Well, yes, maybe. But if I go round for days, stewing in resentment and finding many reasons to justify and perpetuate my anger, how might that affect him too? Moreover, more importantly, how will it affect me?

The direct way means that I am owning the anger as mine. I am taking responsibility for feeling it and for doing something about it. And at the end of it, I feel great. I am no longer angry, and I am glad that I have taken active steps to rid myself of something I no longer want. Yes, I felt he let me down, but he is not the only person who has ever done that. Maybe other occasions will come to mind that make me see that my anger was not just about him, but also about various specific unhealed incidents from the past, which I may choose to work on later. I may realise that I sometimes let people down too. Without the anger, I am much more likely to see the whole situation in a more balanced way.

Besides, whatever happens, I shall see my own emotions and my own needs in a much clearer light. In fact, after expressing the anger towards him, I see that part of it was anger at myself for letting him take advantage of me. People only get away with things if you allow them to. I was blaming him for my own inability to say no, my reluctance to complain if I felt that he had overstepped the mark.

If I do not like something, it is up to me to do something to prevent it from happening again. So, my anger is telling me that there is something I need to change about my own behaviour. I need to act more assertively. I need to state clearly, what I like and what I do not like. Having realised this, when I do speak to Rob, I will be able to tell him, directly, pleasantly but firmly, that it is important to me that he does what he said he would do. I will no longer resent him. I will no longer be carrying that anger around with me. In this sense, I have released myself from the weight of the anger, and I have accessed the energy contained within it to use for productive action. Isn't that what the anger was asking me to do all along?

Of course, different things work for different people. Shouting or stomping, kicking cushions or a mattress or hitting a punch bag can all be effective. You need to find something that works for you, preferably somewhere that is readily accessible and where you are not self-conscious about doing what you have to do. It is not easy. Not least because we are so conditioned to feel ashamed of our anger that we do not really like admitting we have it. And of course, it is easier just to carry on blaming someone else for making us feel that way. Nevertheless, once you start to let go of anger, you wonder why you ever wanted to hold on to it.

WHY DO WE HOLD ON TO ANGER?

THE mind is a very complex organ. It is capable of finding elaborate reasons for something when it has almost no recognition of its true underlying motives, and of forgetting, or excluding from conscious awareness; those things it does not wish to remember. In Freud's view, these mechanisms were the means by which the ego defends itself against anxiety, pain and other unpleasant emotions.

Freud had a lot to say about anger. As mentioned previously, he came upon the idea that we repress unpleasant feelings because we feel powerless to do anything about them.

Repression is the exclusion from conscious awareness of feelings or memories that are painful or anxiety provoking, or that conflict with our image of ourselves. It is as if a part of us is saying, 'I feel bad. I don't want to feel bad, and I don't want to know why I do. I will get rid of these feelings.' Only it does not always work, or it works only partially, because however much we have tried to push those unpleasant feelings out of our minds, they still pop back in.

Eventually, they start to make us feel bad again; we feel angry, anxious, or depressed for no apparent reason. We cannot see the connection between those past repressed emotions and our current emotional state. We do not know why we feel bad. Besides, just as importantly, we still do not want to know why, so we use other defence mechanisms to stop ourselves from finding out.

HOW THE EGO DEFENDS ITSELF

THE ego defence mechanisms include denial, rationalisation, avoidance, displacement, projection, intellectualisation, and regression.

For example, if we feel angry, we will not admit that we do (denial); we bang around in the kitchen rather than saying, 'I feel angry and upset that you were late home last night.' Or we find reasons for being bad-tempered which have nothing to do with the underlying causes (rationalisation); rather than admit that I am angry and hurt that you haven't wanted sex for three weeks, I pick a fight about how you do not do enough to help around the house.

If someone has said something that has triggered a reappearance of our anger, we steer clear of him so we do not have to express how we feel (avoidance). On the other hand, we avoid saying directly what upset us. I am annoyed that you had a good night out with your friend without me, so I am angry and negative about him, instead of owning up to what might seem childish or jealous feelings at being left out.

Rather than face the person involved, we take out our anger on someone who had nothing to do with it — usually someone weaker than the person who originally triggered the anger, and weaker than us; so we know they will not fight back (displacement). I find fault with my partner after being criticised by my boss at work, then I shout at the kids or kick the dog when my partner finally tells me to back off.

We complain at someone else for being in a bad mood, or we start an argument so that we can then blame him for our own unacknowledged bad mood (projection). In fact, any emotion that we do not acknowledge we tend to disown and project onto someone else. Funny how other people are jealous, calculating, negative or aggressive but we ourselves never are!

Or we talk around and about an issue in general, abstract terms while completely divorcing ourselves from our own feelings (intellectualisation); I get into heated discussions about how the company exploits the workforce rather than admit my own issues about authority and personal power in relation to my father or lover.

Or instead of dealing with our anger in an adult way, we have a temper-tantrum or become whining, self-pitying and demanding like a fretful child (regression); I punch my printer when I cannot get it to work and then cry when it is broken.

We use the ego defence mechanisms to protect ourselves from pain. On the other hand not even that, because the pain has already happened. The defence mechanisms are really our attempt to talk ourselves out of the pain that we are experiencing; to shorten it, to reduce its impact, to make it go away. Bit short-sighted really. Because pain does not actually go away until we work at it.

The problem is that the ego defence mechanisms were intended to defend the immature ego. In childhood, we are both immature and vulnerable; we are physically and emotionally dependent upon others. We cannot solve problems. We cannot take responsibility for ourselves, and we cannot think about things other than at a concrete and egocentric level.

The child thinks that the world revolves around him; that everything that happens is somehow related to him. He expects that people will love him and give him what he wants; he is a romantic at heart. In addition, he is an opportunist; all he is really interested in is avoiding pain as much as he can and having as good a time as possible. He is an idealist; he expects that the world should be fair, and is gullible, indiscriminately trusting much of what he is told.

So, that child is going to be inadequately prepared for the unpleasant things that are eventually going to happen to him.

In general, adults are not very good at facing their own problems. Thus, many children emerge into adulthood with little sense of their own feelings or needs, and few strategies for dealing with their problems. It stands to reason that parents can only give to their children what they have been given. If they cannot own up to what they are feeling, if they cannot protect themselves and fulfil their own needs, neither will they be able to teach their children how to do these things. If they have no tools to deal with their anger and pain, neither will their children.

From this viewpoint, we are all needy, and we all need to learn. It is understandable that as children, when our egos are fragile and our skills and resources are limited, we need to have an effective means of minimizing damage. We need to be able to remove pain, anger, and anxiety at least in some measure from our conscious minds. Defending ourselves against the traumas and unhappiness that befall us makes sense. We have enough on our plates trying to forge an identity and find a place for ourselves in a frightening and essentially predatory world, without having to deal with every unpleasant feeling as it arises.

However, there comes a time, and this varies for each individual, when we begin to suspect that the old ways no longer work. We cannot keep using the same strategies now, when we have far more awareness and conscious control than we did when those automatic and unconscious strategies were our only means of survival. We cannot keep thinking that just because we do not want to look at that pain, anger, and anxiety, we are never going to have to look at it.

Because, eventually, the alarms start sounding. The recycle bin is full to overflowing. The defence mechanisms that we relied upon for so long now turn around to attack us. Illness, depression, crisis, unhappiness; numbness, pointlessness — they are all signs that our recycle bins have started to leak. They are telling us that all that was, still is. The problems that were there to be faced still must be faced. In a sense, we have just been living on borrowed time.

The point is that long after those old methods are counterproductive and no longer appropriate, we are still using them. And we really do not want to give them up.

'Give them up?' says our ego, aghast, 'I am not ready for that. I am still fragile.'

'Yeah,' we say, 'I know. But things are going to have to change.'

And that is not easy. Nobody wants to change. It takes a lot of energy to break out of old habits. Our defences make us feel safe; it takes a conscious decision and a lot of courage to give them up. But we know there is no alternative. We have to try to find better ways of dealing with our ongoing anger and pain: that of the present, and that of the past.

How thoughts affect feelings

Shakespeare: *Hamlet:* 'There is nothing either good or bad but thinking makes it so.'

WHAT we believe at least partially determines what we feel. In other words, it is the interpretation that we ourselves put on an event rather than the event itself which causes us to feel a particular emotion, such as anger. Therefore, what is actually happening is that we are constantly talking ourselves into our anger; the beliefs we hold about an event are giving momentum and energy to that anger.

Walen[24] writes, 'Past events may have had an important role in contributing to past distress, but they continue to be a problem only because we continue to think about them in the same way. It is present cognitions, not past events, which affect us.'

We judge everything according to our beliefs – and the vital thing we overlook is that often these beliefs are not actually based on any evidence, so they are not necessarily accurate. Or they may simply no longer be true.

Albert Ellis PhD.[25], the pioneer of Rational Emotive Therapy, writes, 'You create your emotional disturbances by your irrational beliefs, and you keep these beliefs alive by repeating them to yourself, reinforcing them in various ways, acting on them and refusing to challenge their validity.... An irrational belief leads to inappropriate consequences; anger, hostility and desire for revenge. A rational belief leads to more appropriate consequences; disappointment, feeling rejected, loss of opportunity.'

In Cognitive Therapy, first developed by Aaron T. Beck, M.D., the aim is to challenge these dysfunctional beliefs, and to identify and change distorted thinking.

So, by changing our thoughts, we can decrease our anger.

Walen[26] explains that 'Irrational beliefs are the result of dysfunctional thinking; exaggeration, oversimplification, overgeneralisation, illogic, invalidated assumptions, faulty deductions, and absolutistic notions.'

For example, if the guy I am seeing does not ring when he said he would, I start out by feeling a bit disappointed (appropriate). I think perhaps he got tied up at work or went for a quick drink (realistic). Sure, he will call, I tell myself. Or is he deliberately ignoring me? (dichotomous thinking; either/or). Two hours pass, and I am still wanting the phone to ring (get a life!) Miserable sod, I think to myself, he has forgotten about me (illogical conclusion). I am feeling irritated now. He should have sent me a text to tell me what he was doing (absolutistic notion: 'should' or 'must'). I am not being unreasonable, he said he'd phone – only by now I have worked this up in my mind to 'he promised' to phone (dishonesty). He is probably out with some people (invalidated assumption). In fact, I bet he is enjoying himself with some woman (faulty deduction). Bastard (negative automatic thought). Why else would not he phone? (oversimplification). He doesn't care about me (exaggeration). I am really quite pissed off now. I suppose I could ring him. But no, if he can't be bothered then why should I? He is so unreliable (magnification). I hate men like that (over generalisation). And I hate waiting around for phone calls (low frustration tolerance). Things like that make me angry...

Distorted thinking? Irrational beliefs? You bet.

So, challenge them. Instead, I could say to myself: 'Why must he do what I want him to? Why can I not tolerate frustration of my desires? Do not always assume the worst. Do not ascribe motives to him for which you have no evidence. Do not demand that he fits in with your unrealistic expectations. Do not exaggerate one incident into a defect of someone's character. Do something productive; phone him or forget it. If you cannot forget it, sit down and try to find out why you are working yourself up into such an angry state.'

Thoughts, feelings and behaviour are closely intertwined. The things that we tell ourselves can make us feel either worse or better: we can act in ways that either improve or aggravate the situation. The problem is that many of us do not know we have a choice.

CHANGING BELIEFS

THE beliefs upon which we base our view of the world, and from which we operate, are often still hanging around from when we were children. They have never been revised. Automatically, without thinking, we just slip back into those old beliefs and behaviour patterns, even if they are no longer helpful to us.

It is not that some people have irrational beliefs and others do not. We all have irrational beliefs about ourselves, the world and other people. Such as, that we are the centre of the universe and should not suffer pain; that the world is fair and should give us what we want; and that other people should love us and treat us well. In other words, the beliefs of that egocentric, romantic, opportunistic, idealistic, gullible child that we met earlier. The beliefs of the immature ego that the defence mechanisms were set up to protect.

We hear a lot about the inner child, how it needs to be healed so we can be more playful, spontaneous, and creative. And this is certainly true. But there's the flip-side too of the inner child; the part that wants everything without working for it, that sees the world as one big play-pen that exists only for his amusement, and that believes that love must come to him regardless of what he gives to others. Clearly, this part is going to get very angry when it does not get what it wants.

So, we must also heal this needy, greedy inner child. Otherwise, he will never feel truly satisfied. Moreover, his neediness will cause him problems and will alienate other people as long as he continues to demand that everything must come from outside rather than from loving himself and fulfilling at least some of his own needs.

Gary Zukav [27] writes, 'Watch your own needs in action – where they are not real, expect to experience a negative emotion.' In addition, when you experience that negative emotion, challenge the beliefs that support it. 'Why do I think I need this? Why will it be so terrible if I do not get what I want? What is it I am really trying to achieve? Are there better ways of doing it?'

The best way of identifying and challenging beliefs is to write them down. You cannot hold many thoughts in your mind at one time. They tend to go round in circles and you cannot see where you need to get off the merry-go-round.

Allison Price [28] says, 'As your own counsellor, your job is to surprise yourself into an insight to which your old habits of expectation, beliefs, etc. have blinded you. And I know no way of doing it for yourself except by writing... Something happens during the act of writing itself, which seems to tap into an area of consciousness that is not normally available to us. Often, in fact, the words will create, or liberate, a thought you had not even realized you had.'

Writing is also a way of taking your feelings seriously, giving them the time and attention that they require. One of the reasons we get angry in the first place is because we feel that no one is listening or that no one cares how we feel. This is a great example of projection – ascribing our own attributes to other people. The truth of it is that we are not listening to ourselves. We do not care enough about our own feelings to actually do the work of finding out what they are really about. Half an hour of free-flow, or stream of consciousness, writing would do us far more good than half an hour of sulking or complaining or stewing in our own anger.

Body anger is about sensations, images, and feelings. It is likely to need some physical expression for its release, and it may be non-verbal or need only a few key words to focus its energy. Mind anger, on the other hand, is very much tied up in words. The thoughts that go round in our heads, the messages we repeatedly give to ourselves, the entangled web of beliefs and expectations and demands that we have woven in our minds.

To penetrate and disentangle these, we have to use words. Moreover, for some people it may be an easier way in to what is really going on for them than through their bodily sensations. Usually we have to use a mixture of the two. In the end, we have to try many different strategies and see what works most effectively for us; a combination of different methods is likely to yield the best results.

And, it is understood, that the methods we resist the most are probably the ones, which will unearth the most useful insights.

Try writing about some of these:

The last time I got angry.

The angriest moment of my life.

When someone else was angry with me.

Why I get angry ... and why I do not.

What I fear most about anger is...

HOW ANGER AFFECTS THE ENERGY SYSTEM

Bernie Siegel: 'Patients' bodies respond directly to their own beliefs.' [29]

THOUGHTS, feelings and bodily sensations all have energy. Our angry feelings and thoughts automatically activate the physical manifestations of anger, and vice versa. Repeating negative beliefs, letting irrational thoughts go round and round in our mind unchecked, drawing angry memories from the past through present triggers, are all ways in which energy is added to the anger system.

As already mentioned, it is a basic principle of physics that energy cannot be created or destroyed. This is important for two reasons. Firstly, we only have a certain amount of energy at any given time. We may actually feel that we have more energy when we are angry, but if we merely use this energy to keep fuelling the cycle of anger, then instead of acting, we become immobilised, and we have less energy to use in other ways. The second point is that to 'get rid of' anger, we have to transform it; its energy has to be changed in some way in order for it to be released. Somehow, we have to work it out, work it off, and work it through – the important word of course being work.

The root chakra is one of the main power centres of the body; its energy enables us to realise our dreams and put our ideas into action. It connects us to the Earth; when we need energy, we can draw it up from the Earth through our root chakra, and when we have too much energy, we can earth the excess energy down through it. The root chakra enables us to literally ground ourselves; it provides our link with reality. If we have a blockage here, these processes are not able to function properly and the flow of energy to and from the Earth is impeded.

Anger is one of the things that can cause a blockage or build-up of energy in the root chakra. If we cannot express our anger, it tends to build up and draws more and more energy into itself. If our energy were flowing more freely, we would be better able to express the anger, act upon it and let it go: we would not remain angry and energy would no longer be locked in our root chakra.

We saw earlier how anger and other emotions become excluded from the conscious mind and buried in the subconscious mind. This process of repression is the primary ego defence mechanism, and it acts to exclude unpleasant emotions and memories from conscious awareness. In effect, this means that they have become split off; we no longer see them as a part of us. We dissociate from them, and we may have difficulty accessing them.

Similarly, in the energy system, when a particular chakra becomes blocked, it is not working to its full capacity, and it cannot communicate freely with the other chakras. Energy and emotions become trapped inside that blocked chakra, and we may have difficulty releasing the energy or expressing the emotions that are held within it.

A blocked chakra can therefore be seen as the energetic equivalent of an ego defence mechanism. Both act to stop emotional contents rising to awareness; both act to lock emotional energy within them. So, we need to bring not just awareness but also energy to these problems in order to solve them.

A blocked chakra is not communicating freely with the other chakras, which means that it is limited to its own strengths and resources – and weaknesses. Thus when anger builds up in the root chakra, it has the inbuilt characteristics of that chakra behind it; the urge to ground itself, to get things done; the drive to fulfil its basic needs. Without the opposing influences of the other chakras to modify these forces, they may propel us to act even if to do so might be inappropriate; to speak when it would better to remain silent; to push forward when we should have held back.

The root chakra is also concerned with our sense of security, self-esteem, and our will to survive, which are established in the early years of life. Therefore, strong negative emotions and energy blockages affecting the root chakra often strike at the very root of our self-image, causing us to doubt ourselves and even our desire to live. For example, when someone is angry with us, we tend to feel very insecure and threatened, and various childhood memories and fears may be triggered. Conversely, much of our own anger arises as a direct result of our insecurities.

If we are blocked at the root chakra, there will be a poor connection with the other chakras. We may find it difficult to connect with the creativity of the sacral chakra and the personal power and sense of responsibility of the solar plexus. It may be hard to access the love and compassion of the heart chakra, and the acceptance and expression of the throat chakra. We may be less in contact with the insight and clear vision of the third eye and the wisdom and spiritual connection of the crown chakra.

When we are balanced and the energy is flowing freely between all of the chakras, we can draw on the individual strengths of each, thus we are more likely to be able to see the alternate point of view, to be less rigid, more tolerant and expressive, in other words we are more able to act from the whole of ourselves.

It is therefore important to regularly give energy to each of the chakras in turn, and to balance the energy between them, so that they are connected and we are not acting from one isolated centre of energy. One way of doing this is to connect with the energy and bring the infinity symbol down through each of the chakras in turn, with the intent that it cleans and balances them.

By healing and developing the root chakra in these ways, we can release blockages and aid the flow of energy up through the other chakras, allowing them all to interact and work together.

HOW TO HEAL ANGER

Acknowledging and expressing anger

The first step towards solving a problem is admitting you have it. When you feel angry, acknowledge that feeling and make a conscious decision to look at it. Accept yourself and your anger. There is no point in telling yourself you are not angry, or that you do not want to feel angry. If you are, then tell yourself, 'Yes, I am angry. This anger is mine and I want to find out what it is about.' A shift occurs just by honestly owning your own feelings, without judging them or trying to deny them. Denial takes up a lot of energy. Admitting your problem allows self-healing to begin.

Anger is a habit, which we can break - by calming our mind and body – and by listening to our own emotions. We do this partly by learning to relax. We can give energy to the parts of our body where we feel the anger, and send it to the cause of the anger. However, we also need to find some appropriate means of expressing the anger. We could go to a private place and shout, stomp, kick, or hit a punch bag - anything that helps release the anger from our bodies.

When we have done this, we are ready to explore the feelings more. We can find out about the anger by writing, drawing, focussing, or dreamwork. Through words, images or dream symbols, we can follow it to its roots, or we can use visualisation to change the image, bringing in a part of us to help if we like.

Identifying your triggers

We often repeat certain thoughts, behaviour patterns, or cycles of events, until they become automatic. Some of these habitual ways of responding may not be helping us, in fact they may actually do us harm.

So, it helps to identify your own tendencies; where you hold anger in, how you let it out. Whether you push it down into deep resentment or fire it out in random, uncontrolled aggression. Whether you talk yourself into it – or out of it. If we can identify the particular strategies we use, then we can start to break some of these cycles and learn new strategies, which are more productive and less destructive.

Part of breaking the cycle is being honest about why you got in to that particular habit in the first place. Nobody does anything unless they get something out of it.

However unpleasant or uncomfortable anger may be, we still get something out of it.

Being angry can make you feel superior. 'I am right, you are wrong. I am better than you.' It can make you feel that you are doing something about the problem, or it can build a smokescreen around you, hiding your pain, covering up the fact that you have a problem. To get angry with someone else is after all so much easier than admitting that you yourself have a problem. It can mean you get your own way; other people back down or give in. It is usually the bully in the playground who gets all the sweets.

Take a moment to look at your own situation. What are you putting in to your anger? What are you getting out of it? Do you get angry because you have difficulty setting boundaries, asking for what you need or saying no? Do you use anger as a means of withholding affection, approval, acceptance, love or even sex? Is anger your way of keeping distant from people, of avoiding commitment or intimacy?

Anger can be a justification for lack of trust, a way of disengaging and avoiding doing the work of being open and honest with others. Perhaps you use it to punish others, to make yourself feel better at their expense, to assert your power over them or to control their behaviour. If you have grown up amidst anger, it may be that getting angry is the only way you know of relating to others.

We can use anger as a substitute for true power. For all of us, true power can only come through acknowledging our own feelings and needs, taking responsibility for our own lives and being honest with ourselves.

When you feel angry, ask yourself a few questions. Write down your answers. Do not judge yourself or your feelings; just try to find out what is really happening. Why do I feel this way? Why did I do that? How did this happen? When have I felt this way before?

Look at some of the beliefs that lie behind your anger, for example, 'That shouldn't have happened.' Writing them down means that you can then subject them to some reality testing: challenge the thoughts and beliefs that perpetuate your anger. What is the evidence for them? What are the alternatives? Substitute more realistic beliefs that do not continue to make you angry. Once it becomes clear in your mind, you can let it go.

Learning to be assertive
Martin Shepard: 'If you learn to say 'No' when you don't want something, take 'No' with grace from others, ask for what you want and say what you feel, there isn't much leftover tension for aggression to pose any great problem.'[30]

There are various ways of handling your own needs and wants. The problem that many people face is, not actually knowing what they want. This may lead them into passive, aggressive and unassertive behaviours. Being unclear about your goals, you do not make much effort to achieve them. The first step then is to do some inner work to find out what you do want.

When we know what we want, then we have three options: to act passively, aggressively, or assertively to achieve our ends.

The first, passive behaviour is when you go about achieving your wants in an indirect way. You try to get what you want in roundabout, possibly dishonest ways; you manipulate towards your desired goal rather than honestly stating it. And, therefore, you miss many things unnecessarily. Then, because your desires are not fulfilled, you end up feeling anxious, angry or resentful. You do not fully admit your needs to yourself, in fact, you tend to deny that you have needs or wants at all.

The second is when you go about things in a direct but inappropriately aggressive way. Rather than asking, and allowing other people to say no, you try to get your way by browbeating or bullying them into giving you what you want. It is not a give and take situation because you tend to feel that you are right and that your needs take precedence over anyone else's. It is likely that you also find it hard to say no yourself, so you act aggressively instead. You expect others to fit in with your plans and goals, and feel angry if they do not. When your desires are not fulfilled, you tend to blame the other person for your lack or loss because you feel that he should have done what you wanted him to.

You tend to upset other people because getting what you want is more important than the effects or consequences for anyone else: for you, the end always justifies the means. You express your own opinions, demands and emotions strongly yet are indifferent to other people's. You are emotionally honest but often excessively or inappropriately so. You overdo things, and your criticism, forcefulness and anger make people frightened to express their point of view. In the short-term, you often do get what you think you want, but these aggressive attitudes and behaviours may make people resent you, and you may later feel guilty about your hostility.

The third type of behaviour is when you know what you want and know how to get it in an honest, direct, even-handed way, not at someone else's expense. This is assertive behaviour.

Behaving assertively, you acknowledge your desires or goals to yourself, and you actively and positively pursue them. You are honest about your feelings, and you express yourself clearly and directly, but you do not feel the need to justify yourself to anyone, or to explain more than you want to. When you do not want to do something, you simply say no.

You do not need to act aggressively or manipulatively; if things do not work out the way you wanted, you do not blame anyone else, you think of alternative ways of achieving your goals.

You respect other people's values but choose ones for yourself that best suit you. You accept that we all have needs and desires and are each responsible for trying to fulfil them. You also accept that other people have their own goals and that no one is obliged to fulfil anyone else's rather than their own.

Rehearsing strategies for dealing with your own and other people's anger

Imagine talking to the person who has triggered your anger, or the part of yourself with which you are angry. Write a dialogue, act out the different parts (Gestalt), or write a letter to him or her (not to be sent). Just let yourself write, do not let your critical or rational mind interfere, you simply want to find out more about what you are feeling.

Writing a dialogue with the person just let yourself imagine his responses to what you have said. You may find that you are writing very quickly, the words are just tumbling out, without you needing to think about it at all. This exercise can be very illuminating. Often at the end, you will realise that many of the things he said were quite reasonable. You may be surprised at how he saw the situation and what he felt about what you were saying. You can get a lot of insight into the reasons for your own anger, and it helps a lot to see the other side.

Once you have your own feelings clear in your mind, you are in a much better position to confront the other person in real life. You will be able to say much more directly, and with less anger, what it was that upset you about the situation. You may even be prepared to admit that you were wrong.

Another useful technique that we could probably all benefit from is to practise ways of telling someone you are angry. If we are able to say we are angry at the moment that we feel it, then we will not let that anger build up and become unmanageable.

We could practise saying, 'I feel angry that...' 'I have an issue with this...' 'I know it is my problem, but...' 'Hold on a minute, there's something bugging me here...' 'This is to do with me, not you...' Saying the words out loud to yourself when you are alone makes them much easier to say when a situation arises, you are already angry, and you are maybe not thinking so clearly.

If you cannot deal with it at the time that it happens, and your anger has already snowballed, work it out on your own as much as you can, as both will regret it if you explode with inappropriate force or violence. Then make sure you go and tell the other person. Do not put it off. Rehearsing it in your head helps, but it is not enough. So often, we think we have got something sorted out in our minds, and then we talk ourselves out of actually talking it through with the other person, so the issue is never really fully dealt with, there's no closure. It is important to prove to ourselves that we have now learned to satisfactorily resolve angry or unpleasant situations. And we can only do that by doing it.

Once we are more used to saying how we feel, we are also better able to ask others what they are feeling. It becomes easier to respond to other people's anger.

On the phone to a friend once, he was angry about a past situation, in which we had both handled things badly. He sounded negative and resentful, and I could not see any benefit in going over all that old ground. Instead of talking about the situation yet again, I said, 'I can hear you are in pain.' And the whole conversation shifted. He told me later that it was as if all the anger suddenly drained away.

Anger is a communication that is not getting through. It is much harder to deal with than pain. Anger is solitary; it shuts others out, whereas pain allows them in. Having our feelings acknowledged and listened to is sometimes all it takes to break through that protective barrier of anger to get at the pain beneath.

It is important to be able to own up to your own anger, but also not to take on other people's. Remember, if someone else is angry, you are not responsible for it, and need not feel guilty about it. You are not the cause of it even if something you have said or done may have triggered it, and you do not have to respond to it by defending yourself or attacking him.

We can so easily respond to someone's anger by becoming angry ourselves. Instead, we need to be flexible. Acknowledge that he feels bad; listen to what he is trying to say, find out what he needs. Then it may be possible to clarify some of the issues: What exactly happened that made you angry? What are the details? Be specific. Is this what you mean? What was really going on? Somebody said this or did that, so you assume that shows - what? How did you take it?

Maybe something was misinterpreted or misunderstood. Maybe our irrational beliefs have made us angry rather than the other person's actions. Anger implies a judgement about a situation or a person: it assumes that the other person could have acted differently and chose not to, rather than allowing the possibility that he did what he did because he was unable at that time to do anything different.

Healing anger is much more rewarding than holding on to it. Often simply saying sorry to someone can make such a difference. Others are much more likely to realise their part in what has happened if you are willing to take your share of the responsibility.

Often we are actually angry at ourselves, for allowing someone else to act in the way that he did. Forgiving ourselves, we will probably find that we are able to forgive the other.

Ultimately, compassion is the only counter to anger. We can only break the anger cycle by being courageous, by openly acknowledging that anger exists, and that it is our problem too. Moreover by honestly accepting all the different parts of ourselves. For until we do this, these parts will remain in conflict with each other, and it is of course unresolved conflict that generates anger.

CHAPTER FIVE

Understanding Anxiety

INTRODUCTION

EMOTIONS are probably the most important thing in our lives. Most of what we say, think and do is dictated by emotion. Nothing occurs without emotional consequences.

The Latin *movere* means to disturb, and emotion is an 'aroused state involving intense feeling, autonomic (or involuntary nervous system) activation and related behaviour.'

Even back in the 19th Century, the links had been made between our feelings, or emotional perception of an experience; our thoughts, or conscious evaluation of things; and the automatic physiological responses within the body's nervous system.

We all experience unpleasant emotions: fear, anger, anxiety, and worry. The problem is that if we repeatedly either do not express, or express but do not resolve, these emotions, they can create negative energy patterns in our minds and bodies which over a period of time may ultimately lead to illness.

Defining Worry, Anxiety and Fear

The word to worry comes from the Old English word to kill, choke or gobble up. It means to make anxious and ill at ease; allow one's mind to dwell on difficulties or troubles.

We all worry at times. If you are sitting for an exam, taking your driving test, performing in public, moving house or undergoing any major change in your life circumstances, you will probably worry about it. If jobs are being axed at your workplace, you might realistically worry that you could lose your job and be unable to pay the mortgage. To be concerned about this possibility may well help you to organise your thoughts and plan a course of action. In this case, a realistic worry has lead to useful thought and productive action.

However, what if you worry about everything? What if every stressful event sets you off on a cycle of worry that you cannot break? Then every time something unpleasant or unpredictable happens, you immediately escalate it in your mind, into something catastrophic. You turn what actually is 'I might lose my job,' into 'I will lose my job, then I will lose my house, my family, my self-esteem, and my friends too.' You imagine all sorts of other unlikely and unrealistic worst-case scenarios. These awful thoughts go round and round in your head and you cannot stop them - and then you wonder why you have a headache?

Of course, what you actually have is a habit. Something happens, you feel bad, you start worrying, you build it up in your mind into something worse than it is, then you feel worse – and the cycle goes on. Worry has literally gobbled up your time and energy and has made sure you will not do anything to improve the situation.

Unfortunately, like many habits, it is actually an avoidance strategy. When something bad happens, we need to acknowledge it. We need to express how we feel, and calm our body so it will stop sending out those stress hormones that make us feel horrible. We need to calm our mind so it will not exaggerate the problem into a disaster. If we tell ourselves that we are perfectly capable of dealing with this problem, we can then get on and think about the best way to solve it. When we have come up with our best solution – which might take a few goes - we then need to act on it. This is our calm, coping, and problem-solving, feel-better, success cycle.

What we actually do is allow the worry cycle to take control. We probably do not ask for any help, we do not talk it through enough – or we talk endlessly and do not move on to problem solving. We do not express our feelings or find out the real reasons why we are upset. We do not take time to relax our bodies, so physically we still feel horrible.

We frighten ourselves further by exaggerating the problem and understating our capacity to deal with it. Our minds become so clogged up with repetitive worries that it is impossible to think clearly about the problem; so we end up with no plan of action, and even if we had one, we would be so afraid of failing that we would never attempt it.

We tend to avoid what we fear, and every time we avoid it, we reinforce the fear. Fear is a state of alarm or dread caused by a sense of impending danger. Of course, a certain amount of fear is necessary to survival; we need to be aware of actual or potential dangers in order to protect ourselves and the fight or flight response is an automatic, involuntary response of the autonomic nervous system, which mobilizes energy and prepares the physical body for fight or flight whenever we feel threatened.

The problem is that we often feel threatened by things, which do not actually represent any real danger. The autonomic nervous system does not know the difference; it just does as it is told. The fight or flight response is either on or off. You tell your nervous system you are afraid, it springs into action. It has already prepared you to jump out of the path of an oncoming train when all you are doing is sitting at home on your sofa worrying about telling your husband that you bought a new dress. You sit there anxious and sweating, with a pulse of one hundred and twenty and your stomach churning; all because you flipped the fear switch by mistake.

Or, rather, not quite by mistake. Habits take time to build. This worry habit is one we have probably cultivated through the whole of our lives, partly because we do not realise how important it is what we tell ourselves. If we habitually build up a minor irritation into a cataclysmic disaster, then our autonomic nervous system is repeatedly aroused, our body leaps to fear alert and we are flooded with anxiety-stimulating stress hormones.

A certain amount of anxiety is beneficial, in the sense that it allows us to 'be prepared.' It makes us think, plan ahead, anticipate problems and focus our energy. Except, head too far up the anxiety curve and instead of being enhanced, performance starts to deteriorate.

Anxiety is trying to make us do something, yet we are so bogged down with it that we end up doing nothing. We talk of being scared stiff, or petrified (turned to stone), paralysed or immobilised by fear, and all of these are literally true; we are like the startled bunny caught in the headlights— so frightened that we are unable to act. We need to learn how to get out of those headlights.

So, enough of definitions. What we want is a useful working model not an obituary. To conclude, what we can say is that worry, fear and anxiety are all different aspects of the same problem. They all affect the mind, the body and the emotions. They all keep us where we are. They prevent us from thinking effectively, from feeling positively and from acting to resolve the underlying issues.

On the other hand, do they? Because seen from a different perspective, what they actually tell us is that if we want to think clearly, we need to gain control over our worrying; if we want to feel better emotionally, we must face our fears; and if we want to feel good physically we must deal with our anxiety.

What are you really afraid of?

Fear is a headline emotion. It makes us sit up and pay attention. However, attention to what? The apparent surface issue is not necessarily related to the underlying cause. Old roots run deep. Moreover, they take a bit of digging to find.

We worry about all sorts of things: practical and financial problems, the events and circumstances we encounter, the small disasters that make up everyday life.

Common worries are:

> Asking for what we need,
>
> Saying no,
>
> Not being good enough as a worker / parent / lover etc.,
>
> Not being successful,
>
> Not having enough money,
>
> Not living up to the standards set by us and other people.
>
> There are hundreds of different themes and variations.

Beneath these specific worries, there may be a general fear of criticism, failure, rejection, abandonment, change or loss of control. Often we fear acknowledging the way things really are. It is painful to compare your ideal self-image with reality, to admit that you are not everything you'd like to be; to realise that your needs are not being met or that there are major problems in certain areas of your life and relationships.

So why do we worry about other people's opinion of us? Why does anxiety stop us from revealing who we truly are? Why are we afraid of acknowledging how we feel? The basis of these fears seems to be non-acceptance of self.

If we cannot accept ourselves as we are, then whatever our abilities, achievements or successes, we will never be convinced of our own worth. However positive or complimentary other people may be towards us, we will never believe that they really love or value us. We are unable to unconditionally love and accept ourselves in the present, maybe because we have not been shown unconditional regard at vital stages in our past, but probably because that is just the way life is.

We misinterpret it. As children, we do not understand why things happen the way they do. In fact, we are hurt far more than we are able at the time – or willing later – to acknowledge. As adults, the vast majority of us have the feeling, hidden away somewhere in our unconscious mind, that we are not good enough, not deserving or not lovable. It is not logical, not at all rational. But it is there.

How the past affects the present

When I was eleven, my mother went back to work at sea. She was away for nine months of the year. She used to bring me presents, and tell me how much she had missed me, but when she went each time, I was still frightened that she might never come back. At times, I felt totally miserable, rejected and abandoned. If she loved me more, maybe she would not have gone away? Perhaps I had done something wrong. I would go to the docks or to the airport when she was flying out to meet the ship, and stand choking back the tears, waving until she finally disappeared from sight.

It took me about twenty years to realise why, whenever I drove by the docks, or took someone to the airport, I would feel so desolate and lonely. Maybe it surprised my friends, that I would hang around with them in the check-in queue for ages, trying to put off the moment of saying goodbye, and then bolt away quickly with tears in my eyes. I thought I was simply upset at them leaving. But it was not really much to do with them at all, because at that moment I was a little kid crying for her mother. I just didn't know that then.

I didn't know it because I had repressed the pain I felt as a child when my mum used to go. I had forgotten the child-logic which said, 'She is gone so she can't really love you. If she doesn't love you, you are not lovable.' I did not realise that, unbelievably, as an adult, I still believed it. I could not see that friends leaving brought back the feelings I had experienced when she had left.

This is the essence of transference, one of Freud's greatest concepts. It shows how we are prisoners of the past. And, it shows how the energy of old emotions stays with us, ready to be triggered at any moment by somebody or something vaguely similar in the present.

Any of those times at the airport with friends, I could have asked myself simple questions about my own feelings.

'Why am I so upset? Is this all about them?' No, it's about me. 'Is this all about now?' No, it's about the past. 'When did I feel like this before?' When my mum used to go away. 'How did I feel then?' Lonely, frightened, rejected, unloved. Allowing myself to acknowledge and truly feel the pain of those repressed feelings, I could have given myself a chance to release and heal them.

Our unconscious mind knows what we need to heal, because it knows what has hurt us in the past. It wants us to admit that we feel bad, find out what really hurts, and do something about that. It keeps giving us opportunities to do this, and we keep choosing not to take them. I missed the opportunity, time and time again, of healing that old pain.

Transference affects all of our relationships. We think that what we are feeling is about this person, now, in this situation. In fact, this person is just the trigger that brings up the pain we have felt in the past, in similar situations, about other people: often our parents, but not necessarily.

We forget that as children there were many things we just could not handle. Children feel small, powerless and vulnerable - because they are. They are sensitive to the emotions of the people around them, they often feel them - but they do not understand them. They have experienced so little; their frame of reference is so small. Everything that happens in their world has enormous significance, and they are bound to take everything personally.

Mum says, 'Don't do that!'

Junior wants to do it. When he can't, he gets angry. He is furious with Mum.

'I am angry' becomes 'I am angry with you.'

We learn to project all our feelings onto others. I am upset because he said something nasty. I am angry because you will not do what I want. Feelings become seen as a response to someone or something external to us, rather than as an internal response to our own changing world, a way of registering what is going on inside ourselves.

We attach feelings to others, but really, they are ours. They are not caused by other people. They are a whole range of inner experiences that we have never learned to properly interpret or manage; that we have never learned to take responsibility for.

Each person is capable of feeling every single human emotion, from joy and love, to grief and hatred. We each have to find a way of experiencing feelings without being overwhelmed by them. To understand how they drive us, but not to be driven by them. Each of us has to find his or her own way of dealing with the sadness, jealousy, insecurity, fear, anger, loss, loneliness and disappointment that is part of being human, part of living in this world. Emotions are not unique to any individual; yet, each individual, eventually, has to learn to face them. We take everything so personally, yet these emotions are in a sense impersonal, they act within us all.

Deep within us, in our unconscious mind, our intuitive wisdom, we know that this is so. Our unconscious mind keeps engineering situations that will bring those yet unresolved emotions to our conscious awareness again. It keeps giving us a chance to re-experience the pain that we have suffered, so that we can acknowledge it, heal it and let it go.

We are drawn to situations in which these basic emotions and conflicts will be re-experienced. We are drawn to relationships that will bring up our unresolved issues repeatedly. At an unconscious level, we pick people who are going to trigger those emotions we have not yet learned to deal with. For instance, if I am a bully, I will keep being drawn to those who are unassertive. If I am insecure, I will attract those who are afraid of commitment. If I am afraid of expressing my feelings, I will seek out those who are also afraid. Until, finally, I overcome my fears and start doing the things I need to learn how to do.

Of course, when these emotions re-surface, if we do not consciously decide to work on them, then we will just push them back down again, and pretend they do not exist. With no more conscious insight than previously, the unconscious mind has to deal with it in the only way it can, by compelling us to repeat the behaviour of the past, and by bringing out the pain again later, unchanged and still unhealed. This is Freud's idea of the repetition compulsion.

This cycle can only be stopped by a combination of the conscious and the unconscious mind. The unconscious mind brings painful emotions to the surface, and then the conscious mind makes the decision to stay with them and do something about them. Together, the conscious and the unconscious mind can then work on them. In this way, the emotions are released and transformed, and through this process, we are able to change and grow. It is wonderful, really; because knowing this gives us a choice.

If we are not aware that this is what is happening, we probably will not learn as much as we could from relationships. We merely repeat old roles and behaviour patterns from the past; we experience the same pain and feelings of rejection, which then further reinforce our core beliefs about our own lack of worth. The painful feelings trigger the same old negative beliefs about ourselves— however, we do not try to explore the pain, and we do not challenge the beliefs. Feeling bad, and believing ourselves unlovable, we then behave in a way that makes it hard for other people to react positively towards us. We do not say how we feel, we withdraw and sulk or get angry and bully them into rejecting us again so we can say to ourselves, 'Told you so,' and feel even worse.

So, what is the alternative?

The alternative is to make a conscious choice just not to repeat blindly the past but to change and take control of our present experiences.

This means — admitting our past and present pain (that will be upsetting); telling people how we feel (that can be uncomfortable); challenging our beliefs about our unworthiness (that is painful) and learning to like ourselves (that is hard work). If we can take responsibility for our own feelings rather than merely acting them out, then we are not so vulnerable to feelings of rejection, and other people are likely to react to us in a more positive and supportive way.

If we are willing to explore the origins of our feelings, and are able to express those feelings, then we are in fact being given over and over again the opportunity to heal them, and to free ourselves from the pain of the past.

'Know thyself? If I knew myself, I'd run away.'
Shakespeare: *Hamlet:* 'This above all: to thine own self be true, and it must follow, as the night the day, thou canst not then be false to any man.'

Goethe's famous line shows that to truly know who we are is not easy.

As young children, we all had large measures of honesty, spontaneity, curiosity, and faith that we could do anything. We actually believed in ourselves and in our inner world a whole lot more than we do as cynical, outer-world-focussed adults.

Nevertheless, we were also completely dependent on others for everything: warmth, comfort, shelter, food, affection, approval, and love. The possibility that any of these vital nutrients could be withdrawn at any time kept us in a constant state of anxiety. We had to do what people told us to do. We had to become what they wanted us to be, and hide those parts that they did not want to see. The alternatives were too awful to contemplate: loneliness, isolation, discomfort and despair.

Erich Fromm wrote that 'the suppression of spontaneous feelings and thereby the development of genuine individuality starts very early.'[31] It is not a unique, personal thing – in the sense that no particular event was to blame, no particular person or parent or traumatic experience can be pinned down as the one that made us into something less than we might have been. It is the whole socialisation process, and is common to all.

In childhood, we were indeed vulnerable, powerless, and unable to control events. Yet, to change these deep-seated beliefs about our own powerlessness, which persist in many cases unchanged into adult life, we have to accept and heal those parts of us, which have retained the memories of those fears and hurts. We have to accept that we have been hurt. We need to heal the past so that we can free the present.

The problem is that as adults, many of us are emotionally still children. We are terrified still of rejection and abandonment, so we never truly reveal ourselves to others. Unable to separate, we tie ourselves in to negative, unnurturing relationships. Fearing failure, we live below our potential, and do not accomplish the success we are capable of achieving.

We need to learn to nurture ourselves, to build our own positive self-image, so that we are not always dependent on other people's opinion or approval of us and we do not continue to live by other people's values. Otherwise, we will end up not knowing who we really are. This is the common malaise of the twenty first Century: alienation from our inner world.

Pasternak says in Dr Zhivago: 'The great majority of us are required to live a life of constant, systematic duplicity. Your health is bound to be affected if, day after day, you say the opposite of what you feel if you grovel before those you dislike and rejoice at what brings you nothing but misfortune.'[32]

Deep down, I think, we all know this.

The Path to Self-Knowledge
Gary Zukav: 'The journey to authentic power requires that you become conscious of all that you feel.'[33]

So who are you now? Think about it for a moment, because it is probably the hardest question you will ever have to answer.

Jot down a few of the roles you think you play. It is an interesting exercise. Because most of us think that we have one unique personality that is consistent through time and that is determined by a fixed set of in-built characteristics, which are largely unchangeable. Furthermore, most of us think that we know pretty much all there is to know about ourselves.

In fact, nothing could be further from the truth. You might think okay, I am a man, a son, a husband, a father, a provider, a worker – an architect or a builder or a teacher, a brother, a mate, a lover, a neighbour, a sportsman, a gardener, a socialist, a Christian, a beer-drinker, a meat-eater. Then what? Well, I am an extravert, a left-brainer, a good motivator, a clear thinker, and a reliable, honest, and straightforward kind of guy.

Yeah. And the rest. What about all the things you think you are not? What about all those things you don't like to mention - the Trickster, the Betrayer, the Bitch or the Ass-hole? Remember back to when you were a child and you played pretend games and you could be anything you wanted to be and you imagined all sorts of fantastic scenarios where you were the hero, the villain, the wizard and the cowboy all in quick succession? One minute you were Superman, the next you were the evil King who tortured his enemies in dark subterranean dungeons, the next you were 007 conquering the world and getting the girl.

Where did they all go?

In Jung's view, they all went into your shadow. And they are still there. You did not grow out of them, you did not get bored with them (otherwise you wouldn't still dream of them and watch all the movies); you just somehow gave them up. They did not fit in with the 'real' world. Once you became an adult, they were not acceptable things to own up to anymore.

Frieda Fordham wrote that 'the shadow appears in dreams, personified as an inferior or very primitive person, someone with unpleasant qualities or someone we dislike.... It is all those uncivilized desires and emotions that are incompatible with social standards and our ideal personality, all that we are ashamed of, all that we do not want to know about ourselves.'[34]

In order to accept all the different parts of yourself, you have to get to know them. Each character in your dreams is a part of you, so by starting to pay attention to these characters, you can find out more about yourself. That is why writing down your dreams can provide such a vast supply of images, emotions and sub-personalities of which you were previously unaware, all of which represent vital, interesting, important parts of you.

As mentioned previously, some of these inner characters or sub-personalities belong to what Jung called the personal unconscious; all the images and dreams and possibilities which lie in the disowned, undiscovered shadow land within each individual. They represent the vast range of hidden emotions and experiences in each of us. The personal unconscious is a store of unrealised potential specific to you; it is everything that you might have been, could be, or already are.

Some are what he called archetypes: they belong to the collective unconscious, that psychic realm common to all mankind that is represented and lives on in story and myth and fairy tales. It is available to everyone because it exists both outside of us in the universe and inside of us in our inner instinctive knowledge.

All of these things are wonderful because they show us that, in fact, potentially, we are everything. If we just take these potential parts, or sub-personalities, seriously, we can find them again. You can find your villain and your hero, if you are open to seeing them in whatever guise they may appear. You can find your inner healer, or magician, your old wise man or earth mother. You only have to ask.

However, because of what we already believe about ourselves and the world, that is one thing that we probably never do.

How what we believe makes us anxious

The mind actively processes, and therefore potentially distorts, all the information it receives; everything that happens goes through a mental filtering system, and what is in the filter determines what comes out the other end. So that when something happens, we perceive that event in a particular way, we evaluate it according to our pre-existing beliefs, we feel certain emotions about the event, and all of these things affect our final reaction or response to it.

If we perceive an external event as dangerous or threatening, our automatic fight or flight response is immediately activated and we feel physical symptoms of anxiety. This automatic bodily response is one of the things that affect our emotional response to that event. What we feel is also dependent on our memories of past similar experiences, our evaluation of our capacity to deal with them, and our general beliefs about ourselves. These underlying beliefs about ourselves, that constitute our self-esteem or self-concept, are probably the most important determinant of how we feel in any given situation.

We each bring our own unique past experiences, emotions, values, and set of beliefs about the world and ourselves to every situation we encounter. That is why ten people experiencing the 'same' event will give ten different read-outs of it. It is not surprising that 'eye-witness' accounts are so unreliable. In fact, that one event has become ten different events to the various people all experiencing, interpreting, evaluating and responding to it in slightly different ways.

We may think that we each react in a particular way because of who we are, but it might actually be more accurate to say that who we are is what we have come to believe and feel that we are. Many of our beliefs are not actually helping us. In fact, if you look more closely, they are doing just the opposite. They are often quite negative and destructive. Set against a background of negative thoughts about ourselves, we are likely to interpret every event in a way that further reinforces those core negative self-beliefs. Our reactions are therefore, determined more by inner thoughts and feelings than by apparently external causal events.

For example, Graham remembered that when he was a kid he used to ask his dad to play with him. His dad would be tired, lying on the sofa after work, and he would agree to play just for ten minutes. For many years, Graham thought that he was only worth ten minutes of his dad's time. He felt he was not a worthwhile person and not worthy of other people's time, and various later experiences tended to reinforce that belief. However, when he finally challenged that negative belief about himself, he could see that although his dad used to be tired after work, he had still made the effort. Now, thinking back, he feels good that his dad wanted to play with him at all.

So, we constantly need to explore our beliefs. We need to be continuously asking, 'How do I feel? What am I telling myself? What automatic thoughts are going through my head?'

Otherwise, we just react without knowing why, and we continue to feel bad instead of working to change those negative beliefs.

For example, when I was a medical houseman, I was not sure whether a patient had symptoms of a deep venous thrombosis, a blood clot in the leg veins. My boss got angry with me on the ward-round, and, of course, the more upset I got, the less I could say. Then, with the whole team standing round the patient's bed, he said, 'Not only do you not know any clinical medicine, Teresa, you don't know any basic sciences either.' Even the patient winced.

I was wondering recently why that situation had made me so anxious. It was not just fear of getting it wrong, but also the guilt about making a mistake. The judgement and condemnation by others was what upset me the most. The painful image of being blamed kept returning.

It made me see how this has been a pattern in my life. When someone criticises or accuses me, my anxiety makes me panic, my mind goes blank, and so I cannot say what truly happened. I cannot think of the real reasons so I flounder around, get upset, and quickly try to think of some excuse. Then, later, when I realise I have been unfairly blamed, I go over and over in my head what I should have said, I feel a real wimp for not being assertive, and resent the other person immensely.

At this point a thought pops into my mind. I know that an assertive response can reduce anxiety and lead to more effective coping techniques. I read it just the other day. Sounds easy, doesn't it?

So why didn't I act more assertively? Why didn't I say, 'Sorry, I know what I should be looking for but I have a mental block at the moment. Please remind me.'

Of course, it is partly the fear of authority figures. The times when someone in a position of power has been too busy, too angry or just plain disinterested in finding out my side of the story. The times when they haven't listened, and I have wanted to run back and shout, 'It wasn't like that,' only I have been too scared to open my mouth. Or too embarrassed, or upset, or self-conscious. So, they end up thinking I am incapable of doing what I should have done.

Then, in my mind, I blow up this one isolated incident of being ineffectual or incompetent into the statement; 'I am ineffectual and incompetent.' A single action becomes proof of my global unworthiness as a human being. 'My behaviour' somehow translates into 'me.' Now I am convinced that everyone will see me as ineffectual and incompetent.

All roads lead back to past experiences, and most of us will have unpleasant memories of being criticised, blamed and condemned as a person for some unfortunate mistake. For instance, when I was nine, I dropped a tin of white paint on the tarmac outside the front door.

Dad got angry. 'You clumsy idiot. I can't trust you with anything. I will never be able to get it off. You just don't think, do you?'

I felt about an inch high. Miserable. Rejected. Guilty. Ashamed. It is official: I really am the selfish, stupid, worthless worm I always secretly feared I was.

But I didn't mean to do it. I thought I would help by offering to go and get the paint. I just didn't realise the lid was not on properly, and then because I was hurrying, I tripped and then, well, white is conspicuous on black, isn't it?

None of these things was taken into consideration. I could not say them and nobody asked. My knee was smarting from where I hit the ground, and my dad sulked all the time he was scrubbing off the paint. He grumbled about it for days afterwards, telling everyone who came to the house that it was my fault the doorstep was a messy shade of grey.

Sadly, fifteen years later, on the ward round, I still had not cleared up that pot of white paint.

If I had, I might have stuck up for myself better. Or accepted criticism as far as I felt I deserved it, but no more. The problem was that, still believing negative things about myself, I was bound to believe someone else's negative comments about me, however unfair.

The reality is that other people's condemnation of us often says more about them than it does about us. After all, making judgements about someone's personality based on their actions is dangerous. 'I don't like what you are doing' so easily becomes 'I don't like you.' 'You've done something stupid' becomes 'You are stupid.'

Broadly speaking, it is an example of inductive reasoning, which means moving from the particular to the general. But it does not always work. Therefore, when we attribute a person's actions to a defect in his personality rather than to the situation he finds himself in, we are using faulty thinking. We are making assumptions about his motivation without knowing the full circumstances, or inferring something about his character purely from observing his behaviour.

Most of us think we are pretty good judges of other people. We must do, or we would not be quite so quick to criticise and condemn. We are habitually judging others by forcing them into our own stereotypes — over-generalisations that are often built upon no more than physical appearance or racial origin. I mean, are all blondes really stupid? Are all Italians actually greasy? Do a short haircut and a penchant for body art mean you have to be a member of the National Front or have a low IQ?

Of course, most of the time, we are not actually seeing others as they really are; we are putting them into a little pre-packaged box, labelling it, locking it up and throwing away the key. The problem is, once we have put someone in a box, it is very difficult for him or her to get out of it. In addition, we probably only put them in there in the first place because they were different.

We tend to like people who are the same as us, who feel familiar, and whom we like the look of. Those we find unattractive, unfamiliar or different from ourselves, or in other words most of the five billion people in the world, we tend to dislike.

I think what we are actually saying is that we like those things we are prepared to accept about ourselves, and we like the people who reflect these things. All the things we do not like about ourselves and are not prepared to accept we project onto all those others out there who we do not like. Great, we'll keep away from them, bitch about them, focus our aggression towards them, keep our anxiety away from ourselves, and learn nothing.

Listening to all this, it sounds as if we are fairly certain of what other people are, of whom we like and dislike, and of why other people do things. It sounds as if we each know ourselves pretty well. The problem is, I do not think we do know ourselves (and hence others) very well at all.

Compassion for others can only begin when we feel compassion for ourselves, for those unacknowledged parts of us that are mirrored by those others.

That is why it is vital to trace current anxieties back to past situations, and present beliefs back to old prejudices, because we can then see where certain responses first arose. Once we are aware of why we are acting in a particular way, we have the choice to change both the behaviour and the underlying beliefs that reinforced it. We will not have to keep getting hurt – or keep hurting others - in the same way again.

None of us is so very different. Certainly, the one thing we all have in common is pain. So, isn't it time we started doing something about it?

How unexpressed emotions and negative beliefs predispose to illness

Bernie Siegel: 'When we don't deal with our emotional needs, we set ourselves up for physical illness. One's attitude toward oneself is the single most important factor in healing or staying well.'[35]

Freud: 'We must begin to love in order not to fall ill.'[36]

Conventional medicine has proved that certain character traits and personality types are linked with particular physical illnesses. For example, Type A personalities are more prone to heart disease; these are power seekers, people with a low self-concept who are always trying to prove themselves in the external world.

'Type A's express themselves emotionally with an excess of anger and hostility. They tend to be aggressive, hard driving, competitive and impatient. They have problems with intimacy, accepting help, and nurturing others.'[37] It makes sense, doesn't it, that if you do not love yourself enough, you will be more likely to get heart disease.

The typical cancer patient: 'strongly extraverted, dependency on others for validation of his own worth ... poor self-image ... feelings of worthlessness ... restricted in expressing emotion, especially aggressive emotions related to their own needs.'[38] Recently, 'many studies have shown that unresolved grief and depression are related to specific cancers.'[39]

Cancer and heart disease together account for nearly a half of all deaths. Stress has also been implicated in many other physical illnesses.

In relation to mental disorders, the Department of Health survey in the year 2000 (www.statistics.gov.uk) showed that:
16%, or 1 in 6, adults aged 16-74 living in the UK had symptoms of at least one neurotic disorder, such as depression, anxiety or phobias.

9% had mixed anxiety and depressive disorder.

4% of people had generalised anxiety.

3% had depression.

2% had phobia, obsessive-compulsive disorder and panic disorder.

26% had hazardous drinking patterns.

7% had symptoms of alcohol dependence.

5% of men and 2% of women showed signs of drug dependence.

Running through all of these conditions are high levels of anxiety, low mood, low self-esteem, and an external locus of control; that is, a tendency to look to the external world to alter emotions or mood-states rather than looking within.

Thus, it seems clear that our emotions and beliefs about ourselves are affecting both our physical and our mental health.

Recognising Symptoms of Anxiety and Depression

If we can acknowledge how we feel and if we can express emotions such as anger and fear, then we are likely to lead healthier lives. We have processed those emotions, released them and resolved them. They are not hanging around waiting to cause us trouble.

But if we deny what we are feeling, bottle it up, hide it away and pretend everything is ok, then sooner or later those emotions will translate into physical or psychological symptoms. They have to. They have nowhere else to go.

Basically, we are saying that those emotions are not important enough to listen to, which also gives us the message that we are not important. So we just keep experiencing them, keep adding to them, keep building them up, then wonder why we feel so awful.

Tension comes from holding things in; and it comes from the conflicts between opposing or contradictory forces or feelings. Emotional tension leads to physical tension, it causes the release of stress hormones and a weakening of the immune system.

Over a day, we feel all sorts of conflicting emotions: sadness and joy; excitement and fear; love and aggression. If on balance the painful emotions win, we will end up going to bed feeling upset and not being able to sleep. Over a decade, if the negative emotions win, we will probably end up getting ill.

Because over time, the energy of unexpressed sadness or loss can turn into depression—the energy of unresolved specific fears can become generalised anxiety. In fact, anxiety and depression often merge into one another, because the inability to express and resolve feelings often affects not just one but, the whole range of emotions.

Anxiety and depression are defined as disturbances of mood, which have both psychological and physical symptoms. In other words, they affect thoughts, feelings, the physical body and the energy systems.

A depressed person feels low in mood, negative and pessimistic; he cannot enjoy anything, and cannot seem to get things done. He talks and moves slowly, or he may be irritable and restless, pacing up and down or constantly fidgeting and unable to relax. He cannot concentrate and may become forgetful. He appears deflated, as if all the life and energy have drained out of him.

When low mood persists, it gets worse than normal unhappiness, which we all experience at times. The so-called biological symptoms of depression then manifest: poor sleep, loss of appetite, change in weight, decreased libido, variation in mood during the day, constipation and aches and pains anywhere in the body.

Studies have shown that a depressed person suffers a specific type of distorted thinking; he disregards his strengths and achievements, selectively forgets all the memories and beliefs, which would serve to build his self-esteem, and focuses exclusively on negative and gloomy statements. He dreads the future, remembers every little thing that ever went wrong in the past, and feels himself completely to blame for both his past disappointments and his present unhappiness. He has no self-confidence, sees himself as a failure and often feels that life is no longer worth living.

Likewise, in anxiety, a person has a negative view of himself, the world and the future. He feels isolated and helpless, he anticipates danger everywhere, and sees himself as vulnerable and unable to cope.

A person suffering from anxiety feels apprehensive, fearful, and unable to relax. Worrying thoughts keep going round and round in his mind, so that he cannot concentrate properly or think clearly, he often sleeps poorly and may have disturbing dreams. He feels overwhelmed; he focuses on his weaknesses and is unable to see any of his strengths. His physical symptoms generally cause him to worry more.

The physical symptoms of anxiety are due to increased muscular tension, causing headache, neck or shoulder stiffness, or backache; and to increased arousal of the autonomic nervous system. The person is constantly experiencing the fight or flight response, which can affect any or all of the different systems of the body. Dizziness and faintness can also occur as a result of over breathing or panic attacks, in which he feels that he is losing control and may even fear that he is going to die.

An anxious person is shaky, sweaty and close to tears. He startles easily and may be hypersensitive to noise. He may have a dry mouth and difficulty taking in-breaths or swallowing, and may suffer palpitations, pain or a feeling of constriction in the chest.

Symptoms of anxiety include indigestion, epigastric pain, wind, churning of the stomach or feelings of nausea. There may be increased frequency or urgency of urination, diarrhoea, or lack of libido. In anxiety, sexual problems may arise; men may experience impotence or women menstrual pain.

Probably all of us suffer from some of these symptoms at some time or another, and we probably try to explain them away somehow. Maybe we just do not realise where they are coming from or what we can do about them.

To deny anxiety is the best way of ensuring that it will never go away. It also confirms our lack of confidence in our own abilities and lack of faith in the universe.

To accept that you are afraid is in itself an enormous act of courage. The next step is to stay with that fear, try to find out more about it, and then let it go.

Moving on from fear

Everything can change. It is just a question of finding effective ways of working with painful or frightening feelings and images at the time rather than ignoring them or merely continuing to feel anxious.

Emotion is energy. Viewing it in this way means that we can release and transform it. If we see emotions as unchangeable, as somehow happening to us but beyond our control, then it is unlikely that they will ever go away or get better of their own accord. Merely feeling an emotion does not change it. Why should it? Nothing has happened to it. It pops up, I ignore it, distract my attention from it, or let it flood over me, and then eventually it seems to have gone. But, has it?

Look at it from the point of view of the emotion. I start to feel anxious. I don't like it; I do not want to deal with it. I put the TV on, turn the volume up loud, and sit and eat a box of chocolates. After a while, the anxiety gets bored, sick of trying to get me to engage with it, so it sneaks off somewhere to have a nap. I feel a bit better, and I think, oh well, I've got over that one. I go and do the washing-up.

The anxiety wakes up feeling refreshed and ready for action. 'I will just have a snack and a nice hot bath,' it thinks, 'then I'll go and get her again.' By this time, I have had dinner and gone to bed. I wake in the middle of the night, terrified, sweating and shaking, dreaming that a dangerous prisoner escaped and was chasing me.

I go back to sleep, forget the dream, and get up and go to work.

By continually trying to avoid that anxiety, I am actually increasing its power over me. I am also making myself more anxious, because fear comes from helplessness, passivity and avoidance.

Dealing with your own fear means shifting that balance of power. Your power comes from being active, not passive. It means facing your feelings, not avoiding them.

Anxiety and fear stop us from growing. We are scared of believing what our worries are telling us. That we may have to change, that not everything will remain the same, that the world is unpredictable.

All of which are true. However we will survive. Nothing is as bad as we imagine it to be. Because we are scared of being overwhelmed by change, we do not realise how much it could benefit us. Everything is an opportunity to learn.

If a crisis forces us to re-evaluate our priorities— to learn new coping strategies and break some of our habits, well, great. If we learn to draw upon some untapped inner resources and develop new strengths then we are going to have gained a lot. To depend more upon yourself and less on others is after all the whole point of what Jung calls the individuation process.

We can choose to wait for crisis – he is just off taking an extended nap – or we can start doing our work, bit by bit, in our own time, gradually building up our confidence and resources. Not that difficult a choice, is it?

HEALING ANXIETY

Meditation

One of the most effective ways of stopping the anxiety cycle is to practice relaxation or meditation. Research has shown that a person cannot experience two contradictory emotional states at the same time. You cannot be calm and anxious at the same time. You cannot be tense and relaxed simultaneously.

Realising that your mind is in a state of fear, worry or anxiety; and that your body reflects this is the first step. Recognise which parts of your body are most tense: you may be repeatedly getting tension headaches, or a stiff neck. Notice where the autonomic effects of anxiety are most marked: it may be your stomach, your bladder, your bowel, or it may be affecting your whole body.

Make time to relax. Lie or sit down comfortably, take deep breaths and centre on each muscle group, letting go of the tension. Direct your breath into a particular area if you are having difficulty relaxing that area. Be patient. Everything takes time. You cannot expect the habits of a lifetime to disappear after one session of relaxation. And you cannot expect to be able to instantly relax when you are in the midst of an anxiety attack. You need to build it up, do it frequently, half an hour a day is a good way to start. But if you do practice meditation on a regular basis, you'll find you get to the point where you can use it at will to induce a calm, peaceful, physically relaxed state whenever you need to. As your body learns to relax, you can gradually override the physical and emotional sensations of anxiety.

Meditation is not just about allowing the body to let go of its tension and stress. It also gives your mind a chance to be peaceful. Once you feel relaxed, concentrate on your breathing — on the breaths entering and exiting from your nose. If thoughts come into your mind, try to just observe them, without becoming involved. Allow those thoughts to come and go. Do not judge them. Do not try to stop them. Just accept them, and let them flow away of their own accord. Our thinking is called a train of thought, and trains are difficult to stop. Do not have unrealistic expectations. If, in a half hour meditation, you have managed to observe your thoughts for just a couple of minutes, then you have done well.

One of the main reasons that we cannot stop negative or worrying thoughts when they start going round and round in our minds is that the more we struggle against them, the more energy we give them. Trying to actively get rid of these troubling thoughts is the best way of making them stay.

Meditation is also another way to build self-esteem. The message to yourself is simple: by actively doing something about your physical state of anxiety or discomfort, you are showing your body that you care about it. By listening to your feelings, your thoughts and your body, you are confirming that they are important. Besides, the more you listen, the more they will tell you.

Once your symptoms are more manageable, you will be able to consciously work on some of the underlying issues that have generated the anxiety in the first place.

There are many ways of meditating, but features common

to various types of meditation include:

Relaxation of the body.

An attempt to sense the different parts of the body.

An attempt to allow thoughts and feelings from the unconscious to enter the conscious mind. This facilitates access to the higher self, to intuition, creativity, memories and emotions.

An attempt to empty the mind and then observe what is happening, without judging it, without following the train of thought.

The development of a detached part of the mind that simply observes what is happening in the rest of the mind and body, without reacting to it. This is the witness state.

HemiSync

HemiSync was developed by Robert Monroe, who founded the Monroe Institute in Virginia, US. He had spontaneously started having out-of-body and similar experiences, and he found that by playing different frequency sound waves in each ear, he was able to reproduce these experiences and induce altered states of consciousness in himself and others.

Further investigation showed that when he was accessing these deeper levels of consciousness, he was actually synchronising the electrical activity in the two hemispheres of the brain.

This technique can be very helpful in achieving deep levels of meditation very quickly; it enables you to reach more consistently those levels and to return to normal waking consciousness faster.

Reiki

Reiki is a powerful tool for relaxation, decreasing anxiety and tension and calming the mind as well as the body. It acts at all levels – physical, emotional, mental and spiritual. Relaxation is followed by stimulation of metabolic and detoxification processes.

Reiki decreases the physiological fear response, releases muscular tension and leads to a feeling of general well being. If a Reiki session makes you feel energised and alert, then it is best to do it in the morning; if it makes you want to sleep, do it when you go to bed at night.

Either way, it is a good idea to give yourself Reiki every day. If you find it difficult to relax, then Reiki will help you do this, and you can use Reiki during your relaxation session in order to calm yourself enough to gradually relax each group of muscles in turn.

Giving yourself a self-treatment every day, you will soon notice a reduction in your general levels of anxiety. In addition, you may begin to be aware of how some of your symptoms are trying to tell you more about yourself. If your symptoms seem to recur in a particular part of your body, or you notice that you are taking much more energy in one area, it may be there is a blockage or excess of energy in that particular chakra.

Anxiety is often related to the third chakra (solar plexus) issues of self-worth and relationship to others; the fourth chakra (heart), or love of self; and fifth chakra (throat), accepting and expressing your inner feelings and needs. The sixth chakra (third eye) may also be involved because in anxiety (and depression) you tend to focus on your weaknesses and ignore your strengths; you are not seeing things clearly, so giving Reiki to this chakra can bring relief of symptoms and help you to see things in a more balanced way.

If you do not have time for a complete self-treatment each day, then whenever you experience symptoms of anxiety, feel where that anxiety is in your body and give Reiki to that area. Try to feel into your body to find the focus of those feelings of anxiety, so that you can give Reiki to the parts which are most affected. Then, later, send distant Reiki to that worry, fear, or anxiety, and to the cause of it.

The important thing is to get into the habit of giving yourself Reiki as soon as your symptoms start, and as often as you can at other times. When you start to feel anxious, take a few deep breaths, stay with that feeling. Give Reiki to the part of your body that feels worst. Now how does it feel? See what comes into your head: thoughts, images, feelings, and memories. Ask yourself, 'Do I know this feeling? Have I felt this way before? When? What was it that made me feel so bad?' Sometimes it is clear where similar feelings have come from; sometimes it is not. Send Reiki to the cause of your anxiety, using both the distance symbol and the mental / emotional symbol, whether or not you are aware of the cause.

Ask your intuition questions with simple yes or no answers to help you to realise what is troubling you. Send out a thought to the universe, your guides, and your higher self, asking for help. 'What do I need to know now?' Give Reiki to your sixth chakra, or third eye, so that you can more clearly see things as they really are.

Try sending distant Reiki to your problem, 'To help me deal with my anxiety,' or to a positive outcome for the particular situation that triggered this anxiety. Send Reiki to strengthen the part of you that can cope and is unafraid.

Many people who have Reiki simply forget to use it, or do not realise that sending it to emotions or to the cause of emotions can provide relief.

Opportunities frequently arise during the day to give yourself Reiki for ten minutes or so, for instance while you are in a meeting, or waiting for a bus, or even in the queue at the supermarket. You can use these moments to send Reiki to the cause of your worries, whether or not you are feeling anxious at the time, or to give it to the parts of your body where you habitually store tension. Also, as you do not have to concentrate when you are giving yourself Reiki, you can give it while watching TV, listening to music, even while you are in a car, as long as you are not driving.

Meditating with the All-Love energy
Listen to the Shenu meditation CD, or simply sit quietly and invite the All-Love energy to enter into your crown chakra. If you wish, you can bring the infinity symbol all the way down through your body, within the column of light that you are forming.

Sit comfortably with your feet firmly on the floor. Close your eyes, clear your mind and relax. Imagine each chakra as a flower, and visualise it opening, the petals slowly unfolding. Start with the crown chakra on the top of your head. Imagine the brilliant sun above your head, radiating its light, cleansing and filling the chakra with light as petals of the flower open. Then move on to the next, the third eye chakra in the middle of your forehead, open the chakra and visualise the light flowing down from the crown chakra. Do this with each chakra in turn, working your way down the body through the throat, the heart, the solar plexus above the umbilicus, the sacral plexus in the pelvis and finally the root chakra at the base of the spine. Imagine energy coming up through your feet from the Earth into your root chakra, mixing and merging with the light coming down through your crown chakra. Allow the energy from above and below to come together and fill your heart.

Now imagine your aura filling with light, visualising it as an egg or bubble all around you, bigger than your physical body. The outside of this bubble is the interface between you and the rest of the world. It is your protection. Imagine it is strong, vibrant, and filled with light.

Then close the chakras one by one, imagining the petals of the flower gently closing in to a bud again. Start with the root chakra, and work your way up to the crown chakra.

Cleansing the chakras in this way helps to release any blockages, and also strengthens the aura.

Balancing the chakras
This technique can be used to balance your own or another person's chakras. Connect to the energy, keep your hands in each position for a few minutes, or until you can feel the energy flowing equally through each hand.

The positions of the hands are as follows:
One hand on the 6th chakra (third eye) and the other on the 1st chakra (root chakra).
One hand on the 5th chakra (throat) and the other on the 2nd (sacral chakra).
One hand on the 4th (heart chakra) and the other on the 3rd (solar plexus).

It does not matter which hand is used on each chakra.

There is a variation of this technique, in which one hand remains throughout over the 6th chakra (third eye), while the other is placed on each chakra in turn from the 1st (root), 2nd (sacral), 3rd (solar), 4th (heart) and finally the 5th (throat). Each position should be held for several minutes or until the amount of energy flowing through each hand is the same.

Focussing

Emotions are a right-brained function, and are therefore more easily represented in images than in words. The left-brain uses language, is concerned with logic and reason, and tends to question or doubt the images presented by the right brain. 'Are you sure you see that image? Are you sure your age was six? Where's the proof?' None of these questions is helpful in focusing; we have to ask our left-brain to take a short break and simply trust our images.

In this technique, we aim to contact our bodies and our emotions directly. It is not important what image is seen, as long as it is felt that this in some way represents the sensation. Emotions may come from a time before we could speak, and therefore we are unable to describe those emotions in words. The memories of all our emotions are held within our body, our aura, and in our energy systems.

Focusing into the body may access and release such memories so that we can express a particular emotion in an image form and then work to change it. We all have, within us, all the resources we need to solve any problem that we encounter.

First, relax, breathing slowly and deeply in and out, using the abdominal muscles, not just the chest muscles.

Recall the event, situation or dream that made you feel the way you feel. Then start concentrating on your body and feel where the emotion that you are experiencing can be felt in your body. The sensation may be strong or weak, it may be anywhere in the body. Enter into that area of your body. Really, feel as if you are entering into the body. What comes to your mind? Do you see something?

Do you hear something or someone? Do you smell something?

If you do not see, hear or smell something, then ask yourself how old you are? Just accept the first age that comes into your head. Then ask yourself what was happening in your life at that time? Often a memory will come which seems particularly relevant. You may see yourself at a certain age. You can also ask yourself how you are dressed.

Is there something that you want to do with that image? If all you see is black, you may want to bring in a light in some form. It may be that you do not want to do anything with the image, and that is okay as well. You may feel that you can do whatever you want on your own, or that you need help, or some tool. If you need some help, ask for a part of you to come and help you, or ask that the tool you need appears.

Once you have done all that you want to, feel back into your body and see what the sensation is. You may find the sensation has improved. If another part of your body now seems to have a stronger sensation, go into that part of your body next. Then repeat the cycle. It is possible that after you feel back into your body, the sensation has improved greatly and you do not wish to do any more. If that is the case, thank the various parts of you which have helped you, then start to come back to the here and now, moving your toes and fingers and opening your eyes.

During the session, the person assisting you can beam energy to you, or after the session, you may want to send energy to any images that you received.

Example

G: 'I would like you to relax and to breathe slowly and evenly, filling your chest with air, right down into your belly, and then slowly letting it out. Now, I want you to concentrate on the feeling that you felt earlier, when you were upset or felt uncomfortable. Where do you feel that in your body?'

X: 'I feel something in my chest.'

G: 'What do you feel in your chest?'

X: 'A sort of pressing.'

G: 'Go into that feeling. Go into that area of your chest.... What do you see, or feel or hear?'

If the person does not have an image, ask how old the person is. Then ask what was happening in his life at that age. Then try going back into the chest and see if an image comes now.

X: 'I see a little boy with a steel band around his chest.'

G: 'Would you like to do something about that?'

If he does not want to do anything about it, then ask him what he wants to do: he may want to remain relaxed for a while, or he may want to finish the session, or he may feel a strong sensation in another part of his body.

X: 'Yes.'

G: 'Can you do that on your own, or would you like another part of you to help?'

If he cannot do it on his own, then you can ask which part of him he would like to help. If he is not sure, then you could make some suggestions e.g. inner mother, father, magician, locksmith, etc.

X: 'No, I can do it on my own, but I need some tools.'

G: 'What tools do you need?'

X: 'When I look closer at the band, I see that at the back it has a padlock, so I would like the key for that padlock.'

G: 'Ask for the key?'

X: 'Can I do that?'

G: 'If you would like to. Are you sure that you want the key, and want to open up the padlock and remove the band?'

X: 'Yes I am.'

G: 'Are you going to open the padlock and remove the band now?'

X: 'Yes.'

G: (Pause) 'Have you done that?'

X: 'Yes.'

G: 'And how do you feel now?'

X: 'Much better. I feel that I can breathe now, and that the energy is flowing through my body, coursing through me.'

G: 'Do you want to do anything else?'

X: 'No.'

If he wants to do something more, you could ask him what. Also, you could ask him how his body feels now, and if there is any other part that he feels he would like to go into. If so, you go into that area and repeat the process. If he can feel sensations in more than one part of his body, then ask him to go into whichever is strongest.

G: 'Why do not you say goodbye to the boy and say you will go back and visit him later?'

X: 'Okay.'

G: 'Are you ready to come back now?'

X: 'Yes.'

G: 'Then start coming back to the here and now, moving your toes and fingers and then finally opening your eyes.'

The important thing is to find some symbolic representation for your emotion or pain. Then you can work with this image and start to shift the emotions captured within it.

For example, I was on my own, and was feeling anxious, so I stopped what I was doing, and tried to stay with the feelings for a few minutes. Closing my eyes and taking some deep breaths, I relaxed as much as I could. Then I worked through the focusing steps:

What do I feel? I feel anxious.

Where in my body do I feel that? I feel it in my throat, I cannot swallow properly and my throat feels dry.

Focusing on that area, what do I see? I get an image of a chain around my neck, constricting me.

What would I like to do with that image? Maybe I could cut that chain. It is heavy; it is stopping me from speaking properly.

Would I like some help? Yes, I would, I do not have the tools to cut it myself.

Who would I like to help me? I would like my inner magician to help me; he is very powerful.

What tools would I like to help me? My magician has come, I can see him here, and he has brought a huge pair of magical chain-cutters. He is slipping the chain-cutters in place now.

Have I done that now? Yes, he has cut the chain, and I am free.

Is there anything else I would like to do? No, not just now. If I felt uncomfortable in another part of my body, I could repeat the process with the part that is holding this feeling. However, I feel fine, so there is nothing more to do.

How do I feel now? I cough, and move my neck. It feels much better now.

Am I ready to come back now? Yes. I check my body; it feels comfortable. I thank the magician for his help, and he says he is always there if I need some help again. I finish my session feeling calm and peaceful.

Another time, I was feeling anxious but couldn't get any image:

What do I feel? I feel anxious.

Where in my body do I feel that? My throat feels dry.

Focusing on that area, what do I sense? I do not see anything.

How old am I? I suddenly thought of myself at age seven.

What am I wearing? I am wearing a horrible pair of hospital pyjamas.

What was happening in my life at that time? I was in hospital having my tonsils out.

What would I like to do with that image? I would like to make my throat feel better.

Would I like some help? What I would really like is for the nurse to come, hold me, and give me some ice cream to make my throat feel better.

Who would I like to help me? I want my inner nurse; she will come.

What tools would I like to help me? She is there with me now, sitting me on her lap with a huge bowl of chocolate ice cream.

Have I done that now? Yes, I have eaten it, she holds me and comforts me, and the tension in my throat lessens.

Is there anything else I would like to do? Now I feel a little tearful, and I cry a bit, and my throat stops hurting. I feel peaceful, and tired, and I would like to rest.
How do I feel now? I relax for a few minutes, and then I feel much better, as if freed from some old pain.

Am I ready to come back now? Yes, the pain has gone. I thank my inner nurse, and she promises to come back if I need her. I make a mental note to go back to that seven-year old child sometime, and see if she needs my help again. Then my session is over.

Affirmations

An affirmation is a positive statement, which is reinforced and repeated in order to change negative conditioning from the past. We have all experienced painful emotions as a result of negative statements from others, and over time these negative emotions and beliefs become imprinted in our unconscious mind, embedded in our energy system.

We therefore need to tell ourselves positive things about ourselves in order to build our confidence and self-esteem. When you feel good about yourself, you believe in your abilities, and can make positive choices and gain a greater sense of control over your life.

There may be something that you were repeatedly told as a child that has had a negative effect on your self-esteem. For instance, I was always called a creep by other kids. So, a few years ago, I used to shout out loud over and over while I was out chopping firewood, 'I am not a f***ing creep.' There was a lot of anger mixed in with that pain, so the physical exertion and the shouting really helped to release that and I would often end up sobbing. Once I had the anger out, I was able to make more positive affirmative statements.

It may be that you were always being told you were stupid, clumsy or ugly; that you weren't as good as your brother or sister, that you were a mistake or a waste of space.

If a specific negative statement has been reinforced many times in our minds, with all the humiliation and wounding that entails, then we need to bring a lot of energy to the specific affirmation we are using to counter that engrained belief.

If you just whisper it to yourself a couple of times now and again when you are feeling down, it is not going to go far towards bringing you up. You have to actively break the hold that negative belief has over you and put a positive affirmation in its place. For example, stamping your feet in time to loud music, dancing around the room, or speeding on your static bicycle are all good opportunities to say your affirmation loudly with all your energy behind it. You need to say it out loud, with energy, many times, every day for a period of at least three or four weeks.

It may be that you are not aware of a specific negative belief that needs to be replaced, but instead have lots of unpleasant, vague feelings that you are not good enough, not achieving enough, or not coping well enough. In this case you can use general affirmations such as: 'I love every single part of me;' 'I am feeling happier and less anxious every day;' 'My mind and body are healing and being made whole, perfect and complete;' 'I value every part of myself,' 'I am an adult, I am strong and able and can depend upon myself.'

It is best to find a phrase or sentence that sounds right to you, that sums up the things you need to hear in words from your own vocabulary or images from your own imagination. Then you can find a regular time each day to say them to yourself, maybe in the shower, or driving to work, or even as you fall asleep at night.

With regard to improving self-esteem, decreasing anxiety and feeling better about yourself, the simplest affirmations are often the most effective. Say one that appeals to you out loud, with feeling and energy, twenty or thirty times a day. At first, you will probably resist saying it. It will sound strange because deep inside you do not really believe it. But after a week or so, you'll realise that you are actually coming to believe it is true.

Another use of affirmations is when you start to feel an upsetting emotion, and you know it is pointless and painful to let yourself be caught up in it and make yourself feel bad. For example, I know I have a problem with jealousy. So, my lover says something about another woman that starts me off on one of my inner torture cycles; 'I hate her; he likes her; he hates me; I am worthless and ugly; I will lose him; I will never get another man in my life; I will die alone.' Which is about as pointless and painful as they come. There is no benefit to wallowing in that for an hour; there is no insight to be got, believe me. As soon as one little jealous thought pops into my head about him, I repeat quietly to myself, 'I love him and I know that he values me.' After a few minutes, I feel peaceful, calm and full of good feelings towards both him and me. If jealousy pops back, I repeat it a few more times.

This is using an affirmation to challenge a negative

emotion that I know I do not want to experience. It does not take away the need to explore that jealousy problem, but it does stop me from wasting time yet again with the same destructive thoughts going pointlessly round and round in my head. In addition, it makes me realise that I am in control of my own emotional state; I can choose to challenge negativity and affirm positivity.

By committing to positive self-statements and affirmations, you start to change your negative thoughts about yourself. Then, when you are feeling low, anxious or depressed, saying these positive things can shift the energy of that negative emotional state.

The things that we need to do are actually very simple. It is easy to think, yes, I probably would feel better if I said positive things about myself instead of the same old negative stuff all the time, but then never get round to it. So, just start, keep doing it, and within a few weeks, you will notice the difference.

Stream-of-Consciousness Writing

Taking half an hour, each day to write down whatever comes into your head is one of the best ways of exploring your fears and finding out more about the hidden parts of yourself. Writing down your dreams is another.

Often, we resist doing work like this; we do not want to ask ourselves questions because we do not think we will like the answers. But it is actually difficult – and uses up a lot of energy – to avoid hearing at least some of the messages you are trying to tell yourself. So, start jotting down your dreams in the morning, even if you only remember a few isolated fragments, and start doing a page or so of free-flow, stream-of-consciousness writing each day.

In fact, writing anything helps you in your quest to understand yourself. The power of writing is immense. It relieves your conscious mind of the need to keep going over those thoughts, the need to constantly worry around them. It reveals some of the loops we keep re-playing, the core beliefs and negative self-statements that we do not even realise we keep repeating to ourselves. Besides, it frees the creative part of the mind; somewhere in amongst all those worries and that seemingly trivial repetition, sudden flashes of insight and clarity will emerge.

'But I can't write,' you say. Forget it, you are not doing it for the sake of literature; you are doing it for yourself. No one else should read it, or you will start censoring it.

'But it is all negative and whining, that's not really me. It makes me sound like I am a horrible person.' Stop judging and just listen to yourself. Turn off the inner critic and let some of your other voices speak for a change. Even if it is just a few pencilled notes scribbled on the back of an envelope, it is still going to make a difference. Believe me. Writing down your thoughts and feelings is one of the best gifts you will ever give yourself.

People you dislike are another gift. Instead of criticising and judging them, we should actually see them as an opportunity to learn about ourselves. We tend to project onto others all those attributes we least like about ourselves, so if we experience strong negative feelings about someone, or they repeatedly trigger anger or anxiety in us, it is likely that we are reacting to something that exists in at least equal degree within ourselves.

Try writing an imaginary dialogue with someone you really dislike, or a letter (not to be sent) to that person saying how you really feel. These are good ways of exploring your own shadow and bringing to consciousness some of those things that you have not yet been able to own as yours.

We all hide things. We all have negative beliefs about ourselves. We tend to hide parts of ourselves that we think are unacceptable, and their very existence generates guilt, and shame.

It is only by acknowledging them, that we can stop being afraid of them.

CHAPTER SIX

Understanding How
the Mind Works

HOW DO WE LEARN?

A friend's four-year-old daughter asked me, 'How much does your house weigh?' 'Well,' I said, 'I am not really sure.' Unimpressed, she asked what the piano was, then said, 'Why is the piano a piano?'

Now there's a question.

To a four-year old, of course, everything could be just about anything anybody says it is. My house might weigh three hundred tadpoles, or the piano might really be a rainbow.

So, what we learn depends partly on the answers we got to the questions we asked. In those early years, we learned how to label many different things, including abstract things like our emotions. Some of which we have never redefined. That is pretty amazing. I mean, now, as an adult, would you trust a four-year-old's definitions?

Psychology has described how we learn by connecting things together. As a result of our individual experiences, particular thoughts, emotions and behaviours become associated with one another; from these associations we form the mental maps, emotional links and behavioural response patterns that determine our reactions to both familiar and new experiences. We tend to repeat these cycles until we do something to break them.

It is only by exploring and releasing emotions, challenging and modifying thoughts and beliefs, or substituting alternative behaviours, that we can interrupt maladaptive cycles and update outmoded or no longer appropriate learned responses.

The psychoanalytical model agrees with this and describes how our template or blueprint for action, feeling and response in relationships was probably set in the first few years of life. By tracing current emotions and behaviour back to past experiences and events we can reveal the origin of particular habits and responses. What we learned has stuck, so we simply keep repeating it. It is very unlikely to change unless we see the connection.

And we do not just learn via words.

Six-year-old Tom's mother keeps telling him that she loves him, but when he puts his face forwards for a kiss, she turns away.

This is an example of what Gregory Bateson in the 1950s described as the double bind, where verbal communication is contradicted by non-verbal communication. People say things their bodies do not believe; the words mean one thing, but the tone, facial expression or body language tells another story. Each communication apparently negates the other. We have all seen how people say one thing, but do another. For example, your mum says you must tell the truth, but then when you tell one of her friends he is fat, you are told off - even though it is true.

It is not surprising that we get all muddled up in our minds. Words will always have a vaguely hollow ring if they do not match what the body says. The problem is you cannot choose which to believe. The whole point of a double bind is that it is not either/or; it is both. Mixed messages become inextricably linked. Tom's mother says she loves him, but gives non-verbal messages of rejection.

Thirty years later, Tom wonders why he feels anxious whenever his girlfriend tries to get close to him, and why he does not trust her when she says she loves him.

Knowing how those messages got mixed; it is understandable that little Tom learned to associate the word love with being rejected physically and feeling hurt.

The problem is that the adult Tom does not know any of that — not consciously anyway. Until he can recognise some of those connections, by accessing memories from his unconscious mind, he is not going to know how his vision of the world was formed or what certain words, emotions and sensations actually mean to him.

We do not consciously remember how we learned things. We cannot even necessarily put words to what we learned, or we might have made connections before we had words to name them — such as that love means constantly being rejected, or that approval depends on doing what others want you to do.

We are all unique. We have all learned a different version of the world. So, we cannot unravel our own problems by listening to anyone else's definitions, and we cannot refine our own definitions until we know what they are.

MODELS OF THE MIND

THE mind and body are designed to function optimally in a state of balance, and we each have a complex system of interconnected neural and hormonal processes in order to achieve this.

Messages move around the brain and nervous system via electrical impulses and chemicals called neurotransmitters. Depletion or build-up of certain neurotransmitters can lead to disturbances in mood or thought, in how we perceive things or even how our muscles work.

From neuroimmunology, we know that when you think a negative thought, a chemical molecule is produced in the brain, which is released into the bloodstream and travels round your body. This chemical may affect certain tissues or organs leading to abnormal functioning and eventually even physical pathology.

Different regions of the brain are thought to have discrete functions such as sensation, motor activity, memory, emotion and personality, and the interactions between these different areas mediate all the voluntary and involuntary functions of the mind and body.

The brain is composed of two cerebral hemispheres, the left and the right. The verbal motor area, or speech area, is for the majority of right-handed people situated in the left hemisphere, while in a left-handed person, language functions usually involve both hemispheres. Generally speaking, the left hemisphere is more involved in verbal linguistic skills, while the right hemisphere is more involved with visuospatial functions.

For this reason, the left-brain has come to represent verbal, rational, logical processes, and the right brain has come to represent emotional, intuitive and imaginative processes. Wordless visual images, pre-verbal memories, and processes involving shapes and symbols are likely to be localised to the right hemisphere.

The left-brain is biased towards facts, rationality, and reasons. It is concerned with verbal and critical analysis. It will not readily accept anything without proof, which as far as emotions go, is usually hard to find.

The left-brain has the world all mapped out in a neat little logical structure. This means that it will reject experiences or interpretations, which do not fit in with that structure. In other words, nothing new will be allowed in; everything will be much the same as before. The upside of this is that the left-brain is reliable, consistent and efficient; the downside is that it is rarely spontaneous or creative.

Similarly, the right-brain is biased towards emotions and imagination. It blurts things out, ignoring all the rules and beliefs that the left-brain likes to impose. The right brain does not feel the need to explain itself. It is more concerned with its own experiences and perceptions than with reasons or discipline. It can tolerate contradictions and inconsistencies, because it is not always attempting to fit perceptions and concepts into separately labelled little boxes. In other words, it is open to new experiences, but cannot always describe or interpret them once it has had them. The upside of this is that the right brain is sensitive, creative, and capable of making inspired intuitive leaps; the downside is that it is not very organised and not always easy to understand.

In the past, education focused more on facts and rote learning, which are essentially left-brain processes, than on right-brain activities such as imagination and creative interpretation. Our formal education system has recognised only in recent years that children learn in different ways, and that, rather than teaching a specific solution to one particular problem, it is better to teach general problem-solving skills that can be applied in a wide variety of situations.

One model of learning is that people predominantly use certain senses. The sensory systems of vision, hearing, touch, taste and smell all process sensory input in a different way. The fact is that we are highly sensitive sensing organisms. We respond to everything that happens to us – somehow or other. Every stimulus provokes a response. And each processing system responds slightly differently to the multi-layered stimuli we experience.

At school, I had glasses, but, being self-conscious, I did not wear them. Even sitting in the front row, I could not see what was written on the blackboard. So, I learned from what I heard. I still find it hard to visualise. For me, the predominant senses are hearing and inner dialogue—which rely upon words and are therefore, probably mainly coordinated by the left-brain. For someone else the predominant senses could be touch and vision, which are more closely dependent on the right-brain.

Visual people learn best from seeing visual representations of things, and they use images to recall information. Auditory people get most from listening. Others rely on inner dialogue; mentally they go through a series of questions and answers, and can remember the solution later because they understand how they arrived at it. Still others learn though touch and movement and working out how things fit together.

It is not that any one of these processes is better or worse than any other, it is just that different tasks are suited to particular styles of learning. Vision and touch are going to be of utmost importance when stripping down an engine or performing a ballet, whereas solving a maths problem depends largely upon inner mental dialogues.

We each tend to prefer certain styles and we think, often from an early age, that we are no good at the others. Most of us tend to focus or rely on certain qualities, skills or aspects of ourselves to the exclusion of others. However, we all have access within our unconscious mind to all the different types of learning; throughout our lives, we have learned things using each of these various techniques. Besides, we have all had the experience of getting stuck, then finding that a slightly different approach helps unstick you far quicker than keeping pushing harder in the same direction.

It makes sense that my internal representations of things will be different from yours. When my roller blind broke, I said to myself, 'I have forgotten what to do, but I know how this works. I will remember.' My friend opened it up, looked, felt where the short cords connecting the blind to the central roller had come undone, and fixed them back onto the roller. By the time he had finished, I said, 'You have to wind the long cord which raises and lowers the shutter on from the top in order to lift it.' I was logical and left-brained, and he was more creative, and right-brained. With a balanced approach, we got it mended rather quickly.

The model of the conscious and unconscious mind shows that each has a different way of storing and recalling information. In normal everyday life, we generally use less than ten percent of our brain capacity. Our conscious mind contains only what we are focusing on, or paying attention to, at any given moment. This makes life easier, or bearable, as it would be impossible for the conscious mind to be aware of everything we are experiencing, let alone everything we have ever thought or learned.

When you first started to ride a bicycle as a kid, it seemed hard to balance, to remember where everything was, and to focus on what was happening on the road all at the same time. It took concentration and practice; you had to go over the steps repeatedly in your conscious mind. Once you have learned, when the pattern of behaviour is laid down in your unconscious mind, you no longer have to concentrate and this frees your conscious mind for other things. Now, of course, you ride off without a thought.

Similarly, when you are thinking about one thing, there are hundreds of other things, which you are not thinking about. These other things have not disappeared; they still exist within your unconscious mind. In order to remember them or bring them into conscious awareness, you need to access them. Sometimes this is easy; someone mentions an event or fact you had long forgotten and suddenly the details come flooding back to you. At other times, we need to use specific techniques to help the unconscious mind to search for and obtain the required information.

Research has shown that we can consciously handle between five and nine facts or pieces of information at any one time.[40] More than this and we are overloaded and confused.

We make our decisions consciously, based on what we are aware of at the time, i.e. on those five to nine pieces of information. Most of the experience, learning and insights that we have accumulated throughout our lives remain unconscious and not readily accessible because we are not actively aware of them. So, we are only considering a very small amount of the information available to us.

Which means that we are probably not going to know why we end up doing what we have decided to do. Our true motives or driving forces remain unconscious. But we can bring them to consciousness, because everything we have ever felt, thought or experienced has been stored in our unconscious mind. It contains a vast collection of images, insights, emotions, skills and resources, which are all there still, waiting for us to use.

After Graham broke his leg, following weeks of relative immobility he found that he had forgotten how to walk. He had to consciously access the information from his unconscious mind to relearn the steps - and he had been walking for forty years without giving that a thought. His unconscious mind provided the knowledge that enabled his body to walk properly again. The physiotherapist helped as well!

Our unconscious mind is like our disc operating system, the program running in the background of a computer, which affects how we interpret everything that we experience. We make apparently conscious choices without first finding out what our unconscious has to say. This is fine if it is about taking a walk in our own backyard or remembering how to ride a bicycle. But when it is about choosing a career, deciding whom to marry, or making a judgement about whether we need to heal, that gets dangerous. Especially as the conscious mind is a bit of a fibber and can usually come up with some plausible reason for whatever it decides to do.

The point is that the capacities and capabilities of the unconscious mind far exceed those of the conscious mind, despite our conscious minds telling us otherwise.

Another part of the mind is our inner voice, or mental dialogue, which does not easily fit into any category. It is usually a voice, which we may think of as our own thoughts. Strictly speaking, it is not really auditory because it is not heard through our ears. It uses words so is probably associated, for the majority of right-handed people, with the verbal area of the left hemisphere. The inner voice is thus likely for many people to be rational and logical rather than imaginative and intuitive. The inner voice is what we are conscious of at any point in time, so belongs mainly to the conscious mind.

These models of the mind are complementary in that they are all concerned with describing and understanding how we experience ourselves and the world. The sensory-learning model shows that each sensory system has a different way of experiencing and learning. The left-brain/right-brain model shows that each half of the brain has a different way of processing and responding. The conscious/unconscious model shows that although we are not aware of it, we have access to all the different ways of learning and responding that we have ever experienced.

Whatever model we use to visualise the workings of the mind, it is clear that if we are not using all its different parts, we are likely to become one-sided, fragmented, or out of balance. After all, if our right brain really still is that playful, spontaneous four-year old with endless questions, then it stands to reason that we also need the adult left side, which is more sensible and practical, to be able to fully answer them.

The left-brain works in words and the right brain works in images and symbols. So, if you are too left-brained and not in touch with your right-brained emotions, then you will find it difficult to know how you are feeling; it may be hard to be spontaneous, intuitive or creative.

If you are too right-brained and not in touch with your left-brain, then you will find it difficult to understand the emotions that are constantly arising. You may dream up all sorts of good ideas but have difficulty making them into reality.

Ideally, what we need to do is to enhance communication and cooperation between the two. In order to do that, the predominantly left-brained person needs to develop the right brain abilities: such as translating his feelings and thoughts into images and symbols, and become more intuitive and in contact with his emotions. On the other hand, the right-brained person needs to learn to develop his left brain abilities: such as expressing in words what his images and symbols mean, and become more logical and organised.

We can also learn how to bring the unconscious more easily into conscious awareness — through various altered states of consciousness such as meditation, dreams and hypnotic trance. Without the distractions of the outside world, without the interference or resistance of the conscious mind, we can access the knowledge contained within the unconscious mind more easily.

In Milton Erickson's view, all learning and change occur in the unconscious mind, which we cannot consciously control. Just consciously deciding to change is not enough, we have to use the unconscious mind to effect the desired changes.

Combining various learning styles, problem-solving techniques, and creative abilities, we can find all sorts of solutions and answers for ourselves; or, more precisely, within ourselves.

Because different parts of the mind work in specific ways. They are separate yet all part of the whole. All we have to do is join them up, like a four year-old with a dot-to-dot drawing. And we are all doing this continually. If you join certain points, you get one type of picture; if you join others, you see things from a different perspective. Making connections between previously unconnected points, we create a new picture.

In your mind, all the pieces are in place. So, what you get out of it just depends where you make your connections.

Changing Your Mind

IMAGINE you are going to buy a used car. What do you do? Look at the alternatives. Get advice. You test-drive the one you like, check the steering and the suspension and listen to the engine. You inspect it from every angle. Go through a mental checklist of possible flaws. Value it. Consider if it is worth it. Wonder if it will suit you. Your attention is going to be pretty focussed on that car. Automatically, you bring your past knowledge and experience into your conscious awareness so that you can weigh up the situation and carefully decide what to do.

Yet, when it comes to making our own personal decisions and solving our own problems, we do not find that very easy to do. We all have problems, and they are probably best approached from a variety of different angles.

Only the conscious mind is not very creative, it likes to hang on to its old beliefs, even if they have not worked, and it does not understand the language of the unconscious, so it is not very good at finding out what the unconscious mind thinks it should do. The conscious mind tends to thinks that its one angle is the best and it does not really like to change. That is why we tend to be better at buying used cars than we are at solving emotional problems, and why we have many emotions and thoughts that remain unexpressed. Much pain and hurt exists within us, unchanged, that we have not allowed ourselves to heal. And, because of this, there is much joy and happiness that we are unable to experience.

Our conscious mind tells us that all these things do not matter – or worse, do not exist! However, the fact that you do not consciously accept them does not mean they are not there. 'Denying the truth does not change it.'

Every pain, whether physical, mental or emotional, has its source in some experience we have had at some time. When we think of a problem, our conscious mind is searching for that source because it wants to find a reason. Although the reason it comes up with is often just a projection or externalisation. Putting the source of that painful feeling onto someone or something outside of us does not lead to insight or resolution, it is just rationalising it away with left-brained reasons rather than right-brained knowledge – because somewhere in our memory, body or energy system, we know exactly how the problem arose, and what we need to do about it.

Freud pointed out that talking about past traumas always had to involve expression and release of the accompanying feelings in order for those traumas to begin to heal. A purely intellectual understanding of a problem is not enough; we also have to access the emotions. We actually need to use both the hemispheres to heal anything.

So, when we talk through something, we get upset, we suddenly see a link with a past event, or gain some insight into the cause of our distress. And then what? Any inner work is likely to be painful. Telling is an important part of accepting things that we would probably prefer not to accept about ourselves; and it usually brings some degree of relief. However, most of us do not have a supportive, non-judgemental listener — not even inside ourselves. Therefore, much of the pain that we are experiencing is still there, and we need a way of making it feel better.

That is where many of us get stuck. To try to feel better, we use drugs, alcohol, sex, possessions, money, food or whatever else we have habitually used to try to distract our attention. Instead, what we really need is to connect with our own centre, and to the energy outside of us, which can ease the pain, and help us to face the things that we have hidden or that have hurt us. Knowing that we can draw on our own inner spiritual resources gives us the confidence and energy to carry on exploring problems rather than avoiding them.

It is a strange paradox that, if something's wrong in the external world, we usually at least try to do something about it, yet if something's wrong in our internal world, we usually just ignore it; or try to alter something external to ourselves, thinking that this will somehow magically transform our inner experience. For instance, if you are unhappy with your marriage, you might start planning together to build an extension or buy a bigger house. Caught up in the enthusiasm of how great the house will be; you forget that it was your relationship you were worried about – if it appeared in your conscious mind at all.

We end up spending a lot of time and effort trying to change the external world in the hope that this will affect how we feel inside, but all too often, it does not. Instead, we need to focus on the reality of our inner world. We are going to have to consciously decide to give more attention to our unconscious mind, because within it are all the skills, wisdom and resources that we need in order to solve our problems.

But in order to access this information, we would have to acknowledge that some of our conscious attitudes, beliefs and behaviours are not actually helping us. We would have to let go of some of those old habits and learn some new ones. This means change. So why does this seem so difficult?

The problem is that we tend to think that the need to change implies there is something wrong with us. We are sensitive to what we perceive as criticism, and we do not like anyone telling us what to do. Probably because parents, teachers, partners, friends, bosses, politicians, the media and all sorts of other authority figures have been doing it for years. 'You must do this!' 'You shouldn't do it like that!' 'Why can't you be more...?' We are all pretty fed up with that.

Each one of us also tends to see him or herself and his/her personality as consistent, fixed and largely unchangeable. We each think we know what there is to know about ourselves, and even if we knew more we do not believe it would change anything. 'You can't teach an old dog new tricks,' we say; 'A leopard does not change its spots.' It is comforting to think you are a neatly packaged finished product.

Habitually listening to just one of your voices, it is startling to begin to hear all the others. Believing you are just one thing, it is confusing to realise that you are actually lots of other things as well. It is frightening too, because if I am not what I thought I was, then who am I?

The result of all this is that we have come to see change as being negative, difficult or unpleasant - something to be resisted at all costs. Yet let's face it, things could be better for all of us.

We are all grappling with the same basic issues – of unhappiness, confusion and pointlessness. We do not like something about ourselves; we do not like something or someone in our lives; we cannot get over something that happened in the past. We do not really enjoy ourselves, or we continually pursue external things to try to enrich our internal world.

We are in conflict. Part of us says, 'Do this!' another part says, 'Don't.' One says, 'Yes, you can,' the other says, 'No, you can't.' So, we are pushed and pulled in different directions, and we have trouble knowing how we feel or saying what we need. Our unconscious mind is closed off. Our conscious mind is rigidly in control and thinks it knows it all: 'This is the way it is. This is how it has got to be.'

We know there are things we are not happy with, yet we put off doing something about them. We find it difficult to start making the changes that we know we really need.

So think of some of the positive changes you have made, the times when you looked back later and thought, 'Why didn't I do that before?' Throughout your life, you've already changed in lots of different ways: you stopped crawling and started walking, you learned to speak and communicate with the world, you learned to read and write, you passed your driving test, you got your first job, you left home, you fell in love. You've learned and achieved and become so many things that you never thought you would, that at the time you may have resisted - yet that transformed your world.

There are three things that might help us to view change in a more positive light:

No one else has the authority to tell you what to do or what not to do. Only you know what is best for you. Trust yourself.

We are all finely tuned, self-regulatory systems. Your unconscious mind will let you know when there is a problem. It will know what is wrong and what you need to do about it. Listen to yourself. We all say it in different ways; if you are unhappy, if things seem to be going wrong in your life, if you are in pain, depressed, drinking too much or feeling angry all the time, then that may be your way of showing yourself that something needs to change. And, whatever it is you would like to be better at, or do differently, or change about yourself, your unconscious mind already knows how to do it.

Change is necessary. It's normal. It's growth. It's great. Because we have to keep moving in an ever-changing world.

You wouldn't want to be still riding the bicycle that you had as a kid, would you? Or wearing the fashions that were around when you were a teenager?

Yet in a sense you still are. Most people are reliving old painful actions, emotions and negative thoughts. They're living in a time and space that no longer fits them. Problems like depression or addictions or anger are not about weakness, or sickness, or personality defects, it is more that those people are carrying on doing things which were helpful at one point in time and no longer are. If you don't keep up, you get left behind, replaying your own past patterns of behaviour. Many things that worked then simply do not work any more.

For example, I used to like to think of myself as a 'nice person.' So, everything I said or did had to fit in with my predefined 'nice' – and if I did something, which contradicted this, I would feel guilty or ashamed. But I was not even aware of what I meant by nice, or from where that definition came. It may just be a fossil. Maybe when I was five, being told; 'Nice girls don't do that!' So nice means acting in a way that is convenient for someone else: perhaps parents or teachers. Great. I am forty-two and am still trying to gain approval in the manner of a five-year-old. I might think I appear credible, convincing, and spontaneous, whereas all I am doing is wearing very, very old clothes.

Many problems arose in childhood, when we were vulnerable and had few resources, and, as children, we dealt with problems or pain in the only ways that seemed possible to us at the time. Now, as adults, those childhood fears may still exist, of not being able to cope, of being overwhelmed when faced with painful memories or feelings.

Yet, the fact is that we are already at a different level of awareness. Now, as adults, we have the inner resources and knowledge to see that problem differently. Going back to an image from the past, we need not be frightened, because we are now able to solve the problem. We only need to communicate better with our unconscious mind in our everyday thoughts and actions and choices. Every time the unconscious looks at something it sees it anew, unrestricted by what Ernest Rossi called the 'closed circuit of associations'[41] of the conscious mind, and the limitations of the past.

Douglas Adams: 'Clearly I wasn't going to be able to think of anything else until I had the answer, but equally I would have to think of something else if I was ever going to get the answer.'[42]

AS over ninety percent of our brain is not used, we are consciously aware of only a very small part of what is going on around us and inside us. However, our unconscious mind is constantly sensing and experiencing at the physical, emotional, mental and spiritual levels simultaneously. Unconsciously, we are aware of all those things that our conscious mind misses or chooses to ignore.

The unconscious mind is where the answers lie to all those questions we once asked. It remembers everything.

When we go into the unconscious mind, it may seem that we are going backwards, into the past, but what we are actually doing is going more deeply into the present.

From working with energy we know that time does not really mean anything. Sending energy to the cause of a problem in the past helps us to feel better in the present, even if we do not know what the cause was; or when the problem first occurred or indeed what it was. We exist in a past-present continuum, which is populated by feelings, thoughts, physical sensations and energy.

When we look within, we are acknowledging that what we need to see, already exists there. The solutions to our problems lie only within ourselves, not in the external world; and we can find them if we can bring the conscious and the unconscious mind to work together, to be in agreement rather than in conflict. This is very exciting; because it means we all have the capacity to heal ourselves.

The unconscious mind is colourful, artistic and imaginative. It is the realm of emotion and perception unrestrained by conscious rules; it can react in all sorts of delightful and surprising ways. Everything is possible. Faced with a problem, the unconscious mind responds creatively; it can draw upon experience and learning we did not even know we had in order to come up with a new and effective solution.

This happens spontaneously when we get an intuitive answer to a question or problem. Consciously directing your attention to a problem will not always solve it. You think about it, and consciously you are tending to view it from within the confines of your established beliefs, your predetermined mind-set. So, you have no new skills or viewpoints from which to order that information. You have exhausted your conscious techniques or possibilities for problem solving.

However, go away and do something completely unrelated like watering the garden or playing the piano, and often an idea or image suddenly pops into your head. Your unconscious mind, given the specifics or even just the general outline of the problem in hand, goes to work on it in its own way, unhindered by your conscious rules and expectations.

I get some of my best ideas when I get up from work and go to the bathroom. In that short time, my unconscious mind reorganises the information that my conscious mind was grappling with, and comes up with a completely unpredictable and unseen solution.

When your conscious mind is distracted, your unconscious mind is able to work unimpeded by conscious restraint. This happens naturally when daydreaming, or doing some automatic action like mowing the lawn or, more worryingly, when driving a familiar route. We drift off into a reverie or dream-like state, which is different from our normal waking consciousness, and is in fact a light trance. Someone speaks to us in the middle of this, and we say, 'Sorry, I was somewhere else, what did you say?'

Problems are always surmountable. When we say we have a problem, what we really mean is that so far, the methods we have tried have not worked, so we need some alternative strategies. The framework of conscious beliefs we have built around our problem – ideas about why the problem arose or how to solve it - have not worked, so we need some new ones. It makes sense that if our conscious mind could have solved the problem, it already would have done so. Happily, those new strategies and ideas already exist within our unconscious mind.

WHY WE DO WHAT WE DO

AS we have already seen, most of the time we are unaware of the underlying reasons why we feel or act the way we do. Often, we are not sure what we feel, or we do not know why we feel it. Things and events in the external world dominate our conscious mind, and we are not really aware of what is happening inside us at any particular moment. Most of our motivations, beliefs and emotions are unconscious, therefore we are constantly being driven by unknown forces within ourselves.

The conscious mind thinks it is in control. It finds reasons for doing what we are doing, or feeling what we are feeling. But it is very much based in the present, because it cannot remember most of the events and experiences that have lead up to this moment. So it thinks that what it sees in front of its nose is all there is to see.

In a Spanish cafe, my friend Annie asked the waiter for the daily set menu, and he said there wasn't one. Ten minutes later she saw him serve it to some men at another table. 'Look at that!' she said, 'He has given it to them and not to us. I don't like that. He said there wasn't one. I am going to speak to him; I shall be annoyed with myself otherwise. It's bugging me.'

'What is it that annoys you so much?'

'Well, he's treated us like we're tourists, as if we're not important. He lied. I don't like that. He should have told us.'

'Yes, sometimes they just assume you can't speak the language so don't bother. It doesn't really worry me,' I said, 'but you are obviously upset.'

'I am,' she said.

'Why? Did other people lie to you? Has being lied to, upset you in the past?'

She thought awhile. 'When I was little, a girl lied about something she'd done, she blamed me, and her mother came round to tell my father, and I remember my dad just looked at me, he didn't ask me whether it was true. He believed them, and I couldn't say anything. I got blamed for something I hadn't done. That's why I really hate lying.' There were tears in her eyes. 'Oh, you are right, you know, there was something else.'

Later, she said to the waiter, pleasantly, 'I'd have liked the meal they had, but you said it wasn't available.'

'Oh,' he said, a bit sheepishly, 'they're workmen and I did a big pot just for them, you know, stew, the tourists don't usually like it. Next time you come in, you say you want some, and I will bring some specially for you.' He came back with a large brandy for each of us.

Things like this are happening all the time. Something upsets one person; the other cannot really see what the big deal is. The waiter's busy and cannot be bothered to tell us everything on the menu – so what?

On the face of it, Annie is upset that he did not tell the truth. To her conscious mind, that explanation is adequate. She decides to ask him about it. However, even having decided to do this, she can't stop feeling upset and angry.

The real reason she is so upset is actually nothing to do with the waiter. It would have been easy just to be angry with him, take out her feelings on him and leave it at that. It is not so easy to recognise that her feelings are disproportionate to the situation, and to look further than the apparent reason. Her conscious mind repeats a few times, 'He lied, he should have told us.' Then, her unconscious mind, given a few quiet minutes to search for the underlying reason, comes up with the answer. Being open to whatever feelings or images might be triggered, she found the memory of the past event, which for her had brought so much emotional significance to the current situation.

Several things are relevant here. Firstly, owning up to your feelings. They are yours; they are triggered but not caused by someone else's actions. The situation in itself does not make you angry. The same situation made me only slightly irritated. Secondly, you cannot assume why that person did what he did. The waiter may not have deliberately lied. To shout, complain, and be angry with him would have been overreacting after making many unfounded assumptions about his motives. Thirdly, realising that your conscious mind thinks it has got the whole story; you have to enlist the help of the unconscious mind. You have to ask it questions, and give it time to respond. Fourthly, you know the answer is significant because genuine emotion or a feeling of clarity or new understanding accompanies it. Annie was tearful when she remembered how she felt with her father. Realising the true source of her feeling, she did not need to be angry when she spoke to the waiter.

There is a reason for everything; it is usually just not the one we think it is. The conscious mind, being concerned with the minute-by-minute details of the external world, tends to explain internal emotions as a reaction to what's happening outside: so I am depressed because it is raining, I am angry if the waiter lies, I am irritable if the bus is late, I am unhappy because of you. The conscious mind automatically looks for superficial reasons outside itself to explain its inner emotions. This is the essence of projection: it is ascribing to some outer object, situation or person one's own inner personal feelings.

The unconscious mind knows the real reasons. It sees what you are feeling. It remembers all those things you have forgotten. It understands much more about you, and knows far more than you ever give it credit for.

The unconscious mind can access everything that is stored in your memory, your body, and your energy system; in fact, everything that has ever happened to you, every feeling you have ever felt— every pain, every rejection, every failure. And of course, every joy, every success which, just as importantly, you may have forgotten.

We are actually all far more complex than we imagine ourselves to be. Anyone who believes too much in the stories his or her conscious mind comes up with, who seems too convinced of all those nice easy rational explanations, probably has no idea just how small a part of the whole story they really are.

The unconscious mind — reacting to all the thoughts we have ever thought, and remembering all the feelings we have ever felt — is the emotional database that drives our lives. As such, it really works very simply. New data comes in, it is compared with data that already exists, and appropriate data goes out. That is, appropriate to what is already in there. If I have a great deal of angry, painful emotions that are unhealed, then minor irritations will come out as major explosions of rage or upset. If my image of myself is built upon many negative statements that I have believed and stored over the years, then if someone criticises me for a small oversight, I shall probably overreact. Odds are that in my unconscious mind I do not really like myself, however much my conscious mind tells me I do.

Our unconscious mind interprets everything that happens to us, and if we do not make a conscious decision to give close attention to what we are feeling and thinking, then we will interpret any event in a way that just reinforces the beliefs that already exist in our unconscious mind.

For instance, if my unconscious belief is that I am a failure, then if I do well at something, instead of feeling happy about it, I will probably have a sense of disappointment that nothing ever seems to be really rewarding; yet I will not know why that is. When the word success sinks down to my unconscious mind, it meets only fear of failure. There are no positive beliefs to anchor it, only self-doubt and distrust. So, instead of feeling pleased with myself, all I become consciously aware of are critical thoughts: I start telling myself I could have done better, and focus on the bits that went badly. It is a reflex response; automatically the unconscious mind reinforces and finds evidence for the negative beliefs it has accumulated over the years.

It is a tragic waste to keep reacting negatively to positive experiences. That is a habit we need to break whenever it starts to kick in. We can do this by consciously exploring exactly what beliefs, emotions and learning our unconscious mind is contributing at any particular time. Sometimes it is not that easy to be in contact with our hidden beliefs; however, by focusing on feelings as they happen, we can begin to see those little negative thoughts coming into our consciousness.

For example, ask yourself, from where does that thought or feeling come? When did this happen before? See what comes to mind. There may be one particular incident in childhood when we were criticised when we did something well. Odds are it is a series of humiliating and painful experiences that have undermined our faith in ourselves. One man's mother used to hit him over the head with a heavy ring when he was a boy every time he told her one of his ideas. Another man remembered he would show his dad his homework and his dad would say, 'You're never going to be a brain surgeon, are you?'

This sort of thing has happened to all of us far too often and as a result, we have built up an enduring store of negative self-beliefs, which we have never challenged.

So when my unconscious mind responds to my achievement with something like: 'Don't get your hopes up, you loser, that was just a fluke, it won't happen again,' I will realise that I am dealing with some past negative conditioning. First, I have to acknowledge and grieve that pain. Then I'd say to myself, 'No, that critical statement was not true then, and it is not true now. I did well and I deserve the credit for it. I no longer want that old belief that I cannot succeed.'

Or you could imagine you have a stun gun, a laser or whatever weapon you want to use to blast that negative thought to smithereens as soon as it enters your mind.

The advantage of learning to bring our unconscious thoughts and feelings to consciousness is that we begin to see much more clearly, what is going on inside us. With practice, the process gets easier. We need to reinforce and repeat positive statements many times in order to counteract those previously held unconscious negative beliefs, to build on our successes – and to truly enjoy them.

JOHNSON: 'The shadow is that which has not entered adequately into consciousness.'[43]

The shadow is really another word for the unconscious mind. It contains all that we are not consciously aware of: thoughts, feelings, aspects of ourselves, learning, insight and knowledge.

The basic fact of life is that at some time all of us have felt every emotion that exists; anger and fear, joy and sadness, jealousy and compassion. We often have completely contradictory feelings about individuals or events. We can love and hate something simultaneously. We can be drawn to someone and yet repeatedly feel the urge to pull away. We tend to identify with the dominant feeling, or the one we find easier to accept, and it is this that we consciously acknowledge or tell ourselves we feel.

The feelings that we find harder to accept we tend to project onto another person – both in our waking life and in our dreams. Therefore, if you have trouble making decisions, you might tell your partner off for being indecisive. Alternatively, instead of owning your own anger, you might project it onto a frightening or threatening dream character that you see as distinctly 'not you.'

Feelings come and go; they change. We feel confused or ambivalent because we experience contradictory emotions. Our conscious mind likes to have clear-cut, simple answers that fit in with its fixed set of rules and beliefs about ourselves and the world. It wants us to know what we feel and stick to it, but that is not the way feelings work. They are contrary, inconsistent, and irrational. That is why our conscious mind represses, or pushes out of view, all the ones it does not want to acknowledge.

If we constantly overvalue the outer world, at the expense of our inner world, then we tend to use the unconscious mind as just a re-cycle bin; a dumping ground for anything we do not want to think about. We tend to see it as a dark, shadowy place populated by frightening and unpleasant characters. However, of course, it is far more than that.

The shadow contains not just the things we have labelled bad and unacceptable about ourselves, but also all the things we have longed for and never done, the things we dreamed of but talked ourselves out of – including perhaps our creativity and most cherished hopes, or what we admire most in others and deny in ourselves. We are living such a small part of ourselves, and we have done this most of our lives as a learned, protective mechanism.

Clearly, the parts of ourselves that we do not acknowledge or express are not going to be very happy. The part of you that wanted to be a dancer isn't overjoyed that the part that wanted to be an accountant was the only one your conscious mind listened to when you chose your career. Each part has its own needs and desires; it feels differently, it views the world differently, yet is just as valid a part of you as all the rest. Often, these parts are representing diametrically opposite points of view, and there will undoubtedly be conflicts of interest between them.

So how do we resolve this without going mad? Johnson wrote that 'We must be whole whether we like it or not; the only choice is whether we will incorporate the shadow consciously and with some dignity or do it through some neurotic behaviour.'[44]

The answer of course is to be all of who you are – in all your colours. We can do this by accepting the repressed parts of ourselves, by consciously exploring how these various sub-parts are influencing our feelings and behaviour from minute to minute. Because the fact is that, the neglected parts, with all their emotions and urges and disappointments, are constantly being triggered and re-played. We repeatedly act out in current relationships the unresolved parts of our personality.

We are continually being presented with situations that allow us to choose to do something differently. Each moment is a chance to heal an old wound, to start to change an old habit, to redress an imbalance in our personality.

Fordham writes; 'The unconscious can only become known by experience.'[45] Most emotional conflicts recur again and again. Each time they do, we can decide not to back away or ignore them, not to let the moment pass – or we can miss that chance, so the problem is not resolved and is likely to return.

Hermann Hesse wrote that; 'What isn't part of ourselves does not disturb us.'[46] So, when we experience powerful emotions, or pain, or we feel particularly strongly about something, it is probably an issue that has meaning for us and that is asking us to pay attention, listen, and do something about it. We are being given the opportunity to link to our unconscious mind and heal that issue. If emotions come up and we push them away because we do not know what to do with them, then we need to go back later and try to replay those thoughts and feelings, but they are usually best dealt with at the time that they happen, because it is not always easy to find them again.

Ideally, we should be able to live in the present, so that when we feel something, we do not deny it; we consciously register it, we explore it and do what needs to be done.

Recognising the different parts of ourselves that are in conflict, we can do something to resolve that conflict; we then have an option as to how we view the world, and how we act. When we become conscious of what we are feeling, we no longer need to live life unconsciously or automatically. When we are able to truly accept ourselves, both the shadow and the light, we become more self-sufficient and less reliant on the opinion of others. In addition, as our inner conflicts and tensions diminish, we will find that we no longer need to express them in our physical and emotional symptoms and illnesses.

Healing is the process of becoming whole. This then is our aim – to become consciously more aware and accepting of all that we are, so that we are not continually having to deny, reject or repress certain emotions, thoughts, or parts of ourselves. So that we can express ourselves more freely, and can consciously and more effectively choose how to live our lives.

Castaneda: 'Human beings always lose by default. They simply do not know about their possibilities.'[47]

Zukav: 'When a soul decides to evolve consciously through responsible choice, it becomes capable of liberating itself from its own negativities.... The light that flows through you becomes aligned with what you choose consciously, just as they are aligned, before you choose awareness, with what you choose unconsciously.'[48]

ACCESSING THE UNCONSCIOUS MIND

WE are in contact with the immense wealth of information and experience of the unconscious mind when we are dreaming, daydreaming, meditating, being creative, listening to music or working with our energy system or intuition in various ways.

In fact, the unconscious mind is continually sending us messages and giving us opportunities to discover more about ourselves. Sometimes the unconscious speaks in words, when our conscious mind will usually ignore or censor what it hears, but most of these spontaneous messages come in a form that our conscious mind does not readily recognise, because the unconscious speaks a foreign language; the intuitive language of dreams, images and symbols. By this mechanism, the unconscious mind protects itself from the hypercritical conscious mind, and it ensures that only those of us who value the unconscious and are prepared to work with it will discover and receive its treasures.

So, until we consciously choose to give time and attention to our inner world, until we make some effort to communicate with our unconscious mind, it probably will not readily tell us what it is we most want to know. If we have largely disregarded it for years, as we probably have, then it is going to take a bit of encouragement before it yields up its secrets directly to us.

The unconscious mind works best when we are relaxed and quiet and not thinking or doing anything at all. Our thoughts are just slowly drifting, not in any particular direction, just wherever they want to go, and in this dreamy, sleepy trance state we are open to whatever happens inside us, we are receptive to whatever experiences might occur, and to whatever questions or suggestions we might present to our unconscious mind. Because our conscious mind at this moment is submerged, resting, out of sight, giving the rest of us a chance to speak.

And if we fall asleep, our bodies too are resting. Only our unconscious mind is still active, working on the problems we have given it to solve, and taking care always of our body. When we are ill, we sleep a lot, because sleep allows all our energy to be focused on restoring health.

We know that we can heal more quickly and more effectively when we are in a state of relaxed inactivity, not doing anything, not thinking anything, just letting our awareness drift inwards, to whatever part of us that needs our attention. This is the trance, or meditative, state.

A trance, then, is a chance to go within oneself. With no distractions from outside, where else can we go? Moreover, because our unconscious mind knows where our problems lie, and has the tools to solve them, it automatically draws our attention to those things we need to heal. In this calm, receptive state, we are able to heal them. We just need to enter this state long enough to let this happen.

Our conscious mind tries to avoid problems it does not know how to solve, or which might be painful. Our unconscious mind does not want to avoid problems, in fact, every opportunity it gets; it tries to get us to look at them.

Quietly focusing inwardly, certain images come to mind. Just accept them, watch them. Keep critical thoughts and doubts out of your mind; 'I don't know whether I really see it or not.' It doesn't matter. Any image that comes can be worked with. There is no 'right' or 'wrong' image. We worry too much about getting it wrong, or we may view the images of our unconscious mind as too simple, silly or irrelevant to have any real influence on our experiences.

An image is an inner reality, a feeling or memory or representation of something that is causing you distress, that wants you to look into it. Emotions are more easily represented in images than in words, so staying with an image enables you to contact your emotions more easily because that image is how you are choosing at that time to symbolise a particular emotion or cause of conflict. At another time, the same trigger might produce a totally different picture.

By accessing the unconscious mind, by accepting our inner realities, we are making contact with some part of our inner emotional experience and expressing it in the form of an image. We can then use various techniques to work on it and change it; doing this, we also change the emotion.

CHAPTER SEVEN

Dreams and Self-Hypnosis

Shakespeare: 'There are more things in heaven and earth, Horatio,
Than are dream'd of in your philosophy.'

INTRODUCTION

WE are all fascinated by our dreams. Dreams can be beautiful or
terrifying, they can recur repeatedly, or be so vivid they seem more
real than waking life. Whatever your experience, there are some
dreams you do not forget – and that you cannot ignore.

They are the means by which your unconscious mind is
desperately trying to get through to you; they allow buried issues,
emotions and conflicts to surface, and give you the opportunity to
resolve and heal them.

Dreams also show us how wonderfully creative each one of
us is; we create the whole dreamscape and all its characters every
time we dream. Dreams help us to discover more about ourselves, as
every different character represents a part of us, which we can start
to learn about and integrate.

All of us would like to find out more about ourselves, and
what we really want in our lives. After all, knowledge is power.
Knowing ourselves, we can increase our capability, energy and
strength, and achieve our full potential – including our potential to
love ourselves and others.

Dreams are a portal to our inner world, a door to the unconscious mind. We only have to open it.

WHAT ARE DREAMS?

DREAMS are a gift. They are a regular, spontaneous and insightful communication from yourself to yourself about yourself. It is like downloading an exclusive newsletter entitled 'You' every single morning. What could be more fascinating?

A dream (from Old Saxon *joy, music*) is a series of thoughts, images, sensations, or emotions occurring in the mind during sleep.

We spend a great deal of time dreaming; we dream every one and a half hours during the night (whether we remember them or not); we all spend time day-dreaming, where in unguarded moments we drift into a relaxed state. Then there are the things we dream of or long for; the cherished perfect visions of our ideal life. To dream is to envisage, to picture to oneself – and, perhaps most importantly, to believe possible. We know from our own experience that dreams throw up new ideas, they make us feel an enormous variety of emotions; they are a source of imagination and inspiration.

We know from research studies that dreams are an altered state, an alternative perspective of reality that is different from our normal conscious awareness. They are outside of time and space. Past happenings, current preoccupations and future possibilities, all happily jostle along side by side. They are an ever-changing personal landscape, in which we play all the parts and where our experiences and perspectives are constantly shifting.

If you stay awake for days without ever dreaming at all, you get progressively more depressed, disorientated, and eventually show signs of madness.

Therefore, dreams happen for a reason. They are a place where we are constantly sensing and reacting, re-playing and processing our emotions and re-organising our thoughts. It seems then that we cannot live without dreams. After all, being responsive and in a state of continuous motion is what's meant by being alive.

Siegel: 'When we communicate in visual images, we tell the truth, because we cannot manipulate the language as well.'[49]

EXPLORING DIFFERENT LEVELS OF REALITY:

HOWEVER you choose to work with a dream, you will get something out of it, because dreams are sending messages on many different levels simultaneously.

At the physical level, the dream might alert you to a potential problem or might explain some of your symptoms. It could show you what you need to do to deal with pain or to avoid further injury. Physical sensations of pleasure, pain, and sexuality can all be vividly felt within a dream.

In dreams, we also experience the full range of human emotions. We may be feeling peaceful and happy, remembering past joys or achievements, or we may be facing our worst demons and fears. Dreams draw attention to painful emotions, which need to be healed. Everything within a dream belongs to you; the different characters are all feeling your emotions, therefore working with a dream is a direct and safe way of exploring your feelings and beginning to accept them – and yourself.

At the mental level, a dream can provide you with the answer to a question or the solution to a problem; it can help you make a decision, or give you more insight into a situation or relationship. It may help you to access forgotten memories or knowledge.

Before you fall asleep, think of that issue. Put it in the form of a simple question. For example, if I want some insight into my fear of success, I would lie in bed thinking; 'I would like to know more about success. Give me an answer please.'

Repeat your question to yourself a few times before you sleep, and then write down your dreams that night. If you do not remember any dreams, it may be that you wake in the morning with a clearly related recollection - or a surprising thought that may at first glance seem unrelated to your question. Write it down anyway. Do this over several nights if you are not sure whether you yet have the answer.

A dream could enable you to see why you acted in a particular way, or it might shed some light on a part of you that you do not usually like to acknowledge. It may clarify what is happening in a relationship, so that you can be more flexible in the way that you relate to people.

On a spiritual level, dreams can be used for healing the past, predicting the future, gaining access to intuitive knowledge and stimulating creativity. Dreams may be visionary in the sense that, they allow you to clearly see possibilities or outcomes that you had not previously considered. They may provide a link with the universal intelligence - all the wisdom that exists about everything that has ever happened.

Dream characters can have uniquely personal significance and simultaneously be representations of what Jung named the archetypes, figures of symbolic or mythical significance common to all. As such, dreams reflect our separateness yet remind us of the universality of experience, and our togetherness with everything in the universe.

TECHNIQUES FOR GAINING INSIGHTS FROM DREAMS

Gustave Flaubert: 'There is no such thing as reality. There is only perception.'

THE unconscious mind wants to help us; even just having a dream means that work is already being done. However, in order to harvest the unconscious information and emotion fully that a dream contains, you will need the cooperation of your conscious mind. Tell yourself that you want to remember your dreams, and you will. Start using your dreams to find out what is going on in you, and you cannot help but get excited about them.

Dreams are produced in the language of images, they are essentially right-brain phenomena. As such, they are hard to hang on to. When you wake from a dream, talking about it can help transfer it into long-term memory. Writing it down grounds the images and translates them into words, thereby capturing the dream for further work. Drawing something from the dream is another way of recording it, as shapes and symbols are part of the language of the right brain. So, the first vital step is to catch your dreams.

Keep a pen and paper and a torch or small light next to your bed and jot down your dreams as you wake from them. You think you will remember them until morning without writing them down, but usually they have disappeared completely by the time the alarm goes off.

Make sure you get enough sleep, as it is very hard to remember dreams if you are overtired. Various stimulants such as coffee, tea, and nicotine can keep you awake. Depressants such as alcohol, barbiturates and benzodiazepines help you sleep but make your dreams less vivid. If hypnotics have been used over a long period of time, then when they are stopped you may experience a rebound increase in the vividness of dreams, with nightmares and interrupted sleep for some weeks.

When you start to write your dreams down in a dream journal, it is useful to make a list of each image in the dream and jot down some of the first associations you make to it. Everything in a dream has a meaning particular to you, so you are the only one who can determine what the dream means. Your ideas or feelings about a snake might be completely different to mine, and these ideas and feelings can change over time. So, by writing down your first thoughts about each symbol or character, you build up an inventory of your own personal symbols. Dreams are far too complex and individual for the so-called dictionaries of dreams to be more than a rough guide.

Then, reading through the dream on your own, or preferably to others in a dream group, you can pick out the parts that seem to have most emotional significance so that you can work with them; for instance any particularly upsetting or powerful images.

Characters in a dream may represent real people, in which case the dream may shed some light on what is happening in your relationships with those people; they can also all be seen as different parts of you; your sub-personalities. In any event, everything that happens in a dream has relevance to something that is going on in your waking life at the present time now. If it did not, you would not have had that particular dream.

EXERCISES:

Write down your dream. Try to give it a title.

Note your role in the dream: Were you a participant or an observer? How old were you in the dream? How did you feel during the dream?

First Thoughts: make a list of the most important things, places, and images in the dream and jot down first thoughts or free associations to each. This shows what each symbolises for you.

Second Thoughts: do any of the first thoughts you have written down strike a resonant chord with anything in your life at present?

Identify the main characters and write a list of traits for each. Every character in the dream represents a sub-part of you.

Dream Dialogue. Pick a character and begin a dialogue with it. You usually do this as a written exercise. Speak to the character, writing down your question, and then become that character and reply to the question. Then you become yourself again and continue the dialogue, swapping from one role to the other. Find out what it wants to say to you, why it is acting and feeling the way it does. Do not think; just write. Once you are 'in character,' you are in direct contact with your unconscious mind, and if you ask questions about problems in your life, you will probably be amazed at the simplicity and clarity of the replies.

Dream Re-Entry: This is often easier to do with a partner who can ask you the following questions:

Look for the part of the dream with the most emotion, close your eyes and imagine yourself back in it.

What do you feel? I feel a black cloud all around me.

Where in your body do you feel that?

Focusing on that area, what do you see, hear or smell?

How old are you? Just accept the first answer that comes into your head.

What were you wearing?

What was happening in your life at that time? Often a memory comes to you or an image of yourself at a certain age.

What would you like to do with that image? I would like to clear that dense, heavy cloud.

Would you like some help? I need some light or fire.

Who would you like to help you? My inner wizard could bring some light. In addition, I want my inner mother to come and hold my hand; I am scared.

What tools would you like to help you? Maybe a flame-thrower or a laser beam, yes the wizard has a magic flame-thrower.

Have you done that now? Yes, a brilliant white light is flooding into me. The black cloud is being broken up and filled with light.

Is there anything else you would like to do? No, that is enough for now. The black cloud is smaller, less dense, but it is still there. I shall come back to it at a later time.

How do you feel now? Tired, but I am more relaxed. I feel a lot better.

Are you ready to come back now? I am just saying goodbye to the wizard; he will come back again. I am fine now.

This technique can be very powerful, you may feel upset, or cry, as the pain and tension are released.

Reiki: if you are working on a dream with another person, s/he can send Reiki to you during the process. When you have gone back into the predominant emotion in the dream, where do you feel that emotion in your body? Give Reiki to that part of your body.

Send Reiki to the parts of yourself represented by the characters in the dream, which need healing. Visualise the character while you are sending Reiki to it, and watch to see if that image changes after various sessions of Reiki.

Issues raised by a dream: make a note of any characters or images you want to return to later, list the main issues arising from the dream, and jot down any comments.

Remember, there is never just a single interpretation of a dream character or event; you may work with a dream even years later, and find something completely new within it.

EXAMPLE

Dream: Woman in a Body Bag

I was walking through a hospital car park, and I heard a weak voice moaning. I looked around, and found a body bag. The noise was coming from inside, and when I opened it; I found a woman. She was very thin and looked mummified. She was very weak, so I picked her up and put her in my car, as I could not carry her very far. She nearly fell out, as she could not balance. I finally managed to get her into the Casualty department.

My role: I was taking part in the dream, and was my current age. It was horrible, I felt anxious and frightened.

First Thoughts

Car park: Frustrating, busy place where you cannot find anywhere to park your car.

Hospital: A place where you go to get better or die; people look after you; a sad, disturbing place where nobody wants to be.

Body Bag: Like a portable wardrobe.

Mummified: Dried-out, no moisture, preserved.

Second Thoughts

A hospital car park represents a frustrating, busy place that I do not want to be. Does that feel like any part of my life at present? A mummy could be a preserved body, or could represent my actual mother, or my inner mother – or all three at different levels.

Identify main characters: woman in body bag.

Character traits: she is tiny, wasted, shrivelled, weak, mummified, moaning, and out of balance.

Dream Dialogue: with the woman in body bag.

Me: 'I am so glad I saved you.'

W: 'You are so hypocritical; you are the one that put me here! You act all benevolent and caring when you realise I won't shut up, I will keep moaning till someone takes me in.'

Me: 'Someone? You knew it would be me. There wasn't anyone else out there. Maybe only my ears hear you, anyway, because you're mine. No one else can save you. How many people care about me enough to want to save me, let alone a frazzled, dried-up, prune-like part of me that even I don't want to see. Get real.'

W: 'Real? Yes, I could be if you just realised who I am.'

Me: 'Well, who are you?'

W: 'I'm the scared woman inside you. You've pushed me out so many times. I'm mummified, all right, scared to death. The frightened mummy – your mummy maybe, or your granny. Maybe

I'm all of them - generations of small, tired women terrified of their own shadow. Needy, deprived, yet too damned ashamed of themselves to make any demands. They're in you. Mummies. Yeah, that's why I'm dead but I'm not dead, you see, squeezed dry, shrunken but perfectly preserved. Relics that won't go away, handed down from generation to generation – till someone breaks the cycle.'

Me: 'You're right. I've never had a sense of my roots, of where I came from. And I run away from things, always avoiding confrontation. Like with men, pretending I don't have needs, that I don't really exist at all, except as some sort of minor constellation orbiting around their sun.'

W: 'Then you blame them that your life isn't what you want it to be. And you end up embalmed. That's what happens when you keep denying your own nature; it shrivels up, a kind of self-inflicted state of suspended animation.'

Me: 'I can't carry you; you're too heavy. I can't bring you back to life on my own. You have to do it too – and the people in the hospital, they've got to help too.'

W: 'So why don't you ask for help?'

Me: 'I can't, I mean, I do, but who's there to help? ... I suppose I don't feel I deserve it.'

W: 'Hey, it's ok, here, hold on to me. You've got to shake off all this negative, self-defeating stuff, doubting your own worth. You're alive. So, you have worth. Just the same as everyone else. Life is given, you can't get away from it, don't stifle it. Get it out of the bag, give it a hug and say, wow, isn't it great to be alive?'

Me: 'Yes, you're right, thank you for talking to me. I won't forget you.'

Dream Re-Entry:
This involves imagining yourself back in the part of the dream in which you felt the most emotion (for me the most powerful image was the woman in the body bag). You ask yourself the following questions:

What do I feel?

Where in my body do I feel that?

Focusing on that area, what do I see, hear or smell?

How old am I?

What was I wearing?

What was happening in my life at that time?

What would I like to do with that image?

Would I like some help?

Who would I like to help me?

What tools would I like to help me?

Have I done that now?

Is there anything else I would like to do?

How do I feel now?

Am I ready to come back now?

Reiki: Visualising the woman in the body bag, I sent Reiki to her, watching to see whether there were any spontaneous changes in her appearance over a number of sessions. I noticed that she gradually became stronger and looked younger and healthier. The Reiki energy healed and restored this undernourished but 'perfectly preserved' part of me. I could also send Reiki to my inner mother.

Issues raised by the dream: relationships with women, including myself; femininity; the inner mother. The part of me that is starving, asking for help, healing, and returning to health. Who am I carrying? There is a part of me that is weak, out of balance, and being wasted. I find it hard to accept, I am antagonistic towards it at first, because it is so repulsive and scary, yet it ends up comforting me. A seemingly weak part becomes a source of strength.

Working with dreams, you can see that everything that comes from your unconscious mind belongs to you and has significance for you. Our unconscious reality is every bit as important as our conscious reality. Pain, fear, discomfort or disturbing images draw your attention; they are all asking you to help them. They want you to see that they are a valid part of your inner reality. Therefore, by acknowledging them, you validate them. By giving shape to a fear, you can disarm it. By giving attention to a feeling, you help release it.

'When the aha of recognition comes in working with a dream, it means not only that some of the dream's message is "getting through" to consciousness, but also that the dreamer is changing inside at that moment, as the psychological and emotional energies get reorganised and smoothed out in the work with the dream.'[50]

Dream re-entry is going back into a feeling brought up in the dream. Dialoguing with a dream character is asking a part of you what it wants to say. Once these techniques are learned, they can be used in any situation, to work with any feeling, thought, or image. By doing this, you are taking your own mental, emotional and physical experiences seriously, whether they originate from dreams or in waking life, and you can use these techniques with not just dream fragments, but with any feeling in your body, or any image from a meditation. Just finding an image makes you feel better, and working with it will usually lead to some insight into the underlying emotion.

For example, in one of Graham's dreams, he had a mouth full of spiders. He asked them who they were, and they told him they were words he was afraid to say. He wrote a dialogue to find out what in his life right now he needed to be saying, and to whom. Another time, during a dream re-entry, he had the image of himself as a small child, upset and angry. He gave Reiki for ten minutes each day to this little child, and gradually, in his mind's eye, the child grew up and became stronger and able to let go of his pain and rage. In a meditation, he saw an image of his inner father as a dwarf in a coffin. When he sent Reiki to that image, gradually over time, his inner father got out of the coffin and grew into a full-sized healthy man.

Johnson said: 'The unconscious cannot tell the difference between a 'real' act and a symbolic one.'[51] Therefore, acting 'as if,' imagining, and visualising all work because they are making a new reality within the unconscious mind.

The exciting thing is that everything changes the moment we look at it; the very fact that we are in some way re-experiencing it by the process of bringing it to awareness means that it has already changed from what it was. Gaining insight, discovering a link, or just emotionally connecting with a thought, memory or image makes it change, so that it no longer has the same power or hold over us.

The consequence of all this is that we have the choice to do things differently. We can express parts of us, which were being ignored, we can recognise recurring themes, and we can make changes in our waking life as a result of the insights gained from our dreams. We can see how subsequent dreams change as a result, so that nightmares disappear altogether and feelings or outcomes that are more positive occur. In addition, once the inner work has been done and integrated, we begin to see this reflected in new confidence, skill and opportunity in our outer world.

WHAT IS HYPNOSIS?

Milton Erickson: 'Most of us simply do not know how to utilize our individual capacities. ..... the individual's ability to utilize his own unique behavioral matrix and associative processes... is of the essence in creativity and personality development.[52]

WE have seen that dreams are one method by which the unconscious mind spontaneously talks to us. In order to fully understand a dream and benefit from it we need to use a variety of techniques, such as dream dialogue and dream re-entry, firstly to decipher what it is telling us and secondly to release and heal the associated emotions. This takes a conscious decision to work on the dream.

We have seen how meditation, through relaxing the mind and body, enables us to enter a trance-like state of altered consciousness in which we are open to our inner sensations, images and emotions. Passively observing our thoughts and feelings, we stop censoring them, we become more accepting of them, and we can view them with greater detachment.

We have been using focussing, which is sensing into the body. When we experience a particular emotion, we find out where in our body we feel it. This links a physical sensation with an emotion and, if possible, with an image that we can visualise and then work on and change in some way to release that emotion and improve the physical discomfort.

We have also been using affirmations, which are positive suggestions. By actively, repetitively, consciously giving positive messages to the unconscious mind, we reprogram our unconscious negative beliefs about ourselves that have built up over the years and that underpin everything that we do.

We know that all of these methods work in helping to bring about change and healing. However, in addition, the unconscious mind itself has the ability to reorganise and resolve problems using routes and methods that we cannot consciously predict: it remembers events, makes links and associations, and finds solutions in ways we cannot even begin to imagine. Hypnosis, working directly with the unconscious mind, not only combines all the methods outlined above, but also stimulates the unconscious mind to react in other uniquely creative and individual ways to solve our problems and heal our pain.

Hypnosis gives us an opportunity to achieve a meditative state of altered consciousness, or trance state, in which we relax and focus our attention inwards. Going into our body, we direct our awareness to the feelings or physical sensations, which are disturbing us, and we are open to any images, thoughts or memories, which may be associated with those sensations. In this relaxed state of trance, we are receptive to suggestions, which can encourage us to change the way we do things, or the way we think about things. Our unconscious mind is automatically drawn to our physical or emotional distress, whatever the source, and it is able to do what needs to be done, without the conscious mind knowing how or what it is working on.

Hypnosis is a powerful technique for effecting change. It enables us to view painful or distressing emotions and sensations with a greater degree of detachment and calm than in our normal waking state. We determine our own rate of change because our unconscious mind presents only those things that we are able to process at that time.

Hypnosis can act quicker than other therapies because it bypasses conscious resistance and works only with what already exists within — with our own internal images and mind-sets, rather than attempting to introduce new systems of beliefs from outside. It is always better to work from an individual's own inner representations of the world and himself, rather than try to graft alien or inappropriate belief systems which would only meet with resistance.

For all of us, pain, whatever the source, usually leads to avoidance. In a trance, a person can approach his pain in a relatively relaxed and detached manner, and view it with less emotional involvement and hence distress than he could otherwise achieve. He can ask himself, 'What is actually happening here? What's going on for me?' Rather than avoiding what exists within himself, he is acknowledging and taking responsibility for it.

Self-hypnosis does not lead to dependence on any person or external set of beliefs. It promotes self-healing by focusing the individual's attention on his own inner experiences, and it enables him to find for himself the most effective ways of dealing with his problems. Hypnosis is a holistic method of healing because, recognising that pain has more than just a physical element, we give ourselves the opportunity to heal all its components, using the innate powers and abilities of the unconscious mind.

Through hypnosis, we learn to trust that all the answers lie within us, to trust that once the unconscious mind is given the time and space to consider a problem, it will always come up with the best solution for us.

With self-hypnosis, particularly if you prepare your own scripts or have them individually made for you, you can be directly and consciously involved in choosing your own material, thus guiding your own unconscious processes towards those areas that you would most like to change.

TELLING A DIFFERENT STORY

THE unconscious mind uses the language of symbols, images, and metaphors. In any attempt to access or work with the unconscious mind, what we are trying to do is talk directly to it in its own language.

We think we need to know the reason for everything. We do not like it if things are happening that we cannot explain at a conscious level. Yet, in everyday life we are constantly processing information and images that the conscious mind does not really understand.

Stories, pictures, music and poetry are all much closer to the language of the unconscious than factual, logical data or information, which is understood better by the rational, conscious mind. Moreover, as we have seen previously, emotions are more easily represented in images than in words. Through various forms of art, we are transported into another reality, a space and time where things happen differently to our normal waking life. That is why when we are listening to music, hearing a story or watching a film, we are often actually in a light trance state. In addition, we often feel more emotional than at other times.

For example, when we are listening to a story, while our conscious mind concerns itself with the outer story, our unconscious mind searches for the inner meaning and significance of that story. A story is a metaphor; it talks of one thing, but it suggests another. It contains instinctive knowledge that transcends intellect and reason. The unconscious mind perpetually searches for meaning beyond what is immediately apparent; it finds creative ways of applying the knowledge contained within the story for our own personal uses.

A story, whether read, listened to, or watched on screen, imparts emotional wisdom by representing some situation of importance to us all. Besides, it gives us the opportunity to look a bit deeper inside, to question our own actions or motives, because all the time we are listening to someone else's story, our unconscious mind is looking for the emotional relevance for ourselves.

Names, faces, and backgrounds change, details differ, but feelings are universal. The little boy caught telling a lie makes each of us wonder if we are willing to own up to the things we do. The woman who leaves her home and family to join a travelling theatre prompts us to consider what we'd be willing to give up in order to follow our dreams.

In a story or a fairy tale, characters may represent parts of ourselves, or archetypes, such as the King, the Fairy Godmother, or the Wicked Witch; universal figures that have meaning for all of us, and whose conflicts symbolically represent some battle we are playing out within ourselves.

Jeremy Taylor writes; 'The hero/heroine of myth often has to descend into the depths (of the unconscious) to find the 'treasure' (wisdom, courage, strength and creativity) that is needed to revitalize the 'upper world' (of waking life).'[53]

At the end of any story, something has been answered; something significant has been achieved. The character engages in action in the outside world, and through his battles and the obstacles he overcomes, he resolves an inner conflict or gains insight into his own personality or behaviour, which produces movement within.

And that, metaphorically speaking, is exactly what hypnosis aims to do. The outer story triggers inner images, which access emotions, which stimulate unconscious healing processes.

So, in hypnosis, we tell a story, taking the listener on his own inner journey: wherever he ends up, whatever he finds, will have significance for him.

Techniques in Hypnosis

I have suffered with painful periods for twenty five years, yet it was only recently that I decided to heal that pain. I began to send Reiki to the cause of the pain in addition to giving myself Reiki every day. I started to say to myself every night before I fell asleep; 'I am now able to heal myself. Every cell in my body is being made pure, perfect and complete. The whole of my mind and body are being brought into balance and harmony.'

Then I had a session of hypnosis to try to numb the pain by altering my perception of it.

The following day I thought I would practise on my own. I lay down and focussed my attention on the pain in my pelvis. Doing this, I immediately felt anxious, so I concentrated on my breathing and relaxed for a few minutes.

I began to imagine the pain turning into numbness. Suddenly, thoughts started pouring into my mind, in rapid succession and very clearly. It was just as if a voice was talking to me, telling me all the reasons I have had that pain. It went back to when it began, how I felt and what was happening in my life and what the pain was trying to tell me, and why I had needed it in the past. Everything seemed to make perfect sense. I was amazed; it was a wonderful experience.

Then after twenty minutes or so, it stopped. I felt full of energy and very excited about what had happened. I was just about to get a pen to write it all down while it was fresh in my mind, but then I thought, no, I do not need to consciously remember it, because my unconscious mind remembers it all. I can trust my unconscious mind to heal the pain, now that it knows I do not need it any more.

So, I just relaxed and did nothing.

The session of hypnosis had made something shift emotionally. I was beginning to understand how for many years I had been unconsciously associating fear with pain. Because I had repeatedly told my unconscious mind that pain was frightening, it made sure that my body responded with the fear response every time I felt pain. To the point now, as soon as I felt pain, or even thought about it, my unconscious mind responded with fear; my body was flooded with stress hormones, and my muscles became tense, which made the cramps more painful. In other words, my fear and anxiety were making the pain worse.

If I could relax, the stress reaction and the muscular tension would diminish; the pain would lessen, and I could experience the pain simply as pain, separate from fear. Pain itself does not have to trigger fear. Gradually, relaxing out of the fear, the pain becomes less.

After that, I used relaxation and Reiki each time the pain started. I was less tense, and more relaxed; and subsequently needed fewer painkillers and was much less restricted in my activities. Now, I probably experience not even 10% of the pain I had suffered for twenty-five years. I already talk of it as a pain I used to have.

Daniel Benor writes: 'A more relaxed body can function more normally, free of excess stress hormones. People who are more relaxed usually gain access to higher levels of awareness which facilitates self-healing.' [54]

When you are relaxed, your unconscious mind lowers your heart rate and blood pressure; it slows your breathing and reduces muscular tension. The unconscious mind knows how to make you healthy. It knows how to relax and heal your body and mind. Your conscious mind cannot do this.

The point is that we do not consciously know how to change ourselves. For example, I could tell myself I want to increase my self-esteem. However, just making a conscious decision is not enough. I need to engage both the conscious and the unconscious mind. To override my previous negative self-beliefs and feelings, I have to learn a new, positive self-image and reprogram my unconscious mind.

The conscious mind stops us from hearing or acting on anything, which does not fit in with its existing set of beliefs. So, the best way that we can accept suggestions is to bypass the conscious mind. Then the unconscious mind can take control.

Once we remove the obstacles or blocks constructed by our conscious mind-set, we enable the unconscious mind to find new and creative solutions to our problems, and to change anything we need to change.

The unconscious mind automatically gravitates towards the things that are causing us pain. Once it focuses on a pain, it sets off search and retrieval processes to find where and what the pain is – because it may not be what we think it is. It then sends this information back to us in the form of emotionally significant images.

In the sleepy, dream-like trance state, our unconscious mind draws from our vast inner knowledge and experiences and comes up with effective ways of dealing with our pain and solving our problems.

And, once we are more consciously aware of what the pain really is, we can give our unconscious mind positive messages that will help it to heal. We know that learning is most effective when we are in a relaxed or trance state, because we are then receptive to new suggestions.

This is why hypnosis works.

HOW HYPNOSIS WORKS: A SUMMARY

Milton Erickson: 'Patients have problems because their conscious programming has too severely limited their capacities. The solution is to help them break through the limitations of their conscious attitudes to free their unconscious potential for problem solving … circumventing the rigid and learned limitations of the patient's conscious and habitual attitudes.'[55]

HYPNOSIS is a powerful way of effecting internal change. It works by inducing a relaxed trance state. When we are relaxed, we focus within, on our own sensations and images. We are no longer distracted by the world outside.

Revealing the site of pain or discomfort. Quietly drifting through our inner landscapes, we become aware of any tension or discomfort in our body, or any painful emotions or images that demand our attention. We notice any problems or sources of discomfort, yet, calmly relaxed, we are emotionally distanced from them, so we can view them with equanimity, or at least with less pain or distress than they might cause us in normal waking life.

Allowing the unconscious mind to drift towards problems, or, if necessary, guiding it towards them. The aim is to encourage the conscious mind to step aside. 'That's the important use of images; they bind a person's conscious attention while you make other therapeutic suggestions to their unconscious. You don't want them to have conscious control but to allow their unconscious to function smoothly by itself. And then the results of that unconscious functioning can become conscious. But first they have to get beyond their conscious understanding of what is possible.'[56] A story or a metaphor engages the conscious mind while the unconscious mind searches for its inner meaning and personal relevance. For example, a tale of a knight plucking up the courage to fight a dragon might encourage you to face the personal dragons you have been avoiding.

Stimulating the unconscious mind to find its own solutions: a trance gives the unconscious mind the chance to work on whatever it needs to work on, in its own unique, creative ways. Forgotten memories may appear and intuitive insights arise. We begin to see new possibilities: how we could do something differently or how something would no longer be a problem if we could view it in a different way.

Suggesting ways in which we might solve problems. Hypnosis is a means of presenting new material to the unconscious mind or of enabling it to see an old problem in a new light. Indirect suggestions present information in a non-specific, ambiguous, or symbolic way, through a story, anecdote, or metaphor, which allows the unconscious mind to find personally meaningful associations and insights. Direct suggestions are statements, which encourage affirmative self-beliefs and reinforce positive actions.

Protecting the new unconscious learning and insights from the doubts or criticisms of the conscious mind. At the end of a hypnosis session, it is better to talk or think about something else; to distract the conscious mind from analysing what has happened. We tend to think that things we are not consciously in control of, or fully aware of, are somehow not valid, yet intuitive knowledge does not have to be either consciously known, or understood, in order to bring about positive, effective change.

WRITING SCRIPTS

A hypnosis script should describe sights, sounds, smells and tastes, and thus invoke a sensory reality. Preferably, one that is pleasant for the person experiencing it. For instance, someone afraid of water will not find sitting on an island in the middle of a lake very relaxing.

It should use positive statements not negative ones. 'Don't be afraid' immediately makes you think of being afraid, whereas 'relax and feel calm' draws you away from fear or anxiety.

Any direct suggestions it uses should be realistic. If I relax and tell myself repeatedly that I am rich, I will not believe it, because I know I'm not. It is not credible. However, to say I am attracting success and getting closer to wealth every day is certainly believable.

A script would focus first on finding a relaxing place within. It would include some general, direct ego-strengthening statements to encourage self-reliance and trust in the unconscious mind. It would incorporate a story or metaphor which symbolically contains some of the elements within the specific problem to be solved. Finally, it would include some indirect suggestions which merely hint at how to solve the problem, and so allow the unconscious mind to find its own associations and solutions.

There are many excellent hypnosis scripts and enjoyable guided meditations available. However, it is best to write a script for yourself, with your own language and symbols, using images that you like, and expressing your unique views and associations in your own words. Then, everything that you are listening to in the hypnosis session will be directly meaningful to you, and no conscious resistance will be set up.

Speaking your own language - using your own uniquely meaningful symbols and images - you can communicate most directly and effectively with your unconscious mind. You may want to incorporate phrases from your stream of consciousness writing, images from your dreams, or words that you use to explain your problems or symptoms. For example, I like to visualise emotion as water, whereas you might see it as a pack of cards. You might describe your anxiety as a long corridor with closed doors, so the script could guide you to go up or down to another floor, to find a password or key, or another way of opening those doors.

So, write a script to encourage the changes you need to make; record it or get someone else to do this for you; relax, listen to it regularly, and your unconscious mind will do the rest.

Sample Scripts

The two scripts, which follow, are non-specific ego-building and preparing for change.

Preparing for Journeying

Metaphor: 'It is exciting to go to new places, to see old things from different perspectives. Like when you climb right to the top of the hill, and however much effort it has taken to get there, you are still enchanted to see the breathtaking views. High above now, you look at everything with wonder, amazed that it has become so distant, and that just a while ago you were down there, so far below, a tiny figure lost in a familiar landscape.'

Relaxing Place: 'Up on the hilltop, you are aware of so much more. Details fade, yet overall, you can see how the land shapes, how the rivers wind their way along, and you can see the paths you have taken to arrive at where you have come to be. And everything seems to make sense. The obstacles that you could not see over when you were down there on the ground have now disappeared completely. From up here the light makes the shadows fall in a totally different way. Things have changed shape, and they no longer stand in relation to one another as they did before.'

Sensory Reality: 'It is a joyful moment, one that you can be proud about. Your body is tired, your legs are aching, but it is satisfying to know that you have reached the summit; your goal has been achieved. You have gone as high in that moment as it is possible for you to go. Besides, the journey down is so much quicker and easier, back down the hillside, re-tracing your steps along the new trail that you have made.'

Indirect Suggestions: 'Every journey takes its own time, and brings its own reward. And sometimes you discover shortcuts that you never knew existed, or you find signposts that you had never noticed before. As if someone or something is helping you on your way, encouraging you to see the things you need to see, pointing you in the right direction.

'And it is reassuring to know that there is a part of you that always has that mountaintop view. The part that can see where you have come from, that understands the route you took, and forgives all those detours and dead-ends along the way. That higher self, it knows that you already have everything you need for the journey. Because, somewhere within you, are the answers to all the questions you ever asked. Clear, definite, precise. The answers which will free you from fear.'

Direct Suggestions: 'Because it really is easy when you know how. Believing in yourself, accepting all that you are is easier than you ever imagined. Looking back and realising that you have already moved on, enjoying the freedom of new horizons.

'All your life has been a journey, with signposts and milestones and roundabout trails. Filled with feelings and memories, things that held you back, tying you in to the past, old habits that dominated your life. From the hilltop, you see the things you found and the things you left behind. You have changed, haven't you, so many times, and each time you really didn't know it was happening, and sometimes you didn't want to change yet you did, and it happened almost without your knowing.

'And when you want to change, as you do now, and you know, as you know now, that you are ready, then your journey will lead you ever onwards and you'll be safe, trusting that everything is just as it is meant to be.'

SHEDDING A SKIN

Sensory Reality: 'There was a time, long ago, when your skin was soft, and smooth, like a newborn baby, with its tiny fingers reaching out to touch the world. Fragile and trusting, that little creature lived its life through its skin: the soothing warmth of a bath, the cosy comfort of blankets and cradles, lying snugly against his mother's breast, gentle hands in a loving caress. Shrinking sensations, pleasure and pain, the world speaking always through its fingertips.'

Indirect Suggestions: 'In time, you shed that skin — that transparent, vulnerable, defenceless baby-skin. Because we have to grow; we have to move in an ever-changing world. But, when we are scared, or tired, or hurt, we put our hands to our hearts and remember the shared heartbeats of mother-love and baby skin. Now and always, we can go back to that place, feel the body memories and soft sensations of that long-ago time.'

Metaphor: 'Later, you grew a skin that was hard and strong; it kept the world out, it held you in. And in it, you have stored everything; the bumps, the bruises, and the trail of small disasters that make a life. It remembers the light and the shade, the cold chaos of a winter storm, and the searing heat of a summer sun. Your skin then was your bandage, to cover your wounds, a living, breathing, cellular cocoon.'

'The skin does not speak in words. But it tells your story, nonetheless, not just the outermost things; but all those secret things inside. Which piece of music makes you cry in joy, what has moved you to pity, what you have feared and what has silenced you. What has carried you in strong arms and what has traced new rhythms on your soul. The smiles and sorrows that live in the curves and hollows of your face, a lifetime of hopes and passions, all held within, carved now into your senses.

'Follow the you of today back to its beginning, see the fading images that danced in your eyes, the loves and losses and wounded dreams that shaped your now.'

Direct Suggestions: 'And remember, that now is another time. For strength and softness, for memories and new beginnings; a time to move on again, to set aside that old, painful skin that held you in.

'Remember too, that you are not alone. We are all separate and yet together, as we follow the contours of interwoven lives. I cry your tears and your laughter lines my face. We are all echoes of each other; in the other, we see reflections of ourselves.

'Think back, then, to how fragile we were, how vulnerable, how trusting, reaching out to the world, waiting for that first touch. As we wait now, in new hope, opening ourselves, nothing to conceal, shedding those old, worn-out skins, and knowing, deep within, that now is the time to heal.'

CHAPTER EIGHT

All-Love: Final Words

.

INTRODUCTION

ENERGY does indeed work.

We all have the capacity to make a direct personal connection to the energy of Source, or the Creator, without an intermediary. In doing so, we feel an incredible sense of joy and love, that we may never have experienced in quite the same way before. Our very definition of love is likely to change, as we realise that more is possible than we ever imagined. And, as we see aspects of ourselves that we had not seen before, we change.

The energy shows us the love that we are capable of experiencing, and it also shows us the pain that we are holding on to. It brings feelings to the surface, which have been repressed, and it shifts emotional energy that has become blocked or tied up in things, which no longer serve us. Once these feelings have surfaced, we then have to work with them in order to fully release them and heal them.

We repress emotions that are painful, such as grief, and those that we have labelled negative because we judge them to be unacceptable, for instance anger. Yet, emotions are not good or bad in themselves; they arise for a reason, and are telling us something we need to hear. All of us feel the whole range of human emotions. They only become a problem when we hold them in, hide them, or deny them. In the All-Love class, fully expressing what we feel, and being accepted by others in spite of those 'unacceptable' feelings, allows us to release the shame and guilt that have become associated with them. This has a powerful healing effect. When we experience the energy, we feel love and compassion, a sense of connectedness, and we can begin to truly be ourselves.

This book has described various well-tried and tested psychotherapeutic techniques for emotional healing, explaining the psychological theories behind them. They work very effectively to bring about personal breakthroughs and transformations. However, the energy brings an added element. It seems to accelerate the process, so that emotions are more readily accessed. Working with both the techniques and the energy allows you to pinpoint the source of the problem more quickly, and once the feelings have been released, bringing the energy into that blocked area helps to heal the wound and transform the pain into love.

Healing, the journey to being whole, is an ongoing process. We have to be constantly looking inside ourselves: being honest about what we feel, challenging our thoughts, changing our behaviour, gradually becoming more aware of all the different aspects of ourselves. This book suggests various ways in which we can make that process easier. An initiation is an awakening, but afterwards we have to make sure that we stay awake.

Energy works, but we have to work too.

THE AIMS OF ALL-LOVE

PATRICK: 'You can contact the All-Love energy through any of the different emotions: anger, grief, sadness, fear, worry, guilt, shame – and also joy and love. The most healing is going to come through the emotion that you are least comfortable with. But you do eventually have to experience them all. You want to be able to go into all the feelings and experience them 100%.

'You need to experience your feelings fully, and that is why we do the emotional processing work. The clearing work gives you a chance to heal a lot of the big emotionally charged issues that people have. During an All-Love class, we are constantly with people, working and digging, bringing up stuff, and doing a lot of very powerful clearing.'

'When you have an experience, and you totally go into the feeling and feel it one hundred percent, then that comes into completion and it loses its emotional charge over you. This is what brings about what we call an initiation. Let us say that you are experiencing fear or grief. If you completely experience it, that emotion seems to transform and you go into a state of bliss. That is what we are experiencing as a level of initiation.'

'Any experience that you haven't fully experienced gets stored in your unconscious mind. For example, if you lose a child and don't experience the grief fully, it keeps playing out repeatedly until you allow yourself to fully experience it. Once you allow yourself to fully experience that grief, it completes itself, and it then connects you back to that experience of unconditional love.'

'That is what we are doing in our classes. We go into feelings that have not been fully experienced and which have created blockages in our bodies. They have created a separation from the state of unconditional love. We go back in and re-experience that feeling to its fullest, and that opens up the channel and we end up having an initiation.'

'A person who is focussed in on a high mental plane doesn't experience their emotions very much. This is what goes on in the witness state. You get into a pure mind state in which essentially the emotions and feelings do not really matter any more. People could say that that is an enlightened state. You don't really feel the deepness of emotions, and you aren't letting fears and other things affect you. But in a sense, it is just that you have separated yourself from those. In the classes that I have been teaching, the people like that are normally the ones who find it most difficult to get back into their feelings again. You need a trigger to get them back down into those feelings.'

'I think you need to be able to go into the two different spaces. At times, you want to be able to go into the feelings, and experience the feelings hundred percent. But you also want to be able to experience the mind and the witness state fully.'

'If your awareness in the brain is connected strongly with the emotional part of the brain, which deals a lot with fears, then you are going to be getting a lot of feedback from that part of the brain; because that is where the internal dialogue comes from. The fear and the emotional parts could be running through your thoughts all the time. If you could shift your awareness from these, into the witness state, then the thought processes are not filtered through the emotional processing system, so you get to the point where you are having clear thoughts without having past and future fears and feelings connected. You are able to experience a present state more fully.'

'It is our sense of separateness which creates our feelings of loneliness, loss, grief – all those emotions that we then have to deal with. If you could break down that barrier, between you and the world outside, then you might lose that sense of separation. If you look at many meditation experiences, they are changing your brain chemistry, producing natural hallucinogens and endorphins in the brain to the point where the barrier is broken down. You are living more permanently without that sense of separation. You have a kind of natural high more often.'

'You can use meditation techniques to simply bypass some of the emotional states. Essentially, to get into the witness state, you work on focussing your energy and awareness until you get to an observation mode; rather than integrating with the feelings themselves. In India, we did this for ten days. They encouraged silence and we did the Vipassana meditation every day, so we were moving inwards, but they were able to put you into that state fairly instantaneously - even though it was the tenth day that I experienced that. I had experienced this oneness witness state previously, but I am now able to turn it off and turn it on, whereas earlier I would have to really work at it.'

'When I was in India, there were two separate nights where my mind was totally quiet. It was as if someone had come in and turned the switch off. It was a very good feeling. But would I be able to do any emotional healing from this state? I didn't think so. It was as if I was disengaged. So actually, I started concentrating on emotional stuff, and it brought me back. The witness state is nice, but I wanted to see if the emotional stuff was still there, and it was. I hadn't really cleared it; it's just that I had separated myself from it. And a lot of the time that is where illnesses come from; you just separate yourself from emotion, you are not really present with it, but it is still there. The problem too with the witness state is that you also do not feel that deep passion and that deep love.'

'To be in the moment you need to be clear, to lose that internal dialogue, so that you can achieve the witness state, where you are not being caught up in a lot of the emotions. But you also need a God-consciousness, a realisation of God, or Source, so that you can be in that state as well.'

'In the Shenu meditation, when we bring the sun down, we are connecting with our soul star, or higher self, or whatever you want to call it. Some people's view is that we have a number of energy centres above the top of our head. The number varies from 12 to 144 up to 365. Each time that we bring the sun down, we bring down a centre of higher vibration, so that, as one descends, a higher one takes its place; until we eventually come to Source.'

'When I studied a little with Brian Grattan, he would bring in a chakra from above and then replace it with a higher chakra. He would take the crown chakra and drop it down to the root chakra, and he would drop the root chakra way down into the Earth. So, a shift would take place. It doesn't quite fit with what we are doing, but it's an interesting template.'

'The common theme is of bringing higher aspects down from above your head. You could take them all the way down into your root chakra, or your hara; if you want to experiment with it, you can see where it takes you.'

'One of the reasons that I do the Infinity Dance is because that will take the energy down through all the different chakras. Ideally, you want to integrate the higher energy so that, instead of focussing on seven chakras, you are just one big chakra. That is what some people would term the unified chakra.'

'When you have your initiation in All-Love, you are actually bringing that sun down into your heart and experiencing a whole heart opening. But that doesn't mean that you can't bring it in again; the next time, you bring in another aspect. Essentially, you are connecting with higher parts of yourself; — your higher self, then your higher, higher self. You just keep bringing a little bit more in, another aspect, and this process gradually brings you closer to God.'

WHAT IS ENLIGHTENMENT?

THERE are several aspects to enlightenment. To enlighten means to shed light on, or illuminate; to gain spiritual knowledge or insight.

Firstly, there is knowledge of self. Knowledge means consciousness or awareness. And that has to start with the self. We cannot begin to be conscious of anyone else's feelings, thoughts, motivations or perceptions if we are not aware of our own. Our need in life is not to judge – or even to understand – anyone else. It is primarily to become aware of what is going on within us.

This book talks a great deal about consciousness. It looks from various angles at how we can come to live consciously, in the present moment, so that we are no longer being driven by unconscious forces – thoughts, feelings, energies - deriving from the past or being projected into the future. The aim of doing our own personal work is to become more aware of what we are doing, more conscious of what's happening in our inner world – after all, it is the only one we have got.

There are several aspects to this, because we exist on the emotional, mental, physical, energetic, and spiritual levels simultaneously.

In relation to emotions, being able to live in the present moment does not mean that you don't feel anything. On the contrary, it means that you can feel intensely, and respond spontaneously and authentically to what is happening here and now, uncluttered by all those feelings you experienced in the past. You have a sense of immediacy and aliveness. Your feelings arise; you do not judge them, you simply feel them, express them, act on them, and then let them go. They are not stored up for the future, and they are not throwbacks to the past. They simply are, and then they are not. You feel them and then move on to the next.

Mentally, to be consciously aware does not mean that you don't have any thoughts; it means that your thoughts have clarity. You have examined the beliefs that you hold, so that they are not just all jumbled up and you don't know where they came from. They are no longer unconsciously driving the way that you are acting and reacting. You see how you are thinking, and you consciously choose what to believe. You are able to see more clearly, what is happening inside of you and outside of you.

Physically, to become aware of yourself means to be in touch with the physical sensations and tensions that you experience. You notice how your body reacts to stress, pleasure, and pain, and how your physical state is affected by your thoughts and feelings. You come to know what your body needs in order to function optimally, and what you need to do so that it does not hold on to tension.

Energetically, to become conscious of your own energy system means that you are aware of blockages, and you recognise that energy is bound up with thoughts, feelings and bodily sensations. You can sense, and connect with the energy of the Universe, or Source.

Spirituality is the awareness that we exist at different levels: we have a mind and a body, we have feelings and energies and we are also spirit. These are not separate and disconnected; they coexist together, interconnecting to form the whole.

Enlightenment suggests that you are aware of yourself on all levels; that you are aware of what you are thinking, feeling, and sensing, and that you have more control over what you are experiencing in the present moment.

You have not got rid of your thoughts and feelings, you have not stopped your internal dialogue – that is, after all, what makes you alive. You are able to experience the whole range of feelings, from love and joy to sadness and anger, without being consumed by them. You can readily access both the rational, logical part and the creative, imaginative part of your mind, so that you have an interesting and productive inner dialogue.

When your mind and your emotions are clear, you are able to connect more easily with your higher self, your intuitive wisdom, and also with knowledge and wisdom outside of yourself, the Universal wisdom, if you like. This is knowledge, not of the self but of what exists beyond the self; this leads us to the second point. This is consciousness of the Creator, of Source, or God – whatever you want to call it. In other words, knowing that God exists in yourself.

There are many different ways of arriving at that knowledge: through an intense feeling of love or joy; through appreciation of the beauty of Creation; through apprehending, by intuition or thinking, certain truths or insights; through sensing the vast and powerful energy of the God-force. In fact, any of our senses and abilities, our thoughts, feelings, energies, our mind, body, and spirit, can all lead us to a direct awareness or experience of the energy of Source.

KEEPING YOUR FEET ON THE GROUND

PATRICK: 'Some people, when experiencing the energy, have difficulty bringing it down from their heads into their hearts. They can feel the light, and the joy, but they stay in their headspace and can't seem to integrate the energy into their bodies. They aren't going anywhere with the energy because they don't want to go inside themselves.'

It is easy to think that spirituality is separate from, or somehow better than emotion. Or to believe that because you have an initiation or a light experience, that you no longer have any emotional problems.

We all tend to delude ourselves at times. Whether through egotism, or greed, or self-righteousness, we lose contact with reality.

Sometimes you can look at someone who says pretty often that he is a very spiritual person, and you feel that he does not really seem to care about anyone or anything but himself. His actions simply do not support his statements. He can say, 'I have done lots of work on myself, the Universe is showing me I am on the right track, I have sorted out my emotions,' yet all around him he is leaving a trail of upset and discord. He claims his personal power at everyone else's expense – in every sense! – and shuts off from the parts of himself that he does not want to see. With Jekyll and Hyde, Robert Louis Stevenson brilliantly showed just how powerful these mechanisms of dissociation and projection can be.

Such people can be successful, even within the field of healing, simply because others around them have given away their power.

Paradoxically, the proof of spirituality is in how you live your routine day to day life, not in how strongly you have felt the energy or how many initiations you have had. Some of the most spiritual people live quiet lives, simply taking responsibility for themselves, and being honest, modest, and kind to others.

Patrick: 'The (healing) systems themselves attract many well-intentioned folks as well as some less desirable folks. You might ask why is that. Because the energy does not discriminate.

'There are many in the healing field who deceive and use people for their own selfish goals. I do think that people need to be aware that these people exist. Keep in mind that they exist in almost every facet of life; why should the spiritual healing field be any different?

'My first spiritual teacher was an ex-con and a con artist, but he taught some really good information which he borrowed from the Tibetan and Buddhist culture. Through my own searching, I found some more credible sources. In many ways, we do need people who can get the word out. Many times a more spiritually oriented person is less interested in all the expensive advertising and promotion that goes along with establishing a successful business.'

Which makes it vital that we do not give away our power – to anyone or anything. We must be constantly looking at motives, not taking for granted anything that anyone tells us – whoever they may seem to be or whatever authority they claim.

We all need to take responsibility for ourselves. That means making your own decisions, taking credit for your successes, and being answerable for your mistakes. As Fritz Perls said in his inimitable way 'You have to learn to wipe your own ass.'[57]

Three things help you to do that. First, the fact that you are the one, not anyone else – who has to live out the consequences of whatever you do. Second, no one else knows what is best for you. Your own mind and heart are your best guides. Third, the knowledge that you already have within yourself everything that you need. You only have to find it.

NEW DEVELOPMENTS IN ALL-LOVE

PATRICK: 'Many changes are happening with All-Love now, and it's wonderful that more and more people are being drawn to the system.

'One of the major points of my philosophy is that people are able to make the connection to Source themselves — so that they can receive the energy, the feelings of love and joy, and the beginnings of what we might call an enlightened state, simply through opening their hearts.

'When I was in India, I was connected with their enlightenment activation energy and I now carry that with me, just as when you experience an initiation in All-Love, you carry that energy with you. But in India, their whole philosophy is that you don't really have to do anything. They said, "You just have to let us do the work for you." So I thought, "OK, I'll try that, I'll sit back and let them do it." I wanted to experience that, and I learned a lot, but I have found that it has been more powerful on my own than with what they were doing. When I have done retreats on my own, I've just locked myself into my bedroom and meditated for a week, and I was able to get to deeper states.

'I feel that we need to be able to fully experience the physical, the emotional, the mental and the spiritual. We need to root ourselves in the physical, and integrate the energy into the whole of our body. We need to make the heart connection, and fully experience all of our feelings. We need to be able to enter the witness state, and experience that stillness and clarity of mind. And we also need to experience the energy of Source, inviting in the whole of our essence, our divine being, so that we feel the soul actually connecting with the body.

'I know that we are eventually going to be doing longer retreats. We may start with a five- or seven-day retreat where we really work with the energy. In a longer retreat, we will be able to spend a day dealing with each of the major emotions. We can do the emotional clearing work, and then work on achieving the witness state. I think it is also important to really be on your own. That is one of the things I want to work on. Considering what we are already achieving in a two-day workshop, I feel that we will be able to get some very powerful results.

'We are not alone. We are all in this together. Enlightenment is not so much an individual effort. All of what we are doing will help the shift of consciousness that is occurring on the planet.'

CLOSING MEDITATION

PATRICK: 'Just be comfortable. Connect with your breath. Now connect with your heart, feeling your heart centre.'

'Feel that connection to the top of your head. Feel the flower opening.'

'Connect with the brilliant sun above the top of your head.'

'Just invite the rays of that brilliant sun to come down into your heart.'

'It's first just being aware of its presence.'

'Bring that column of light down from that sun, connecting into the Earth.'

'Feel the whole connectedness from Heaven descending down into Earth, and then bring the Earth energies up into your feet, into your heart, forming a cross, the energy expanding out to your shoulders and your hands. Just feel that.'

'Breathe with it. Breathe into it and feel.'

'Now connect back up to the brilliant golden sun above your head.'

'This is where we begin to invite the descent of our soul essence — our higher self, to come down through the crown and first just let it descend into the crown.'

'Feel your connection with that clarity, with that universal mind, so that you can have that clarity of the mind and be in the witness state.'

'Just be in the witness state now, while it is at the crown of your head, being completely in the present, completely connected to Source.'

'Now, for a few days, you can do this every day, just bringing it down into the top of your crown and connecting now with the mind. Eventually, what we are going to do is to allow the sun to drop down into the heart, and to begin to breathe that connection down. But first, I would like you to experience that witness state in the mind. It is going to take a bit of practice over a few days that you do this.'

'Then we can integrate it down into the heart. So, you go from the mind to the heart. You begin to do this heart-head connection, and feel the descent of that sun so that it really begins to radiate in your heart.'

'And while you are in the heart, allow yourself to really begin to feel the love that is there. Begin to breathe it in, and have it descend down in.'

'Ask for your higher self to descend more fully into your heart.'

'Breathe and feel. And just stay in that state, knowing that you can come back to it whenever you want, and for as long as you want.'

'All-Love.'

REFERENCES

1. Reprinted from Companion to Psychiatric Studies, 4th Edition, Walmsley T. Historical Introduction, p.1. Edited Kendell, R.E. & Zealley, A.K. © 1988, Elsevier Ltd. with permission from Elsevier.

2. Freud, Sigmund. (1910) Two Short Accounts of Psychoanalysis. Standard Edition. London: Hogarth Press, 1957.

3. Smith, David L. 'Psychodynamic Therapy: The Freudian Approach,' in Handbook of Individual Therapy. Ed. Windy Dryden. London: Sage, 1996. p.27. Reprinted with permission from Sage.

4. Smith, David L. 'Psychodynamic Therapy: The Freudian Approach,' in Handbook of Individual Therapy. Ed. Windy Dryden. London: Sage, 1996. p.30. Reprinted with permission from Sage.

5. Edinger, Edward F. Ego and Archetype. Boston & London: Shambhala, 1992. p.52. Reprinted with permission from Shambhala.

6. Casement, Ann. 'Psychodynamic Therapy: The Jungian Approach,' in Handbook of Individual Therapy. Ed. Windy Dryden. London: Sage, 1996. p.78. Reprinted with permission from Sage.

7. Fordham, Frieda. An Introduction to Jung's Psychology. Middlesex, England: Penguin, 1986. P.136. Reprinted with permission from W.A.D. Hoyle.

8. Fordham, Frieda. An Introduction to Jung's Psychology. Middlesex, England: Penguin, 1986. P.88. Reprinted with permission from W.A.D. Hoyle.

9. Casement, Ann. 'Psychodynamic Therapy: The Jungian Approach,' in Handbook of Individual Therapy. Ed. Windy Dryden. London: Sage, 1996. p.83. Reprinted with permission from Sage.

10. Jung, Carl G. (1923) Psychological Types. Translated by R.F.C. Hull. Routledge, an imprint of Taylor and Francis Books Ltd. 1992. p.568. Reprinted with permission from Taylor & Francis.

11. Casement, Ann. 'Psychodynamic Therapy: The Jungian Approach,' in Handbook of Individual Therapy. Ed. Windy Dryden. London: Sage, 1996. p.83. Reprinted with permission from Sage.

12. Edinger, Edward F. Ego and Archetype. Boston & London: Shambhala, 1992. p.4. Reprinted with permission from Shambhala.

13. Fordham, Frieda. An Introduction to Jung's Psychology. Middlesex, England: Penguin, 1986. P.95. Reprinted with permission from W.A.D. Hoyle.

14. Casement, Ann. 'Psychodynamic Therapy: The Jungian Approach,' in Handbook of Individual Therapy. Ed. Windy Dryden. London: Sage, 1996. p.92. Reprinted with permission from Sage.

15. Perls, Fritz, quoted by Parlett, Malcolm, & Hemming, Judith. 'Gestalt Therapy,' in Handbook of Individual Therapy. Ed. Windy Dryden. London: Sage, 1996. p.208. Reprinted with permission from Sage.

16. Parlett, Malcolm, & Hemming, Judith. 'Gestalt Therapy,' in Handbook of Individual Therapy. Ed. Windy Dryden. London: Sage, 1996. p.206. Reprinted with permission from Sage.

17. Parlett, Malcolm, & Hemming, Judith. 'Gestalt Therapy,' in Handbook of Individual Therapy. Ed. Windy Dryden. London: Sage, 1996. p.199. Reprinted with permission from Sage.

18. Parlett, Malcolm, & Hemming, Judith. 'Gestalt Therapy,' in Handbook of Individual Therapy. Ed. Windy Dryden. London: Sage, 1996. p.205. Reprinted with permission from Sage.

19. Parlett, Malcolm, & Hemming, Judith. 'Gestalt Therapy,' in Handbook of Individual Therapy. Ed. Windy Dryden. London: Sage, 1996. p.203. Reprinted with permission from Sage.

20. Parlett, Malcolm, & Hemming, Judith. 'Gestalt Therapy,' in Handbook of Individual Therapy. Ed. Windy Dryden. London: Sage, 1996. p.209. Reprinted with permission from Sage.

21. Parlett, Malcolm, & Hemming, Judith. 'Gestalt Therapy,' in Handbook of Individual Therapy. Ed. Windy Dryden. London: Sage, 1996. p.208. Reprinted with permission from Sage.

22. Parlett, Malcolm, & Hemming, Judith. 'Gestalt Therapy,' in Handbook of Individual Therapy. Ed. Windy Dryden. London: Sage, 1996. p.210. Reprinted with permission from Sage.

23. Parlett, Malcolm, & Hemming, Judith. 'Gestalt Therapy,' in Handbook of Individual Therapy. Ed. Windy Dryden. London: Sage, 1996. p.212. Reprinted with permission from Sage.

24. Walen, S.R.; DiGiuseppe, R.; Wessler, R.L. A Practitioner's Guide to Rational Emotive Therapy. Oxford, England: Oxford University Press, 1980. p.19. Reprinted with permission from Oxford University Press.

25. Ellis, Albert. Anger: how to live with and without it.

26. Walen, S.R.; DiGiuseppe, R.; Wessler, R.L. A Practitioner's Guide to Rational Emotive Therapy. Oxford, England: Oxford University Press, 1980. p.2.

27. Zukav, Gary. The Seat of the Soul. New York: Simon and Schuster, 1989. p.216.

28. Price, Allison. Writing From the Source: Techniques for Rescripting your Life. London: Thorsons (Harper Collins), © 1999. p.19. Reprinted by permission of HarperCollins Publishers Ltd.

29. Siegel, Bernie S. Love, Medicine and Miracles: Lessons Learned about Self-Healing from a Surgeon's Experience with Exceptional Patients. London: Arrow, 1988. p.38

30. Shepard, Martin. DIY Psychotherapy: A Practical Guide to Self-Analysis. London: Vermilion, 1973. p.78.

31. Fromm, Erich. The Fear of Freedom. London: Ark Paperbacks, Routledge, an imprint of Taylor & Francis Books Ltd. 1984. P.208. Reprinted with permission from Thomson Publishing Services.

32. Pasternak, Boris. Dr Zhivago. London: Collins Harvill, 1988. p.432

33. Zukav, Gary. The Seat of the Soul. New York: Simon and Schuster, 1989. p.243

34. Fordham, Frieda. An Introduction to Jung's Psychology. Middlesex, England: Penguin, 1986. P.50. Reprinted with permission from W.A.D. Hoyle.

35. Siegel, Bernie S. Love, Medicine and Miracles: Lessons Learned about Self-Healing from a Surgeon's Experience with Exceptional Patients. London: Arrow, 1988. p.76

36. Freud, Sigmund. (1914) On Narcissism: An Introduction. Standard Edition. London: Hogarth Press, 1957.

37. Schultz, Mona Lisa, MD, PhD. Awakening Intuition: Using Your Mind-Body Network for Insight and Healing. New York: Three Rivers Press, 1998. p.232

38. Siegel, Bernie S. Love, Medicine and Miracles: Lessons Learned about Self-Healing from a Surgeon's Experience with Exceptional Patients. London: Arrow, 1988. p.92

39. Schultz, Mona Lisa, MD, PhD. Awakening Intuition: Using Your Mind-Body Network for Insight and Healing. New York: Three Rivers Press, 1998. p.121

40. James, Tad; Shepard, David. Presenting Magically: Transforming Your Stage Presence with NLP. Crown House Publishing. 2001. P.124

41. Erickson, Milton H., Rossi, Ernest, Rossi, Sheila I. Hypnotic Realities: The Induction of Clinical Hypnosis and Forms of Indirect Suggestion. New York: Irvington Publishers, 1992. p. 28

42. Adams, Douglas. Dirk Gently's Holistic Detective Agency. New York: Pocket Books, 1987. P.216

43. Johnson, Robert. Owning Your Own Shadow: Understanding the Dark Side of the Psyche. New York: Harper Collins, 1991. p.4

44. Johnson, Robert. Owning Your Own Shadow: Understanding the Dark Side of the Psyche. New York: Harper Collins, 1991. p.26

45. Fordham, Frieda. An Introduction to Jung's Psychology. Middlesex, England:

Penguin, 1986. p.80. Reprinted with permission from W.A.D. Hoyle.

46. Hesse, Hermann. Demian. New York: HarperCollins, 1978. Reprinted with permission from HarperCollins Publishers.

47. Castaneda, Carlos. The Fire From Within. New York: Simon and Schuster, 1984. P.118

48. Zukav, Gary. The Seat of the Soul. New York: Simon and Schuster, 1989. p.171, p.110

49. Siegel, Bernie S. Love, Medicine and Miracles: Lessons Learned about Self-Healing from a Surgeon's Experience with Exceptional Patients. London: Arrow, 1988. p.115

50. Taylor, Jeremy. Where People Fly and Water Runs Uphill: Using Dreams to Tap the Wisdom of the Unconscious. New York: Warner Books, 1992. p.149

51. Johnson, Robert. Owning Your Own Shadow: Understanding the Dark Side of the Psyche. New York: Harper Collins, 1991. p.21

52. Erickson, Milton H., Rossi, Ernest, Rossi, Sheila I. Hypnotic Realities: The Induction of Clinical Hypnosis and Forms of Indirect Suggestion. New York: Irvington Publishers, 1992. p. 29

53. Taylor, Jeremy. Where People Fly and Water Runs Uphill: Using Dreams to Tap the Wisdom of the Unconscious. New York: Warner Books, 1992. P. 19

54. Benor, Daniel J. Spiritual Healing: Scientific Validation of a Healing Revolution. Healing Research Volume 1. Southfield, MI: Vision Publications; 2001. p.31. Reprinted with permission from Vision Publications.

55. Erickson, Milton H., Rossi, Ernest, Rossi, Sheila I. Hypnotic Realities: The Induction of Clinical Hypnosis and Forms of Indirect Suggestion. New York: Irvington Publishers, 1992. p. 29

56. Erickson, Milton H., Rossi, Ernest, Rossi, Sheila I. Hypnotic Realities: The Induction of Clinical Hypnosis and Forms of Indirect Suggestion. New York: Irvington Publishers, 1992. p. 24

57. Perls, Fritz. 'In and Out the Garbage Pail.' Highland, NY: Gestalt Journal Press.

BIBILOGRAPHY

Andreas, Steve; Faulkner, Charles. NLP: The New Technology of Achievement. New York: Quill, William Morrow, 1994.

Andrews, Ted. Psychic Protection. Jackson, Tennessee, U.S.: Dragonhawk Publishing, 1998.

Bays, Brandon. The Journey. London: Thorsons, 1999.

Benor, Daniel J. Spiritual Healing: Scientific Validation of a Healing Revolution. Healing Research Volume 1. Southfield, MI: Vision Publications; 2001.

Berne, Eric, M.D. Games People Play: The Psychology of Human Relationships. London: Penguin Books, 1968.

Borysenko, Joan. Minding the Body, Mending the Mind. New York: Bantam, 1988.

Brennan, Barbara Ann. Hands of Light: A Guide to Healing Through the Human Energy Field. New York: Bantam Books, 1993.

Castaneda, Carlos. The Fire From Within. New York: Simon and Schuster, 1984.

Clare, Anthony. Psychiatry in Dissent: Controversial Issues in Thought and Practice. Routledge, 1988.

Chopra, Deepak. The Way of the Wizard. London: Rider, 1996.

Doi, Hiroshi. Iyashino Gendai Reiki-ho: Modern Reiki Method for Healing. Coquitlan, British Columbia, Canada: Fraser Journal Publishing, 2000.

Dryden, Windy. (Ed) Handbook of Individual Therapy. London: Sage, 1996.

Eden, Donna, & Feinstein, David. Energy Medicine. New York: Penguin Putnam Inc. 1998.

Edinger, Edward F. Ego and Archetype. Boston & London: Shambhala, 1992.

Ellis, Albert. Anger: how to live with and without it. Revised Edition Citadel Press, 2003.

Ellis, Richard. Reiki and the Seven chakras: Your Essential Guide. London: Vermillion, 2002.

Erickson, Milton H., Rossi, Ernest, Rossi, Sheila I. Hypnotic Realities: The Induction of Clinical Hypnosis and Forms of Indirect Suggestion. New York: Irvington Publishers, 1992.

Erickson, Milton H. M.D., Rossi, Ernest. Experiencing Hypnosis: Approaches to

Altered States. New York: Irvington Publishers, Inc., Reprint Edition 1992.

Estés, Clarissa Pinkola. Women who Run with the Wolves. London, UK: Rider, 1992.

Fordham, Frieda. An Introduction to Jung's Psychology. Middlesex, England: Penguin, 1986.

Freud, Sigmund. Two Short Accounts of Psychoanalysis. Standard Edition. London: Hogarth Press, 1957.

Fromm, Erich. The Art of Loving. New York: Bantam Books, 1963.

Fromm, Erich. The Fear of Freedom. Ark Paperbacks, 1984.

Geldard, Richard. The Vision of Emerson. Shaftesbury, Dorset, UK: Element Books, 1995.

Gerber, Richard, M.D. Vibrational Medicine: The Number One Handbook of Subtle-Energy Therapies. Vermont, USA: Bear & Company, 2001.

Goldberg, Natalie. Writing Down The Bones. Boston, U.S.: Shambhala, 1986.

Goldman, Jonathan. Healing Sounds: The Power of Harmonics. Rochester, Vermont, U.S.: Healing Arts Press, 2002.

Gordon, Richard. Quantum-Touch: The Power to Heal. Berkeley, California, US: North Atlantic Books, 2002.

Griscom, Chris. The Healing of Emotion: Awakening the Fearless Self. London: Bantam 1992.

Havens, Ronald A.; Walters, Catherine. Hypnotherapy Scripts: A Neo-Ericksonian Approach to Persuasive Healing. New York: Brunner/Mazel; 1989.

James, Tad; Shepard, David. Presenting Magically: Transforming Your Stage Presence with NLP. Crown House Publishing. 2001.

Johnson, Robert. Owning Your Own Shadow: Understanding the Dark Side of the Psyche. New York: Harper Collins, 1991.

Johnson, Robert A. She. London: Harper and Row, 1986.

Jung, Carl. Man and his Symbols. London: Picador, 1978.

Jung, Carl G. Four Archetypes. London: Ark Paperbacks, 1986.

LaBerge, Stephen, Ph.D., Rheingold, Howard. Exploring the World of Lucid Dreaming. New York: Ballantine Books, 1990.

Laing, R.D. The Divided Self: An Existential Study in Sanity and Madness. Middlesex, UK: Penguin, 1987.

Lubeck, Walter. The Complete Reiki Handbook. Twin Lakes, WI, USA: Lotus Light Publications, 1990.

Lubeck, Walter; Petter, Frank Arjava; Rand, William Lee. The Spirit of Reiki. Twin Lakes, WI, USA: Lotus Press, 2001.

Macquarrie, John. Existentialism. London: Penguin, 1987.

Milner Kathleen. Reiki & Other Rays of Touch Healing. U.S.: Atlantic Books, 1994.

Monroe, Robert A. Ultimate Journey. New York: Broadway Books, 1994.

Murphy, Joseph, PhD, DD. The Power of your Subconscious Mind. Revised by Ian McMahan, PhD. London: Pocket Books, 2000.

Myss, Caroline, PhD. Anatomy of the Spirit: The Seven Stages of Power and Healing. London: Bantam, 1997.

Northrup, Christiane. Womens' Bodies, Womens' Wisdom: Creating Physical and Emotional Health and Healing. Bantam Dell Publishing Group, 2002.

Nirula, Nalin & Nirula, Renoo. The Joy of Reiki. New Delhi, India: Full Circle, 1996.

Oschman, James L., PhD. Energy Medicine in Therapeutics and Human Performance. Philadelphia, U.S: Elsevier Science, 2003.

Price, Allison. Writing From the Source: Techniques for Rescripting your Life. London: Thorsons (Harper Collins), 1999.

Rand, William Lee. Reiki; The Healing Touch. Southfield, MI, USA: Vision Publications, 1991.

Schultz, Mona Lisa, MD, PhD. Awakening Intuition: Using Your Mind-Body Network for Insight and Healing. New York: Three Rivers Press, 1998.

Shealy, C. Norman, M.D., PhD. & Myss, Caroline, PhD. The Creation of Health: The Emotional, Psychological, and Spiritual Responses that Promote Health and Healing. Walpole, New Hampshire: Stillpoint Publishing, 1988.

Shepard, Martin. DIY Psychotherapy: A Practical Guide to Self-Analysis. London: Vermilion, 1973.

Shewmaker, Diane Ruth. All-Love: A Guidebook for Healing with Sekhem-Seichim-Reiki and SKHM. Washington: Celestial Wellspring Publications, 1999.

Siegel, Bernie S., M.D. Love, Medicine & Miracles: Lessons Learned about Self-Healing from a Surgeon's Experience with Exceptional Patients. London: Arrow Books, 1988.

Siegel, Bernie S., M.D. Peace, Love and Healing: The Path to Self-Healing. London: Arrow, 1991.

Stein, Diane. Essential Reiki: A Complete Guide to an Ancient Healing Art. Freedom, CA, USA: The Crossing Press, Inc., 1995.

Taylor, Jeremy. Where People Fly and Water Runs Uphill: Using Dreams to Tap the Wisdom of the Unconscious. New York: Warner Books, 1992.

Walen, S.R.; DiGiuseppe, R.; Wessler, R.L. A Practitioner's Guide to Rational Emotive Therapy. Oxford, England: Oxford University Press, 1980.

Zukav, Gary. The Seat of the Soul. 1989. New York: Simon and Schuster, 2001.

Zukav, Gary, & Francis, Linda. The Heart of the Soul: Emotional Awareness. New York: Simon and Schuster, 2001.

ACKNOWLEDGEMENTS
AND THANKS TO:

Patrick Zeigler, a talented and compassionate healer, for inspiring, guiding and supporting us, and for sharing his insights, knowledge and experience with generosity and humour.

John Hunt, for his appreciation, enthusiasm, and professionalism,

Our many patients, for helping us to understand,

Our Reiki and SKHM students, for being able to help each other along our paths;

Marcus Vinnicombe, Katja Kaiser, Shaila Hernández Gonzaléz, Silvia Morales Alonso, Vicky Barnes, Rachel McCormack, Janie Forbes, Michael Heemskerk, Pilar Holgado Catalán, Jayne Forsyth, Pedro De las Heras Garcia, Teresa Arias Alonso, Annie Jury, Linda Newman, and Paz, for contributing their personal accounts.

Thanks from Teresa to:

Graham Crook, without whom this book would not have been written. For his love, support and interminable questioning, and for helping to make the last two years the best ever.

Marcus Vinnicombe, the best intuitive hypnotherapist I know, for his guidance, support and unconditional friendship.

Sue & Dave Brotherton, for helping me to stay down to earth, and for their encouragement, love and unending patience.

Tanya Luider de Hillman, my first Reiki Master, for showing me another way.

Jean Kendall, for her sensitivity and kindness.

Annie Jury, my personal life coach, for always knowing what to say.

Greg Dark, for being a great writer, editor and endless source of help and good advice.

Tim Cotton, the best GP I know, for his positivity and encouragement.

Anna & Jeff Sirl, for their love, generosity, understanding and support.

My father, who first inspired me to write, think and question; and my mother, for her unfailing love and support. Thank you both for giving me so much.

Thanks from Graham to:

Mary & Danny McLean, my grandparents, for all their love,

Mary MacKay, my sister, for her sensitivity, caring, love and generosity,

James Crook, my big brother, for his loyalty, love and support,

Catriona Crook, my daughter, I love you,

Anne Hodges for the many years of love, support and security,

Dr John Lieper, my childhood inspiration to become a doctor,

Dr Peter Brunt, for showing me what a good doctor should be,

Air Cde Graham Turner for his integrity, caring, and his ability to correct and guide gently and sensitively,

Dr Andrew Hopkirk, an excellent clinician, for giving unstintingly of his time and knowledge, and for being my first mentor,

Dr Julio Simó, for his generosity and help, and for showing me a way of healing outside conventional medicine which started me on my present path,

Amanda Reynolds, my first Reiki Master, for helping me to realise and have confidence in my own abilities,

Juana Rodriguez, my friend and Reiki Master, for her openness, sharing and trust in the Universe,

Dave Kemp, for his kindness, caring and humour, and for many years of friendship, trust, and shared joy of music (Caravan!),

Jeff Sirl for sharing ideas, confidences, and trust,

Araceli Arenas Romero for many special memories,

Katja B. Kaiser for her love and caring, and our connection on many different levels,

And lastly to Teresa Parrott, my co-author and best friend, for her intelligence, hard work, discernment, and desire to clarify, and for her many years of love, help, and support. For making it a joy to write this book!

Contact Us

For further information and details of All-Love workshops:
www.reikiworld.net
www.abouthealing.net
www.skhm.org

'Even though mental, emotional, and physical healings do take place, the All-Love class is not recommended for people who are currently being medicated, or for those who have serious mental and emotional problems. The class is designed for mentally healthy people who wish to strengthen their awareness to Source.'

© 24 April 2005
Teresa Parrott & Graham Crook

O

is a symbol of the world,
of oneness and unity. O Books
explores the many paths of wholeness
and spiritual understanding which
different traditions have developed down
the ages. It aims to bring this knowledge
in accessible form, to a general readership,
providing practical spirituality to today's seekers.
For the full list of over 200 titles covering:

Please visit our website,
www.O-books.net

SOME RECENT O BOOKS

Aim For the Stars...Reach the Moon
How to Coach Your Life to Spiritual and Material Success

You can be your own life coach. This is a do-it-yourself handbook for anyone who is genuinely passionate about living a successful life. Using spiritual awareness as a starting point, it takes you on a journey through the emotions and mind, arriving at a life that is full of power, fulfilment and worldly achievement.

You will learn to manifest what you want and enjoy whatever you manifest. Succinctly and powerfully expressed, this is a manual for 21st century living.

A fascinating, intelligent, and beneficial tool and method of programming your mind for success. The techniques are fast to achieve, motivating, and inspiring. I highly recommend this book. Uri Geller

Without heart, success is just about toys; without love and self love, success is meaningless. Conor does a great job of reminding us to find our heart and build our success from that place within us. Nick Williams, founder of Heart at Work and author of *The Work We Were Born To Do*

Conor Patterson developed the content of this book after fourteen years of research around the world studying with living masters, shamans and yogis. He is the youngest internationally-recognized spiritual teacher and personal Life Coach on the public circuit in England, with a full schedule around the world of talks, workshops and seminars.

1 905047 27 4
£11.99 $19.95

The Fall

The Evidence of a Golden Age, 6,000 Years of Insanity and the Dawning of a New Era
Steve Taylor

The Fall is a major work that overturns mainstream current thinking on the nature of civilization and human nature. It draws on the increasing evidence accumulated over recent decades that pre-literate humanity was relatively peaceful and egalitarian, rather than war-like and crude. It is not "natural" for human beings to kill each other, for men to oppress women, for individuals to accumulate massive wealth and power, or to abuse nature. The worldwide myths of a Golden Age or an original paradise have a factual, archaeological basis.

Taylor's ideas are provocative, and never fail to captivate the reader. It is my fervent wish that this important book will have a wide audience and reach the individuals and institutions that mould public opinion and behaviour. In a world where the very existence of humanity is threatened, Steve Taylor offers a visionary yet practical path out of the morass that distorts human nature. Dr Stanley Krippner, Professor of Psychology, Saybrooke Graduate School, California.

The Fall *is an astonishing work, full of amazing erudition, all brilliantly organised and argued. The argument that human beings have not always been - and do not have to be - such a psychological mess is presented with a beautiful inevitability and logic. The book is a remarkable feat.* Colin Wilson

The Fall *is a fascinating heretical work which demonstrates that the myth of the golden age reflects an archaic social reality. Read it and be cured.* Richard Rudgley, author of *Lost Civilizations of the Stone Age*

A fascinating, enlightening and inspiring investigation into the roots of human consciousness and a much needed proscription for a truly human future. Gary Lachmann, author of *A Secret History of Consciousness*

A thought-provoking diagnosis of the causes of warfare, patriarchy and materialism which holds potential for bringing humans

more in harmony with each other, nature, and themselves. Tim Kasser, author of *The High Price of Materialism*

Well-argued, thoughtful, provocative and a pleasure to read. Christopher Ryan, Institute of Advanced Medicine and Advanced Behavioral Technology, Juarez, Mexico

Steve Taylor is a university and college lecturer in Manchester, England, and spent seven years researching and writing this book. He has written many articles and essays on psychology and spirituality for mainstream magazines and academic journals.

1 905047 20 7
£12.99 $24.95

The Invisible Disease

The Dangers of Environmental Illnesses caused by Electromagnetic Fields and Chemical Emissions
Gunni Nordstrom

Millions of people today, particularly in the West, know they are ill even though their doctors can't make a proper diagnosis. Environmental illnesses are known under a number of names, like Multiple Chemical Sensitivity, Chronic Fatigue Syndrome (ME), Immune Dysfunction Syndrome, Fibromyalgia, Electro-Hypersensitivity, Sick Building Syndrome.

This is the first book to make the connections between the range of illnesses and chemicals used in the manufacture of modern appliances that we mistakenly consider safe. They're not.

Gunni Nordstrom is an investigative journalist in Sweden, the world-wide centre of the mobile phone industry, where much of the research on Environmental Illness has been carried out.

1-903816-71-8
£9.99 $14.95

In the Light of Meditation

Mike George

In the Light of Meditation offers an introduction to the art and practice of meditation while laying down the foundations for ongoing spiritual development. A series of ten lessons provide specific insights into Raja Yoga, with practical exercises to complement and to help your understanding of the method and underlying teachings.

Accessible, powerful and challenging, this book shows how meditation is more an experience than something that you do, more a process than an achievement, more an ongoing inner journey than a destination. Take your time, be patient with yourself and always be ready to go back to basics, to lesson one, the true identity of the self, which is the foundation of everything.

Beautifully illustrated in full colour, it comes with a CD.

Mike George is a spiritual teacher, motivational speaker, retreat leader and management development facilitator. He brings together the three key strands of his millennium-spiritual and emotional intelligence, leadership development, and continuous learning. His previous books include *Discover Inner Peace, Learn to Relax* and *The 7 Aha!s.*

1 903816 61 0
£11.99 $19.95

The Japanese Art of Reiki

Bronwen and Frans Steine

Reiki techniques originated in Japan, in an intensely spiritual period of that country's history. This fully-illustrated book traces the system's evolution from a spiritual self-development system to a direct hands-on practice. The journey moves from Japan to the USA, out to the world, and back to Japan.

Focussing on the basic elements in their historical context, this guide contains beautifully grounded information that captures a unique sense of the system's traditional Japanese roots. The clarity and accessibility of the teachings in the book redefine and strengthen the concept of Reiki as it is practised today.

Reiki Masters *Bronwen* and *Frans Steine* are the founders of the International House of Reiki. They have worked with Reiki and researched it for many years, their particular passion being the recovery of traditional Japanese Reiki. They live in Sydney, Australia.

1 90547 02 9
£12.99/$19.95

Mastering E-motions
Feeling Our Way Intelligently in Relationships
Richard Whitfield

Human feelings and emotions are the revolving doors to intellect, action and spirit. Guided by the reality that humans are much more driven by their emotions than by the intellect, this book gives readers both insights and know-how for improved personal emotional management.

Using a clear conceptual structure, the practical emotional growth promoted here can benefit every aspect of life, including intellectual and work performance, personal contentment and quality of relationships.

The author writes from wide experience, and a deep educational concern for holistic models for human development and functioning. The text takes much of the mystique out of 'emotional intelligence', and, with associated insights from brain science, enables readers both to shape and to 'get a life'.

Central to it are the age-old "golden rule" wisdoms, which are not innate at birth but must be learned and handed on by experience. It offers challenging and practical solutions that require responses in lifestyle and outlook. Then our collective democratic consciousness may awaken to the massive evolutionary risks that we face unless we "mind" our emotions.

Richard Whitfield, Professor Emeritus of Education, is an international lecturer, teacher and consultant. He has previously been University Lecturer at Cambridge, Dean of Social Sciences at Aston University, UK Director of Save the Children Fund, and Warden of St George's House, Windsor Castle.

1 905047 26 6
£11.99 $19.95

The Ocean of Wisdom
Alan Jacobs

The most comprehensive anthology of spiritual wisdom available

The first major anthology of this size and scope since 1935, *The Ocean of Wisdom* collects over five thousand pearls in poetry and prose, from the earliest of recorded history to modern times. Divided into 54 sections, ranging from Action to Zen, it draws on all faiths and traditions, from Zoroaster to existentialism. It covers the different ages of man, the stages of life, and is an ideal reference work and long term companion, a source of inspiration for the journey of life.

Frequently adopting a light touch it also makes a distinction between the Higher Wisdom, which consists of pointers leading to the understanding of philosophical and metaphysical truth, and practical wisdom, which consists of intelligent skills applicable to all fields of ordinary everyday life. So Germaine Greer and Hilary

Rodham Clinton have their place alongside Aristotle and Sartre.

The carefully chosen quotations make this book the perfect bedside dipper, and will refresh the spirit of all who are willing to bathe in the ocean of the world's wisdom.

Few individuals have as wide an acquaintance with the world's traditions and scriptures as *Alan Jacobs*. He is Chairperson of the Ramana Maharshi Foundation (UK), editor of *Poetry of the Spirit*, and has translated *The Bhagavad Gita* (O Books), *The Principal Upanishads* (O Books) and *The Wisdom of Marcus Aurelius* (O Books).

1 905047 07 X
£19.95/$29.95

The Secret Journey
Poems and prayers from around the world
Susan Skinner

A gift book for the young in heart and spirit

These prayers, verses and invocations are drawn from many faiths and many nations but they all reflect the same mystery: the mystery our passage from birth, through life, to death. We are born from the unknown. Our life, except perhaps to our friends and family, is a secret journey of joy and sorrow. Our death is shrouded in questions.

In the words of St Paul, "now we see through a glass darkly.." But we *do* see some things, if we respond to the spirit within. Most faiths, personal or communal, acknowledge the inspiration of the spiritual life founded on truth, love and compassion.

This anthology is a small reflection of the inspired and enlightening words that have been passed on down the centuries, throughout the world. They sing to the child within us all, to the spirit which always remains open and free and clear-sighted. In the words of Master Eckhart: "The eye with which I see God is the same eye with which God sees me."

Each reflection is stunningly illustrated in full colour, making this an ideal gift book for the young and anyone starting on the spiritual journey, or seeking images and verses for inspiration and meditation. A map and short introduction to the world religions, along with notes on sources, make it a useful addition to all libraries in homes and schools.

Susan Skinner is an artist who has made a life long study of world religions, working their themes into exquisite images. She lives near Hastings, England.

1 905047 08 8
£11.99/$16.95

The Wave

A life-changing journey into the heart and mind of the Cosmos.
Dr Jude Currivan

Pioneering science and the wisdom teachings of many traditions agree – consciousness expresses itself as energy. All energies are manifested as waves – and it is from the vast and ever changing interaction of these waves of energy that the entire Cosmos, at all levels of experience, is continuously created.

In easily accessible terms, *The Wave* explains the profound interconnectedness and harmony of the universe and reveals its underlying principles. Powerfully combining leading edge research with the perennial wisdom of all ages, it reconciles science and spirit into a universal model of consciousness. It describes how we co-create our realities and how the Cosmos affects all life on Earth. It rediscovers the ancient knowledge that birthed feng shui and astrology and perceived the harmony of sacred geometry, music and number. It clarifies the meaning behind a multitude of metaphysical teachings and the common principles underlying the many techniques of energy healing.

The Wave offers not only an explanation of how the universe is as it is, but why the world is as it is and how we can live in harmony with it and ourselves.

Above all, *The Wave* explains the power of love, and in marrying heart and mind, it births a creative and empowering spirituality from their union.

Dr Jude Currivan has a Masters Degree in Physics, specialising in cosmology and quantum physics and a PhD in Archaeology, researching ancient cosmologies, and has studied consciousness and metaphysics from childhood. Moving on from a highly successful international business career in the mid 1990s, she has worked with the shamans and elders of many wisdom traditions, is a healer and teacher at the College of Psychic Studies in London and a master dowser. She travels and teaches worldwide.

1 905047 33 9
£11.99/$19.95